PRAISE FOR *THE KING OF MADISON AVENUE*

"This brilliant biography is like the tip of a gorgeous iceberg. It dazzles and below is a mass of weighty research. Kenneth Roman enchants us with his account of the life and times of David Ogilvy, who towered above the world of advertising. Below is the hitherto hidden work of a wartime agent. Churchill, we are reminded, galvanized an entire wartime navy with words written on one side of a small sheet of paper. Ogilvy excited the public with similar brevity. The story is told swiftly. The voluminous research will fascinate those who want to know why it was vital to paint a background of grave historical events in this portrait of a singular man. It should be read by all, in or out of salesmanship."

—William Stevenson, author, *A Man Called Intrepid*

"At last! The definitive biography of the most influential advertising executive with whom I had the pleasure of working. Ken Roman has brought more of David's uniqueness to light. A great read."

—Jack Keenan, former CEO, Kraft Foods International and Diageo PLC Wine and Spirits

"A great biography of a truly great man. David Ogilvy rewrote the book on modern advertising. With *The King of Madison Avenue,* Ken Roman tells his story in a fashion that is worthy of David's accomplishments. Extensively researched and very well written."

—Philip Carroll, former CEO, Shell Oil

"A terrific read! David Ogilvy was unquestionably the King of Madison Avenue. This intimate portrayal makes clear Ogilvy's inspiring leadership of his agency. Ogilvy's convictions about what made for effective advertising—it sells—are clearly described as is his brilliant personal salesmanship in winning new clients."

—Ron Daniel, former managing partner, McKinsey & Co.

"A most interesting book. It is a sensitive account of the career of this complex man who so successfully melded intuition and analysis. It should be compulsory reading for anyone contemplating a career in advertising or communications."

—Sir Michael Angus, former chairman, Unilever

"David and Leo were very different types but great mutual admirers. Ken Roman's book is thoroughly researched and very well written. The boss would be proud of him."

—Cap Adams, former CEO, Leo Burnett Co.

"A wonderful job recounting the life of so complicated a person. Beautifully written."

—Harold Burson, founder, Burson-Marsteller Public Relations

"A surprisingly interesting book about one of the most remarkable characters in advertising history."

—Martin Mayer, author of *Madison Avenue USA*

"A fascinating portrayal of a unique life and the contribution made to an evolving industry. Really well done."

—Carlo Vittorini, former publisher, *Parade*

"Ken Roman has drawn a vivid, flesh-and-blood portrait of one of the giants of twentieth century business, and reminds us that David Ogilvy's revolutionary insights into the souls of consumers are still worth more than all the advertising algorithms underlying the Internet."

—Randall Rothenberg, President & CEO, Interactive Advertising Bureau,
former *New York Times* advertising columnist

"Nobody ever need write another word about David Ogilvy, now that Ken Roman has written *The King of Madison Avenue.* It's the definitive biography of the most amazing man the advertising business has ever known. This is the fairest, most thoughtful, most complete and most human biography of that flawed genius we are ever likely to get. *The King of Madison Avenue* is to other biographies as David Ogilvy's advertising was to that of other agencies: simply superior. Everyone who ever knew David Ogilvy will find something about the man they didn't know, and those who never knew him will have a rollicking good time getting to know him. This has to be the most readable book ever written about advertising."

—Bruce McCall, *New Yorker* writer and illustrator

"Having read *Confessions of an Advertising Man* at least seven times, I thought I knew all there was to know about David Ogilvy. I was wrong. In *The King of Madison Avenue,* Ken Roman has shown me a David Ogilvy that no one has ever seen before. It's a must read for anyone in or out of the advertising business. Ogilvy was brilliant and surely one of the original 'Mad Men.' My only regret is that Cary Grant has passed on. He would have been a great David Ogilvy in the movie that will surely be made of *The King of Madison Avenue.*

—Jerry Della Femina, Chairman and CEO,
Della Femina/Rothschild/Jeary & Partners

∾

PRAISE FOR KENNETH ROMAN'S
PREVIOUS BOOKS

Writing That Works
"I don't believe you can get to the top today in any organization if you can't express yourself clearly. And here's the only guide you'll ever need. *Writing That Works* works."

—John Mack Carter, former President, Hearst Magazine Enterprises

"Clear, concise communications that make the right point will launch your career or business to new heights."

—Robert Seelert, Chairman, Saatchi & Saatchi PLC

"In advertising, the challenge is to find the one simple, inspired thought. . . . This book helps all of us."

—Peter Georgescu, Chairman Emeritus, Young & Rubicam Inc.

"Roman and Raphaelson offer an abundance of practical tips for helping your written and oral communications."

—William C. Steere, Jr., Former Chairman and CEO, Pfizer, Inc.

How to Advertise
"Worth its weight in gold."

—David Ogilvy

"Without pulling any punches, the book tells readers what works."
—*Dallas Morning News*

"*How to Advertise* is a timeless treasure of the enduring principles that everyone in the advertising supply chain—those who create, place, manage, review and approve—should read over and over again. It's the definitive roadmap to creating great work."
—James Speros, Former Chairman, Association of National Advertisers

"*How to Advertise* is comprehensive and practical. The experience of the authors is evident on every page. I would certainly recommend it to anyone who wants to get a real-world understanding of the many issues involved in using advertising effectively."
—Don Sexton, Professor of Business, Columbia University

ALSO BY KENNETH ROMAN

How to Advertise, with Jane Maas

Writing That Works, with Joel Raphaelson

THE KING OF MADISON AVENUE

DAVID OGILVY AND THE MAKING OF MODERN ADVERTISING

KENNETH ROMAN

First published in 2009 by PALGRAVE MACMILLAN® in the US-a division of
St. Martin's Press LLC, 175 Fifth Avenue, New York, NY 10010.

Where this book is distributed in the UK, Europe and the rest of the world, this
is by Palgrave Macmillan, a division of Macmillan Publishers Limited, registered
in England, company number 785998, of Houndmills, Basingstoke, Hampshire
RG21 6XS.

Palgrave Macmillan is the global academic imprint of the above companies and
has companies and representatives throughout the world.

Palgrave® and Macmillan® are registered trademarks in the United States, the
United Kingdom, Europe and other countries.

ISBN-13: 978–1–4039–7895–0
ISBN-10: 1–4039–7895–6

Library of Congress Cataloging-in-Publication Data
Roman, Kenneth.
    The king of Madison Avenue : David Ogilvy and the making of modern ad-
vertising / by Kenneth Roman.
        p.   cm.
    Includes bibliographical references and index.
    ISBN-13: 978–1–4039–7895–0
    ISBN-10: 1–4039–7895–6
    1. Ogilvy, David, 1911–1999. 2. Advertising executives—United States—
Biography. 3. Advertising agencies—United States—History—20th century.
4. Advertising—United States—History—20th century. I. Title. II. Title:
David Ogilvy and the making of modern advertising.
HF5810.O34A3   2009
659.092—dc22
[B]

                                                            2008040118

A catalogue record of the book is available from the British Library.

Design by Letra Libre, Inc.

First edition: January 2009
10 9 8 7 6 5 4 3 2 1
Printed in the United States of America.

PHOTOGRAPHS AND ART CREDITS

~

TEXT PERMISSIONS

For Ellen,

who married the agency

as well as the author

CONTENTS

AUTHOR'S NOTE

*D*avid Ogilvy was very much on the scene in 1963 when I joined Ogilvy, Benson & Mather, a medium-size advertising agency with a large reputation. He was 52 and famous. I was 33 and a junior account executive. Early on, he wrote a letter to one of my clients. After listing eight reasons why some ads prepared by the company's design department would not be effective, he delivered his ultimate argument:

> *The only thing that can be said in favor of the layouts is that they are "different." You could make a cow look different by removing the udder. But that cow would not produce results.*

So began my "David" file. Almost everyone who worked at the agency kept one.

At Christmastime my first year, all 600 of us marched up Fifth Avenue to the Museum of Modern Art for our annual staff meeting. Very classy, I thought, like the red carpets that lined the halls of our otherwise understated offices. "Look at my new Sears suit," Ogilvy exulted from the stage as he spun around, a dramatic touch to underline his loyalty to clients—and a charge for everyone to use their products.

Over my next 26 years, there were more such lessons, countless meetings with him around the world, and *many* more memos and letters. Eventually, when I became his third successor as chairman, I no longer reported to him technically, but he was always a formidable presence, and we all thought of the agency as his company.

While Ogilvy disclosed much about his life in three books and several hundred interviews, what he could not do is assess his own legacy and its relevance today. This biography, the first, aims to provide that perspective and impart a sense of his quotable brilliance. Ogilvy's insights go beyond advertising to leadership and apply to almost any professional services organization. I also try to bring alive his idiosyncratic and vivid personality.

I started with a rich bank of personal recollections, papers, and tapes, and added to these from more than 100 interviews and his 30,000 papers in the Library of Congress, plus several other libraries and private collections, countless books and articles, and visits to his schools in Scotland and England and his homes in New York, Lancaster County, Pennsylvania, and France. This research filled in many of the gaps and added dimension and color. Almost everyone who brushed up against the man has a David story.

From time to time in this book, when I report on events I participated in, I will drop my biographer's objectivity and offer the reader a first-person point of view.

Kenneth Roman
New York, 2008

THE
KING OF
MADISON
AVENUE

THE KING OF MADISON AVENUE

*M*adison Avenue is to advertising as Hollywood is to movies or Fleet Street is to London newspapers, as much an identity as a place. It conjures images of gray flannel suits and two-martini lunches. For many years, Madison Avenue was the address of many advertising agencies. Even though most have since fled to less expensive office space, "Madison Avenue" is still shorthand for American advertising.

World War II had been over for only three years when 39-year-old David Ogilvy, an English émigré with almost no experience in advertising, implausibly opened shop in 1948. Although his offices were, in fact, on Madison Avenue, the rulers of the realm at the time had no reason to take notice of him. Within a few years Ogilvy was counted as one of them.

By 1953, the trade magazine *Printer's Ink* was ready to declare that Ogilvy had "become at once the conscience and catalytic agent of Madison Avenue." By 1958, he was being described in breathless terms: "No single figure has come across the American advertising horizon in the past 50 years who has created the sensational impression which the puckish, fortyish Britisher, David Ogilvy, has. Only in the agency business here nine years, the colorful Ogilvy, practically a character out of Dickens, has been the most discussed and publicized ad-man in a generation."

In 1965, *Fortune* magazine asked, "Is Ogilvy a Genius?" and concluded that he might be. (Ogilvy wondered if he should sue about the question mark.) *Time* magazine called Ogilvy "the most sought-after wizard in the advertising industry." Asked to form his all-time agency team, Ed Ney, who led Young & Rubicam, said: "I'd start with David Ogilvy. He's outrageously brilliant. Bernbach was OK, but David was the best of the best." (It was always *David.* That was made clear in the agency's newsletter: "Use of Dave is an almost certain sign that the speaker has never met Mr. Ogilvy, and an absolutely certain sign he has never addressed him by his Christian name.")

Ogilvy's best-selling book, *Confessions of an Advertising Man,* published in 1962, was described as "the only civilized, literate and entertaining book ever written about advertising—a magic distillation of learning and wisdom."

At the height of his career, Ogilvy was invited to the White House, offered the lead in a Broadway play, and cited as the measure of fame in Tom Wolfe's 1964 essay the "Mid-Atlantic Man":

> He always made a big point of telling everyone that he was expecting a call from New York, from *David*—and everyone knew this was a big New York advertising man—David!—David!—New York! New York!—hot line to the source!—land of the flamingo legs and glass cliffs!

Ogilvy would later become by far the best-known advertising man in Asia as well as in Europe, Canada, and South Africa. In India, he was treated like a movie mogul; a magazine listed Ogilvy with Pope John Paul II and Princess Diana among those who made news in the country in 1982. At that year's thirteenth Asian Advertising Conference, the trade's bible, *Advertising Age,* reported Ogilvy "came as close to being anointed king of the Advertising World as it is possible for a mortal to come."

That same year, Ogilvy sent a memo to the fellow directors of his agency, citing the French magazine *Expansion* that had named 30 men who contributed most to the Industrial Revolution, among them Thomas Edison, Albert Einstein, John Maynard Keynes, Alfred Krupp, Lenin, Karl Marx, and, in seventh place, David Ogilvy:

"the Pope of modern advertising." The memo concluded: *Will the College of Cardinals please come to order?*

~

In the early years of the agency, Ogilvy affected a full-length flowing black cape with a scarlet lining. A young employee thought he looked like Heathcliff coming off the moors. Cape off, he appeared the English country gentleman with a bow tie, a foulard in the pocket of his woolly tweed suit, vest with lapels, and thick rubber-soled shoes. In later years, these were replaced by a double-breasted dark blue blazer (scarlet-lined) and traditional striped tie held in place by, of all things, a Bulldog paper clip. He almost never wore a standard "business suit." On state occasions, he would don a royal blue velvet vest of vaguely ecclesiastical derivation. At a time of gray flannel suits and button-down shirts, Ogilvy stood out as exotic.

His wavy hair, "flaming red" in early descriptions, changed over time to dark-blond and then rust and pepper. His blue eyes twinkled. He had a ruddy complexion, aristocratic features, and spoke with an Oxford English accent. A maid named Bridey Murphy served tea in his office every afternoon. Many photographs show him with a pipe, which seldom left his lips, but he also smoked (but seldom bought) cigars and cigarettes.

"Pencil slim" when he first arrived in the United States, Ogilvy grew more stocky with age. As he matured and filled out, the impression was that he was big. He stood about five feet ten inches and had a big head, big shoulders, big hands—"big agricultural hands," says a former colleague, who remembers Ogilvy in his 60s picking up a great stone he wouldn't think of raising and heaving it over a hedge.

He was strikingly handsome. A female friend who knew him as a student at Oxford recalls, "He looked a tiny bit like Rupert Brooke, so he was always running his hands through his forelock, and showing his profile to advantage. He'd turn his head so we could all see what a good profile he had." He adored pretty, intelligent women and made them feel special. "He was very, very sexy and incredibly charming," says a former copywriter. Another agrees: "On my second day in the office, suddenly David walked in. I was struck dumb. It was as though a movie star was in my little office. He was bigger than life, tall, handsome. I almost asked him for his autograph. It was as though everything was in black and white and he was in Technicolor."

A disarming presence, Ogilvy would pop into offices unannounced, sit down, and commence his grilling. You became the focus of his attention. He'd look straight at you and ask direct questions. When he was done (or bored), he would get up and bolt as suddenly as he had entered. Novices thought this meant they somehow angered him and brooded over it until they discovered he behaved the same way with big shots. He was always springing up, remembers a colleague. He was not a getter-upper, he was a springer.

To understand the man, one has to grasp first that Ogilvy was an actor. There was a theatrical delivery to his cultured English accent. He had a sense of center stage and a sure instinct for the memorable gesture. When he spotted his octogenarian client Helena Rubinstein getting out of her car near a puddle, he ran across the street to lay down his jacket for her to walk on. He made his points with dramatic flourish and often dressed for his parts. At black-tie events, he might show up in a kilt. "Perhaps a bit of self-advertisement," he explained. "If you can't advertise yourself, what hope do you have of being able to advertise anything else?"

He had the actor's gift of entrances and exits. Instead of coming into a conference hall while the chairman of another agency was speaking, Ogilvy waited until the man had finished and gone, so all eyes would turn to him. A speech consultant considered his showmanship in so little need of improvement that if he came to her for help, she'd tell him, go home! He was driven around New York in a Rolls-Royce before many were around. It was quite a show.

Ogilvy was not above embellishing his picaresque life story. He told the head of British American Tobacco that his first job had been with BAT. A few months later, he told *another* CEO that his first job had been with that man's company. It was all part of selling himself. Ogilvy's trouble, wrote *Printer's Ink,* is that "he is overcome by an irresistible impulse to say what he thinks will make good listening or good reading. The impulse makes him add things, so he never tells the same story twice: it's *almost* the same—but it has been adorned a little." Like any actor, he wanted to give himself better lines.

One characteristic of geniuses, said Einstein, is they are passionately curious. Ogilvy's great secret was an inquiring mind. In conversation, he never pontificated; he interrogated. At dinner with a copywriter and her husband who worked in the oil business, Ogilvy quizzed the man at length about the oil situation in the Middle East. He queried the 15-year-old daughter of an executive about playing the flute in the school band. "How many flutes? How many piccolos? Why are there always so many more flutes than piccolos?" A woman who sat next to him at dinner said that by dessert, he knew more about her than her mother. At another level, he was an inveterate gossip. He would pump people for information. "Give me the *dirt*." "What do you think of Blank? Is he up to the job?"

A zealous student of the business, Ogilvy claimed he had read every book about advertising—and disdained others who felt they didn't need this knowledge. There were piles of books all over his house, most about successful leaders in business and government. He was interested in how they used their leadership. How they made their money. And particularly how rich people used their wealth.

He knew a lot about a lot of things, and used his knowledge to establish common ground with a wide variety of people. Talking with the British Philatelic Bureau, a client in London, Ogilvy asked, "Tell me, what ever happened to George V's stamp collection?" He loved Mozart, Brahms, and the Baroque composer Henry Purcell, and went often to New York Philharmonic orchestra concerts. Once he corrected a creative group on their use of a line from a Gilbert & Sullivan operetta. Another time he put a prospective hire at ease with a discussion of abstract painting and politics in Czechoslovakia. But "culture" bored him. His comment on an agonizingly long French documentary film: "My bum fell asleep."

Like most snobs, Ogilvy loved to name-drop. According to him, one of his friends in Chicago was a former king of Yugoslavia. He enjoyed telling colleagues he was going to dine with the king. "If there's anything David likes, it's royalty," says a friend, "and a king is best." Yet in business he was democratic. When he entered New York advertising circles, he was shocked to find how separate the Jewish community was from the non-Jewish. "I told our small staff that I wasn't going to play that game. A lot of our clients were Jewish—e.g., [Helena] Rubinstein and later Seagram. And our senior executives were also a mixture, which was certainly not the case at JWT [J. Walter Thompson] or any of the other big agencies." It didn't occur to Ogilvy that race or religion should be an issue in hiring the best people.

He put a high value on caring for people and practicing good manners. "We don't take people to the elevator—we take them down to the street." When he heard a young writer had lost his parents in a plane crash, he invited the man (whom he did not know) and his wife to his house for dinner. A member of the staff who lost her husband to cancer was deeply touched by his three-word note: "You poor lamb."

He cultivated and flaunted his eccentricities, not all of which were attractive. The worst was his appalling behavior in restaurants, where he often seemed to go out of his way to create a scene. He'd listen to a recitation of the house specialties and order Grape-Nuts cereal, or a plate of ketchup or a jar of jelly, as his entire meal. At a pre-Christmas dinner with British clients, he rejected the menu and asked for two small mince pies as a starter; for the entrée, again two mince pies; instead of dessert, two more mince pies.

Ogilvy's fear of flying was not an eccentricity—it was terrifyingly real. He went to bizarre lengths to avoid getting on an airplane and much preferred traveling by train, even for very long journeys. An entertaining train companion, he had an endless supply of anecdotes and observations, and people welcomed the concentrated time with him.

Almost everyone felt that his wit and charm outweighed his occasional rudeness. "He was famous for his eccentricities," conceded David McCall, one of Ogilvy's successors as the agency's copy chief, "but it was the orthodoxy of his working mind that made him an irreplaceable pioneer in a business that needed him badly."

∽

A large part of Ogilvy's success came from the energy he put into getting what he wanted. He would start by mentioning an idea, more or less casually, then follow up with a memo or letter, clips of articles, more memos—a tsunami of communications. An ordinarily purposeful person might follow up an idea with a second note or a call; the more dogged might come back several times before moving on. Ogilvy *never* gave up.

In conversation, if he agreed, he would nod. If he disagreed, nothing. But he'd go back to his office and write a memo—often fierce, sometimes vicious. Ferocious in writing, he tended to be cowardly in person. One account man felt he could win any argument simply by taking three menacing steps toward Ogilvy.

His ideas gained power from a terse, compact writing style. "I believe in the dogmatism of brevity," Ogilvy explained. He registered key thoughts with underlines in memos and letters, verbal emphasis in conversation and speeches. His speeches were riveting; audiences didn't talk while he was speaking. Like a professional actor, he could film a talk in a single take.

He collected and repeated aphorisms to make his points. On compensation: "Pay peanuts, and you get monkeys." On checking expense accounts: "Even the Pope has a Confessor." On leadership:

Search your parks in all your cities,
You'll find no statues of committees.

Points were made memorable by vivid metaphor. Discussing which of two commercials to show first to a client, Ogilvy told the creative team: "When I was a boy, I always saved the cherry on my pudding for last. Then, one day, my sister stole it. From then on, I always ate the cherry first. Let's play the best commercial first." The client liked the first commercial.

"He had a near-psychopathic hatred of laziness in all its forms," says a former copywriter. "He was the least lazy person I have ever encountered. His advertising philosophy was shot through with intolerance of sloth. Lazy people accept mediocrity, which he hated." No matter how good, everything had to be *better.*

Walter Cronkite, who lived next door to Ogilvy in New York, said he could see him working at his desk by the window, night after night, hour after hour. In the morning, letters had been answered, plans outlined, staff memos written. Ogilvy was indefatigable, routinely working in the office until 7 P.M., then packing his unfinished business into two briefcases to finish at home (which didn't help his second marriage). Weekends were for more work, not play. "This weekend I went over 375 pieces of paper," he wrote his directors. "The Duke of Wellington never went home until he had finished all the work on his desk."

~

When the Association of National Advertisers asked Ogilvy to address their 1991 convention, the 80-year-old advertising luminary came up on the platform and sat behind a low coffee table that had been put there for him. After an introduction, he stood up and removed his blazer, exposing his red braces (not "suspenders," which are ladies' garters in England), and dropped it on a nearby chair. He sat again and looked out at the audience.

> The last time I addressed the ANA wasn't exactly yesterday. It was 37 years ago, in 1954. You didn't invite me back for 37 years!

Off to a good start. The audience of marketing executives loved it.

> I'm going to tell you about a crusade on which I have embarked, and about some bees in my bonnet. My crusade is in favor of advertising which sells. My war cry is, "We Sell. Or Else."

He described a reel of television commercials that had won awards but struck him as "pretentious and incomprehensible nonsense," and piled on the stinging adjectives: "obscure," "self-aggrandizing," "high-brow," "ignorant."

> When I write an ad, I don't want you to tell me you find it "creative." I want you to find it so persuasive that you buy the product—or buy it more often.
>   This has been my philosophy for 50 years, and I have never wavered from it, no matter what the temptations have been to jump on the fashionable bandwagons which afflict the ad business.

Coming to the end of his talk, Ogilvy told about being applauded on another occasion. He said the applause had struck him as insufficient and so had made a slight upward gesture with his hands, prompting the audience to rise to its feet and express more enthusiasm. Now he did it again. *Advertising Age* reported a standing ovation for "advertising's greatest living legend."

Most of Ogilvy's notable advertising campaigns were produced during a ten-year spurt early in his career. He called them Big Ideas (always in capital letters). "Unless your advertisement is based on a Big Idea, it will pass like a ship in the night." His Big Ideas went beyond memorable advertisements. (He resisted the use of "ads" as not professional and deplored "creativity," a word he professed not to understand.) Ogilvy's goals were wildly ambitious: nothing less than to change the advertising business and make it more professional. One of his Big Ideas was the now-pervasive concept of brands. He was early in recognizing their importance and the crucial role advertising plays in building them. Before he was finished, this immigrant Englishman would improbably rewrite many of the rules of Madison Avenue and become a brand unto himself.

ONE

AN ECCENTRIC
CELTIC MIXTURE

*O*ur chairman "is *definitely* descended via five different lines of descent from Charlemagne,* King of the Franks and Emperor of the West," obligingly reported *Flagbearer,* the agency's employee newsletter, in the 1970s. A relative investigating the family's roots was said to have made the discovery. To help tighten the connection, the article was accompanied by side-by-side pictures of Charlemagne and Ogilvy, "to demonstrate the similarity in facial characteristics."

The fourth of five children, David Mackenzie Ogilvy was born in 1911 in West Horsley, a rural agricultural village between Guildford and Leatherhead, in Surrey, 30 miles southwest of London. His birth date, June 23, was, incredibly, the same as his father's and grandfather's. It was also the date of George V's coronation and the year that Ronald Reagan was born.

While the population of West Horsley had recently boomed, to 750, there were still more horse-drawn vehicles than motorcars, and the village smithy didn't shut down until 1920. The area has a history going back to the Romans, who were replaced in A.D. 410 by

---

* He also noted a relationship to the Empress Eugenie of France, the beautiful and fashionable wife of Emperor Napoleon III, through his great-great-great grandfather.

invading Saxon mercenaries, then by Danes and Normans. The word "Horsley" is Saxon for "a clearing for horse pasture." The town was bypassed by the Industrial Revolution, so the landscape remained unspoiled by factories or rows of houses.

The Ogilvy home, Wix Hill, was an old estate with a timber-framed manor house dating back to the fourteenth century. The family had moved there from East Horsley. The house was clad with bricks in the eighteenth century to make it look more up-to-date. The name "Wix" comes from "Wick," a corruption of the Latin *vicus,* meaning "an inhabited place where victuals could be obtained," important to anyone on a long journey in a sparsely populated countryside.

Ogilvy reminisced about the Surrey of his early youth: "a paradise of plover's eggs, cowslip wine, charcoal burners, gypsies in caravans, thatched haystacks and governess carts." Plus a witch called Dame Feathers. When his advertising agency created its "Come to Britain" campaign for the British Travel Authority, he personally selected the lush color photographs of the English countryside, picking those that reflected the England where he grew up. "I suppose I ought not to tell this around. I ought to pretend I based my selection on research." It was a world of well-off families with servants, much like that depicted in the movie *Mary Poppins.* With a chauffeur, nanny, undernurse, and two other servants, Ogilvy started off solidly upper middle to upper class.

Little genealogy is disclosed in his 1978 autobiography, *Blood, Brains and Beer.* The title came from his father's bizarre directive when David was six to drink a glass of raw blood every day (for strength) and eat calves' brains three times a week (to expand mental faculties), all to be washed down with bottles of beer. Some locals in West Horsley still remember the "eccentric" father at Wix Hill.

Reading that short autobiography is like having dinner with a charming raconteur. It is thin on family details. We never learn the names of Ogilvy's father or mother. He describes his father as warm-hearted, affectionate, and a failure. His Scottish grandfather is portrayed as cold-hearted, formidable, and successful—and his hero. Ogilvy had three sisters and an elder brother but names only his sister Mary and his brother Francis. His youngest sister, Christina, was so furious with Ogilvy for the way he described their father in the book that she didn't speak to him for 15 years.

A sickly child, afflicted with asthma that dogged him to the end of his life, Ogilvy said his nurse was scornful of him "because I was a mollycoddle, a milksop, a nyaah-nyaah, a sort of sissy because my sister Mary could beat me at everything—at wrestling, at every imaginable game, at climbing trees even. And I grew up to think I was a boob. And I thought so well into middle age." This led him to psychoanalysis in his middle 40s and, with the help of the analyst, deciding he wasn't such a boob as he'd thought.

The memoir portrays a young boy stumbling "bone-idle" through schools, meeting interesting people who fascinate him, and making his way through a variety of jobs that prepare him inadvertently for success in advertising. It drops an assortment of famous names: George Bernard Shaw, Harpo Marx, Albert Einstein, Leonard Bernstein, Lady Astor, Henry Luce, Edward R. Murrow, Alexander Woollcott, George S. Kaufman, Ethel Barrymore, Robert Moses, David Selznick, Charles Laughton, Loretta Young, Alfred Hitchcock, Thornton Wilder, Samuel Goldwyn, Walt Disney, Aldous Huxley. They all somehow crossed Ogilvy's path, and he didn't mind letting you know.

As successful as Ogilvy's other books would be, he admitted this one was "a bust." He said he knew the reason. "When you write a book about advertising, you're competing with midgets. When you write an autobiography, you're competing with giants." He also acknowledged the title was repulsive, "and so was my egotism."

~

Ogilvy always described himself as a Scot, yet he was born and raised in England, and his mother was Irish. His father was a Scot. "That's all that counts," say the Scots. His Scots Irish parentage—"that eccentric Celtic mixture," as one English colleague put it—was a product of three families coming together, like a merger of industrial giants: the Ogilvys and Mackenzies in Scotland, and the Fairfields in Ireland. Ogilvy was firm on the subject: "I'm a Celt, not an Anglo-Saxon."

His ancestral claim was later laid out in a toast to the Scottish Council, as the youngest member of its U.S. Committee: "I had the misfortune to spend the first twelve years of my life in the South of England—which my Spartan Scottish father inflicted on me as a trial of character." He was proud of his Highland relatives in the north of Scotland and sent a teasing telegram to his friend George Lindsay, a director of his agency: "Well, your poor devil came from the low country."

He paraded his Scottish pride in a 1962 address to the Saint Andrew's Society in New York and was introduced as a graduate of Fettes College in Edinburgh. [Cheers and applause.] After noting the society's purpose—to raise money to take care of indigent Scots (he observed there were lots of them)—Ogilvy told jokes, dismantled Scottish stereotypes, and recounted the story of Ralph Waldo Emerson walking through the Scottish countryside with Thomas Carlyle. Seeing the poor soil, Emerson asked Carlyle, "What do you raise on land like this?" Carlyle replied, "We raise men." [Applause.] He talked about his agency's campaign exhorting American tourists to visit Britain—"I mean Scotland"—and quoted Benjamin Franklin: "The time I spent in Scotland was six weeks of the densest happiness I have ever met in any part of my life."

He wrote to one Richard Ogilvie, Sheriff of Cook County in Chicago, saying they were likely to be kinsmen, since the two spellings of the name did not firm up until about 1800, and telling him about another Scotsman, Alan Pinkerton, who uncovered an early plot to assassinate Abraham Lincoln in Baltimore and was made head of the secret service. It was Pinkerton's successor who failed the president, said Ogilvy. "I have always believed that, if Lincoln had kept Pinkerton, he would have averted the tragedy that took place in Ford's Theatre." He also pointed out that this Scotsman was "the father of the F.B.I., the O.S.S., and the C.I.A."

∼

The main seat of the Ogilvy clan is at Cortachy Castle, on the northeast coast of Scotland. The current head of the clan, David George Coke Patrick Ogilvy (the thirteenth Earl of Airlie), saw his namesake in New York walking down Madison Avenue in the 1960s and accosted him: "I must introduce myself. My name is David Ogilvy." Quick as a flash came the reply: "Nice to meet you. What is it like to be mistaken for me?"

He was named for his great-uncle David Ogilvy, who enlisted in the French army in the Franco-Prussian war and was killed in a skirmish. His great-great-grandfather, a merchant, was also named

David Ogilvy. He had no known connection with another branch of the Ogilvys—the Earl of Airlie, Princess Alexandra, and others—says his friend Louis Auchincloss, "unless you go back to Adam and Eve. That really pissed him off. They were very famous."

If great-grandfather Thomas Ogilvy was not one of the royal Ogilvys, he was clearly well off, a "landed proprietor" and a man of status (a justice of the peace). He was born in Inverness, in the Highlands, and for a time was a merchant in Liverpool before moving to London. The Scottish General Registry lists six servants—a house servant, nurse, maid, wet nurse, cook, and housemaid. His 1796 will ran to 55 pages.

Ogilvy's admired grandfather Francis (Frank) Mackenzie Ogilvy, was a sheep farmer by trade but an adventurer at heart. Born in Scotland, he moved to London and, at 24, emigrated to South America, where he led a swashbuckling life, fighting in the Argentine war against Paraguay. He also managed an estancia for a group of Scottish investors. When the estancia failed, grandfather Ogilvy, out of work with a large family to support, tried prospecting for gold in New Zealand. When that failed, he returned to London, where he got a job as secretary in the English Bank of Rio de Janeiro. "Four years later," writes Ogilvy, "this uneducated sheep farmer became manager of Brown Shipley, where he trained the future governor of the Bank of England. He was able to send all seven of his children to private schools and universities" and "lived like a Forsyte."[*] The banking experience led him to advise his grandson to study the firm of J.P. Morgan, pointing to the Morgan criteria for partners ("Gentlemen with brains") and clients ("Only first-class business and that in a first-class way"). Both later became part of the Ogilvy agency's credo.

His father, Francis John Longley Ogilvy, was born in Argentina on a sheep ranch but remained a British subject. A classical scholar who taught himself Gaelic and read Greek in the bathroom, he played the bagpipe for his son. David had to call him "sir" when with other people and would later say his father bequeathed him two things: a scatological sense of humor and a penchant for smoking a pipe.

An agnostic, Ogilvy's father brought his son up under the most stringent Victorian morality. "My dear boy. You do not have to be a

---

[*] Three Forsyte Saga novels by John Galsworthy chronicle an upper-middle-class family keenly aware of their status as "new money."

Christian to behave like a gentleman." Young Ogilvy became a fervent atheist, and debated religion with a colleague, a former theologian, who saw Ogilvy as an intensely rational man who couldn't relate to the idea of a Being able to alter human destiny. Ogilvy confirmed his lack of belief. "The idea of eating the body and drinking the blood of Jesus struck me as repulsive. I could not believe in the Creation, the Virgin Birth, the Ascension, Heaven, Hell or the Holy Ghost."

Ogilvy's father had been averagely successful as a stockbroker. When David was just three, England declared war on Germany, markets collapsed, and his father lost everything. Five servants were let go, and the family had to leave Wix Hill and move in with his maternal grandmother in London for a period before moving to Guildford, where his parents bought Lewis Carroll's house. He said he knew Alice Liddell, the original Alice in Wonderland. Beatrix Potter, the pet-loving author of *The Tale of Peter Rabbit,* visited his next-door neighbor, bringing a tame hedgehog called Mrs. Tiggy-Winkle. Potter's famous gardener, Mr. McGregor, was thought to be based on the bad-tempered gardener at the local Woodcote Farm. "Her England is the England I remember," Ogilvy recounts.

But from then on, they lived in genteel poverty. "We were a very poor family," said Ogilvy. "My father's total income was less than $1,000 a year." His grandfather turned down an appeal from his father for a loan, and his father tried to commit suicide by cutting his throat. Although Ogilvy adored his father and thought him a great gentleman, he recognized he was a scholar, not a businessman. He saw his grandfather as the exact opposite. "He was hard as nails, but a very successful businessman. I couldn't make out whether I was going to be like my father or my grandfather."

When fathers fail, their children are often driven to be successful. The son would always be motivated to achieve—and obsessed with money.

~

The other Scottish strain, the Mackenzies—as in David *Mackenzie* Ogilvy—entered the family when grandfather Frank Ogilvy married Kythé Caroline Mackenzie in 1865. The Mackenzie history goes back to 1494, when King James IV awarded Hector Roy Mackenzie a "writ of fire and sword" to 170,000 acres of land, with 90 miles of seacoast, mountains, lakes, and streams—on the condition of providing jobs for the natives. The grant was a remote Highland estate on the west coast of Ross-shire. From 1494 to 1958—464 years—there was an unbroken succession from father to son of 15 lairds of Gairloch.

Sir Hector was a fearless (and almost incessant) warrior, but not as menacing as his half-brother Kenneth of the Battle, who once felt himself to have been insulted by his wife's cousin. Kenneth decided to return insult with insult by returning his wife (who had only one eye) to her family. He sent her back on a one-eyed pony, accompanied by a one-eyed servant, and followed by a one-eyed dog, naturally provoking some carnage.

Ogilvy, who described himself as a "perfervid" Mackenzie, persuaded his equally ardent sister Christina to publish the memoirs of their other Scottish grandfather. Dr. John Mackenzie was a reformer. He got his medical degree at the University of Edinburgh, where final examinations were conducted in Latin. As a young doctor, he worked in the slums of Edinburgh. Since most of the poor went to an apothecary, "the poor man's doctor," Dr. John abandoned medicine and returned to his beloved Highlands. It was the time of the Highland Clearances, with families being evicted to make way for sheep farming. Dr. John tried to persuade the crofters to modernize their methods of farming. He preached education for children, self-improvement for young men, slum clearance, public health, and abstinence from alcohol.

Ogilvy's gardening gene may have come from a Mackenzie relation. Osgood Mackenzie, Scotland's most famous gardener, developed a great garden at Inverewe in Northwest Scotland, now part of the National Trust.

∼

Ogilvy's mother's side of the family, the Fairfields, were of Anglo-Irish descent but had lived in County Kerry for 400 years. In centuries past, many land-owning English and Scots were encouraged to buy land in Ireland to counter the Irish unrest. Ogilvy's Irish grandfather, Arthur Rowan Fairfield, was listed in the public records as a "Gentleman" (i.e., rich). A friend of George Bernard Shaw, grandfather Fairfield lectured his grandson (at age four) on the Armenian atrocities and the villainy of Liberal Party prime minister William Gladstone, "a cousin on the other side of my family."

Ogilvy's mother, Dorothy Blew Fairfield, called Dolly, was so tiny she was known as the "pocket Venus." A beautiful girl with brown eyes and freckles, she was intelligent, high strung—and ambitious. An 18-year-old medical student when she married her 33-year-old husband, she would grow frustrated being a wife and mother rather than a doctor, as she had planned. Without her medical career, and bored by her husband, Dolly fulfilled her ambitions through her children. She wanted them to make their marks in the world, and drove them to use their brains.

The marriage between Francis Ogilvy and Dorothy Fairfield produced two sons, Francis Fairfield Ogilvy and David Mackenzie Ogilvy, and three daughters: Kythé, Mary, and Christina.

David described his mother as a very hard Irishwoman and very eccentric, having come from a crazy Irish family. "People today would say nutty as a fruitcake. Didn't like me very much. Thought I was very materialistic."

There was a one-sided rivalry with David's elder (by eight years), high-achieving older brother. Francis would become by far the most important of the siblings in David's life, both fraternally and professionally. He was a star at school and established as an advertising agency executive in London when his young brother was still finding his way. Francis thought his brother was a genius and opened doors for him at every key juncture, a helping hand David barely acknowledged in his autobiography.

Ogilvy considered Christina the cleverest of his three sisters. A senior officer in military intelligence during World War II, she invented a device for reading people's mail without their knowledge. Her invention was a glass rod with a hook on the end that was slipped into the unlicked part of an envelope; the letter was extracted by rolling the rod and then replaced the same way after it was read. He was closest to Kythé, his eldest sister—tall, interesting, and extravagant—and he liked her husband, Sir Philip Hendy, the longtime head of the National Gallery in London. The second sister, Mary, became a social worker, then a housemother at a famous progressive school.

Dolly left some inherited money to her daughters because she thought women were too dependent on their husbands. She was known for stirring up the family with intellectual arguments, getting each member to take a different point of view, and her children grew up to be highly competitive, in the world and with each other. "They tended to get what they went after," said a friend.

A Fairfield cousin, Rebecca West, one of mid-twentieth-century Britain's most influential intellectuals and writers, changed her name from Cicely Isabel Fairfield because she thought nobody would take seriously a person with such a prissy name. Although her affair with the married H. G. Wells was open and emancipated, Ogilvy's parents refused to let David visit Wells, who in their view had seduced West. Ogilvy later became a good friend of West's, who told him his grandmother's side of the family was Jewish. "A big thrill," Ogilvy commented, "but Rebecca was an incurable liar, so I'm afraid it wasn't true."

Ogilvy was always proud of his heritage but inconsistent as to its public display. When Queen Elizabeth came to New York on a visit, he gave his agency staff the afternoon off and instructed them to stand outside the Waldorf-Astoria Hotel so she would have an appropriate crowd. But a gaggle of bagpipers hired by the Chicago office to introduce him at a meeting provoked a protest: "Shut down that awful sound. That's the reason I left Scotland."

～

Ogilvy was married three times: first to Melinda Street, who was from one of Virginia's first families and the mother of his only child, then to Anne Flint Cabot, who had been married to one of the blue-blooded Boston Cabots, and finally, to Herta Lans de la Touche, born in Mexico of German Dutch and Swiss English parentage, whom he met in France; they remained married for the rest of his life.

Unlike his brother, Francis, who flaunted his liaisons, whatever Ogilvy did romantically outside his three marriages was discreet. He loved women and was attracted to them (and they to him). At parties, he would hone in on the prettiest girl in the room, engage her in conversation, and charm her, but there was little public evidence of what his friend Jock Elliott called his "lustiness."

Ogilvy spent happy times with his stepchildren from two wives, pushing them to be naughty to see how far they could go. In his 80s, he adored his blond, blue-eyed step-grandson Francois—"his last love," says Herta. But the person he cared for more than anyone was his and Melinda's son David Fairfield Ogilvy—"Zucky" in early days, "Fairfield" until adulthood, now "David" or "David Jr." to friends and clients of his successful real estate firm in Greenwich, Connecticut.

Ogilvy doted on his son from birth, but then became an inattentive or, at times, a too directive parent during the boy's early years, when he was building his agency. Fairfield was 16 when his parents divorced, and he was raised by his mother with help from her brother-in-law, the advertising agency executive Rosser Reeves. He went to Hotchkiss, a boys' school in Lakeville, Connecticut. At lunch with his father and David McCall, a Hotchkiss grad and then copy chief of the agency, the young Ogilvy was sullen. When his father described the sort of school he would run if headmaster, the boy looked up with chilly eyes and said, "That would be a dreadful school. I would never go to such a school. It would be cruel, hateful." His father advised him to be careful in what company he said things like that. "Mr. McCall *goes* to such a school."

As a teenager, made to wear a dress kilt for a ball, he spent the evening venting about how much he hated wearing a kilt, hated advertising, hated everything. Fairfield was a wonderful kid, thought a colleague, but having David as a father was "a cruel, cruel mix." After graduating Hotchkiss and the University of Virginia, Fairfield gave his father new concerns. "What am I going to do with my son?" worried Ogilvy. "He's so frivolous, and he should be getting a job." Following his father into advertising was never an option; Fairfield made it clear that was something he didn't want to do.

On his son's twenty-first birthday, perhaps in part to assuage his guilt about his absence as a parent, Ogilvy assigned him the royalties from *Confessions of an Advertising Man,* assuming they would not amount to much. He regretted that decision when the book turned out to be a best seller and rued that his son used the funds to finance a brief period as a "ski bum" in Europe, but was proud of his later success as a real estate broker. On one visit to Greenwich, when Ogilvy produced his American Express Card at the local hardware store, the merchant asked, "Are you *the* David Ogilvy, the famous real estate man?" Ogilvy told the story often, with evident pleasure.

Whatever issues he had with his father growing up, it is apparent to everyone that the son is nice and normal, as well as successful. Ogilvy did recognize one special skill: "It's amazing that this young man, who I think is so frivolous, if anyone in our family was having a problem, or people are disagreeing with one another, Fairfield comes in and makes it go away. He puts a salve on everything."

Father and son were estranged for a period after Ogilvy divorced Melinda, but later reconciled and became quite close. They kissed when meeting, prompting an observer to hope he and his son could have a similar relationship. When Ogilvy retired to France and took his son to the train to return home, he had wet eyes. On one visit, when Fairfield was unavoidably delayed, his father waited all day by the gatehouse. "He wouldn't have done that for anyone else," said a friend. "He cared for his son more than anyone." Ogilvy wrote proudly of his son: "He has become a champion realtor and my infallible advisor on matters great and small."

As Ogilvy was dying, Fairfield flew to France from the United States almost every week to be with him. After he died and Fairfield remarried following a divorce, a daughter was born—Ogilvy's first grandchild, Melinda Fairfield Ogilvy (known as Field)—the ninth-generation Melinda on his mother's side of the family. Descended from Charlemagne?

TWO

"I FAILED EVERY EXAM"

*O*gilvy was just ten years old when his parents received a report card with these teacher comments:

> He has a distinctly original mind and expresses himself well in English. He is a little bit inclined to argue with his teachers and try to convince them that he is right and the books are wrong; but this perhaps is only a further proof of his originality. It is a habit, however, which it would be wise to discourage and I hope he will try and restrain himself in this respect in the future.

His arithmetic teacher agreed: "He takes the subject seriously and works well, except for periods devoted to attempted discovery of methods superior to those of his instructor."

Having an original mind does not always correlate with doing well in school. Ogilvy's formal education began on a low note and concluded the same way. When he was six, his Scottish father sent him to a London kindergarten in a kilt. Embarrassed and teased by classmates, Ogilvy punched one of his tormentors. On his mother's advice, he learned to fight future foes with his tongue.

But the crowning horror of his school years began when he was eight, at the infamous St. Cyprian's School, at Eastbourne in Sussex, on the south coast of England. Accounts by other St. Cyprian's students—including authors George Orwell and Cyril Connolly and fashion photographer Cecil Beaton—confirm that Ogilvy's traumatic experiences were not unique.

St. Cyprian's was typical of boarding schools in England that started in the 1850s, when Brits were sent to India and other faraway places to run the British Empire in the army and civil service. Parents sent their sons, ages 9 to 14, back to England to be educated. These exclusive boys-only boarding schools, generally in country houses, prepared students to go to Eton, Harrow, and other leading "public" (private in the United States) schools. Beyond supplying a good education, these schools also assumed the responsibility of molding character: instilling in their charges the ideals of duty, discipline, service, and respect for the virtues of the Empire. Typically these schools were run by a headmaster and, very often, his wife. It was a bit Dickensian. In many cases, a strong-minded wife effectively ran the school. If she was a warm, motherly type, lonely boys felt they had a mother to look after them. If not, they had a rotten time.

It was the luck of the draw, and Ogilvy was unlucky. St. Cyprian's* was run by Mr. L. C. Vaughan Wilkes, nicknamed by the students "Sambo" (for reasons unknown), and his wife, Cicely Ellen Philadelphia Vaughan Wilkes, known unofficially as "Flip" (referring to a well-developed bust that bounced as she paced the corridors) and known officially as "Mum." The character of Big Brother in *1984,* George Orwell's novel of psychological manipulation, is said to have been based in part on Mrs. Wilkes, who mercilessly humiliated the boys while her husband merely exhorted them to avoid romantic attachments and not pollute their bodies by masturbation.

Orwell described the school as "a world where it was not possible for me to be good," and vented his bitterness in an ironically titled essay "Such, Such Were the Joys," considered so libelous at the time it was published only after his death. Cecil Beaton remembered "the schoolrooms smelt inky and dusty, the swimming pool was stagnant, the lavatories cold and damp." He said of Mrs. Wilkes: "the escape from Flip when at last we left St. Cyprian's was one of the great milestones in my early career."

---

* No longer in existence.

St. Cyprian's was too expensive for the recently impoverished Ogilvys, but the school agreed to accept David at half the fee, with the hope that his father's honors at Cambridge would be replicated by the son, who soon shared Orwell's views of the school.

> The horror was Mrs. Wilkes, the headmaster's wife. This satanic woman carried the art of castration to extraordinary perfection. Like a chess master playing simultaneous games against several opponents, Mrs. Wilkes played games of emotional cat-and-mouse against every boy in the school. Each was alternately in favor or out of favor, like the courtiers at Versailles. . . . boys whose fathers, like mine, were neither artistic nor rich were always out of favor; for four years I lived in a black cloud of rejection.

Ogilvy remembered the day Mrs. Wilkes refused to let him buy a peach, reminding him that he was poor and attending on a scholarship.

> "How dare you?" she shouted, loud enough for the whole school to hear. "Your father is so poor that we are obliged to keep you here for almost nothing. What right has the son of a pauper to spend money on luxuries like peaches?"

His parents could not afford the price of a birthday cake—or even a single visit during the four years he was there, although they lived less than 50 miles away. He was "wretchedly homesick" and looked forward to letters from his family and weekends with school friends and their families in between holiday visits at home. His best friend, Johnnie Rotherham, became an Air Vice Marshall in the Royal Air Force; Johnnie's sister Jean was Ogilvy's great love between the ages of 12 and 15.

At St. Cyprian's, the Bible was taught intensively. Students had to learn a chapter every day and recite the verses at breakfast. If they made more than two mistakes in the recitation, they had to stand for all meals all day. "So I learned a lot of the Bible by heart in four years," said Ogilvy, pointing out that although he had "absolutely no religion at all," he knew the Bible better than most Christians he knew.

Ogilvy wrote that Mrs. Wilkes made exorbitant profits by starving the students, some 90 in all, so much so she was able to rent grouse-moors in Scotland during the summer and send her sons to Eton. "She and her husband never ate our food, but those who were privileged to sit next to Mr. Wilkes at meals pinched food off the plate of that absent-minded and henpecked man." Ogilvy was once sent to bed without supper for saying that Napoleon was a Dutchman. Sometimes he went to sleep at night sucking on a tiny hole in a can of Nestlé's condensed milk ("tastes like mother's milk") and when that ran out, he sucked toothpaste from free samples.

Living away from his parents, being publicly humiliated as a scholarship student, going to bed hungry. It was a miserable, lonely experience that fed his insecurity as a young boy and could have destroyed his confidence as an adult.

$\sim$

Ogilvy's next school had a fictional student, secret agent James Bond. In his spy thriller *You Only Live Twice,* Ian Fleming reveals that Bond left Eton under a cloud. Bond's aunt manages to get him into Fettes ("his father's old school"), reasoning that the Calvinistic atmosphere of the school, plus its rigorous academic and athletic standards, would put young James on the right road.

That would be Fettes, a preparatory school just outside Edinburgh, where Ogilvy was enrolled at age 13. At the time, being an English gentleman and being educated in Scotland was seen as an almost perfect combination. The Scottish educational system was possibly the best in the world in those days, and Fettes was its top public school. Fettes's baronial gothic main building, ornamented with pinnacles, gables, buttresses, and gargoyles, is said to be the architectural model for the Hogwarts School of Witchcraft and Wizardry in J. K. Rowlings's Harry Potter books.

Fettes (pronounced Fet-tes) was demanding—"homework, homework, homework" says a former student—and formal. In Ogilvy's day, the students wore top hats and tailcoats when they went to town for church; they still wear chocolate-magenta striped blazers to classes and attend daily compulsory chapel. As recently as the 1950s, Fettes was an austere place with classic public school virtues: cold showers in the morning, sports in the afternoon, corporal punishment, and "fagging" (doing small chores for senior boys, known as prefects.) All good character-building stuff, says a former student.

After St. Cyprian's, almost any school would have been an improvement. Ogilvy relished the food at Fettes: "delicious Scottish porridge, three times a day, Scottish roast beef, and Scottish mutton pies. For the next five years I lived like a fighting cock." He loved chapel with its magnificent preachers, and singing he found almost equally inspiring.

Again Ogilvy came with a scholarship. His father had no choice. With a depression on the London Stock Exchange and losses on his railway investments in the Argentine Republic, his already modest income had dropped nearly 90 percent. Fettes was something of an Ogilvy family preserve, the obvious reason young David qualified for financial assistance. The school was, he says, "in my blood." Ogilvy was preceded there by his brother, Francis, their father, and their grandfather, who attended in the first decade after Fettes opened in 1870. His great-uncle, Lord Inglis of Glencorse, was one of the school's original trustees and served as chairman for 48 years, being succeeded in that position by his son-in-law.

Ogilvy's family predecessors at the school were "Foundationers," meaning their tuition was paid by the Fettes Foundation. They were big shots, said Ogilvy. "They won everything. I remember my first term and the boys saying, 'You can't be Francis Ogilvy's brother.' It was bad for my morale." His father had been head of school and captain of Rugby, first team in cricket and fives (a predecessor to squash racquets), and winner of four trustee prizes. Brother Francis was also head of school and captain of rugby and of the shooting team as well as winner of the shooting cup and two governor's prizes.

In marked contrast, David described himself as too odd to be popular. Because of asthma, he did not participate actively in sports. At one point he became so ill he was removed from the school hospital in the "death cart." But he recovered and had a moment in the sun in athletics, when the captain of football (soccer) put him on "Big Side" and he was suddenly one of the lords of creation. Not that he was any good at it—he and the captain had discovered they shared the same taste in poetry.

Music was the center of Ogilvy's life at Fettes. He played the double bass in the orchestra, and his best friend played the violin.

Henry Havergal, the music master, and his wife took an interest in young Ogilvy, and they remained friends for 60 years. Ogilvy also liked history, taught by Walter Sellar, who wrote *1066 and All That,* the renowned parody of history teaching in English schools at that time. Young Ogilvy led the Debating Society and got appointed head fag and house prefect; later he claimed to be the first prefect not to beat little boys. But he said he was too lazy to take classical studies and follow in the footsteps of his father and brother, and resented the Fettes class aristocracy (although he spoke with an upper-crust accent and admitted that he looked down on people who didn't, until he went to America and "grew out of it.")

One skill Fettes instilled in both Ogilvy brothers was a solid foundation in writing and speaking clearly. Then a predominately "classics" school, with inspirational teachers of Latin and Greek, it did not teach English as a separate subject; *all* teachers of whatever subject were expected to teach English. While writing was not taught in a planned way, the atmosphere underlined the "pleasure and importance" of the written and spoken word, explains former headmaster Cameron Cochrane. It was said of one teacher that every classics lesson was an English lesson, a history lesson, and a geography lesson, in addition to setting standards for living. Standards were high; minor infractions were punished by "lines"—copying prose of biblical or classical origin, 25, 50, or 100 lines per lined page. Handwriting had to be precise: lowercase to touch both lines, top and bottom. A math master was known to assign 12.5 lines.

"If you really want to be an English literature scholar," says Cochrane, "you should have studied the classics at school. Perhaps the reason for so much slovenly use of the English language, written and spoken, today is that fewer and fewer students study Latin, almost none Greek." The silver-tongued former British prime minister Tony Blair is one alumnus who benefited from the Fettes curriculum.

Ogilvy summarized his five years at Fettes when he returned to deliver the 1968 Founder's Day oration. He took the occasion to berate the school for not admitting girls (it now does) and to remind everyone that he was not a big shot at school.

> I wasn't a scholar. I was a duffer at games. I detested the philistines who ruled the roost. I was an irreconcilable rebel—a misfit. In short, I

was a dud. Fellow duds, take heart! There is no correlation between success at school and success in life.

Invited back in 1974, he offered an inventive litany of ideas to develop a unique image for the school: hire a great French chef; train students to be first-class plumbers, carpenters, electricians, painters, and gardeners; hire a dancing master so boys would be able to dance with the boss's wife; teach typing and shorthand (he could do neither); make attendance at classes optional and make the boys pay to enter the classroom ("This will enrich masters who teach well. The bores will starve to death."); establish a "marsupial" relationship with Edinburgh University; and start a branch in France (where he had retired).

Ogilvy also proposed revamping the entire theory and practice of instruction.

> The masters have to cram you full of facts, so that you pass those odious examinations. This is like cramming corn down the throat of a goose to enlarge his liver. It may produce excellent pâté de foie gras, but it does the goose no permanent good.
>
> The mission of a great school is not to cram you with facts so that you can regurgitate them a few weeks later at an exam. [It] is to inspire you with a taste for scholarship . . . which will last you all your life. Dr. Potts inspired that taste in my father—he read Horace in the lavatory to his dying day.

In between provocative talks, Ogilvy felt free to offer proposals on how to market the "Fettes Product." In later years, the headmaster was able to write "rich old boy" David Ogilvy: "My dear David, you are stinking rich. We need a minibus. It will cost you 7,000 pounds." Ogilvy sent a check with a terse note: "You bastards! Here it is."

Faced with choosing a school in the United States for his 12-year-old son in 1955, Ogilvy said he doubted that any could teach children how to read and write to his standards. "That is the trouble with most American schools—they turn out people who are perfectly adjusted but illiterate. The opposite of Fettes."

~

Ogilvy left Fettes in 1929, when he was 18, and worked briefly at a Boys Club in the slums of Edinburgh before resuming his schooling.

Finishing Fettes with top marks in modern studies and an endorse-ment of "excellent character," he applied to Oxford, "thereby avoiding competition with my father, my brother Francis, and the rest of the family, who had all distinguished themselves at Cam-bridge." His application essay impressed the chief examiner at Ox-ford, who awarded him a rare open history scholarship on the theory that scholarships should be awarded to those who showed the greatest future promise rather than to those who scored well in examinations.

Oxford's Christ Church college was Ogilvy's choice "because it had produced more Prime Ministers, Viceroys of India, and Arch-bishops of Canterbury than all the other colleges put together." Often described as the grandest, most aristocratic and church-minded of all the Oxford colleges, Christ Church is very traditional. Its striking buildings at the top of High Street, along the Thames River, are some of the best in Oxford. The grand dining hall, seen in the first two Harry Potter movies, displays portraits of several of the 13 prime ministers educated at the college as well as its founder, King Henry VIII.

Ogilvy entered Christ Church in 1929 as a scholar, which meant he had to take an examination to receive financial support. At din-ner, scholars sat in an area slightly higher than the large space occu-pied by commoners, who paid the full tuition fee. It was a literal hierarchy; dons (faculty) sat on a still higher level. Formal academic dress—gowns over dark suits known as *subfusc* ("under shade")—is still compulsory for dinner, tutorials, and lectures. Scholars like Ogilvy wore long black gowns, distinguishing them from the short-gowned commoners. Tuxedos for dinner four times a week; white tie for special occasions.

England was very snobbish then, Christ Church especially so. A fellow classmate said Ogilvy's first question to him was "Did you go to a good school? There aren't many of them." Ogilvy was warm and friendly and "sort of odd," says Margot Wilkie, an American who was taking courses at Oxford and became a lifelong friend. "He was-n't the usual Oxford undergraduate. He was lots of fun, and he was funny. I remember sitting in somebody's digs with David and a cou-ple of other young men, and they had a servant that brought every-thing in. It was very impressive to American women. He used to take us punting [boating on the river]. He was young. I was 17, so he was 18. And I think he was insecure, a little bit, too."

He got off to a good start with his first tutor, who found him "a very interesting and powerful person," but he never felt at ease in the academic atmosphere and fought it at times. He was perpetually late to classes. Once, when he came in during a lecture in a large amphitheater, the professor stopped speaking to draw attention to his tardiness. Ogilvy broke the silence: "If you insult me again, I will not return to this class."

But he lacked direction. In his second term, he transferred from modern history to medicine, having decided for the moment to be a surgeon, like his grandfather. "He was always very self-dramatizing," says Wilkie, who remembers a bull session with him leaning against the mantel and romanticizing about his desire to be a doctor. "He stressed his Scottish inheritance, and to be a Scottish surgeon was a real career. There was a whole line of doctors and surgeons behind him, and he was going to be the flower of them all." When later he found himself working in a French kitchen, he wrote Wilkie: "Well, I thought I'd be doing something with human bodies, but I'm in a French hotel cutting up chickens and doves."

Ogilvy's tutor was skeptical of the switch in studies. "He starts science completely from scratch, and made a very good start. If he can force himself and try to become professional in his work, he might do well. At present he is rather in the clouds. He impresses me as an interested amateur." His problems grew worse in the next several terms, as his tutors recorded. "He finds the transition difficult and painful. He is also much worried by financial straits," wrote one. Another recorded: "He is too blasé to take his coat off and do a job of work. But this, I fancy, is due to his literary antecedents. He has got a job in the long vacation." Alarms were sounded by the third: "I am very doubtful he will pass [chemistry]. He works well but I don't think Science is his line yet. A very nice man."

Then, at midterm, new problems: "He worked quite eagerly, though troubled by illness," wrote his tutor. Asthma was keeping him awake at night, propped up on pillows so he could breathe. If that was not enough, he also suffered with a painful infected double mastoid that made it hard to study or read. Before entering Oxford, Ogilvy had lodged for a year in Cambridge while he had two mastoid operations. His landlady, Appy Sewell, a young widow, became a friend (and his brother's first wife). In those days before antibiotics, infections in the mastoid bone behind the ear were scraped away, often with a small chisel and mallet. Anesthesia, probably ether, took the edge off the pounding near the brain, but it must have been a terrible experience. For almost a year, while the incision was draining, Ogilvy had to swath his head in a turban-like bandage. The surgery left a large hole behind his left ear for the rest of his life, which Ogilvy kept hidden by wearing his wavy hair long. It also impaired his hearing, requiring him to turn his entire body to hear someone on his left.

Ogilvy's various medical problems didn't help his studies, and he barely got by. "I don't think he will fail his subject in Mods [modern studies] this term," wrote his tutor. "He has of course a long way to go. I am satisfied with this term's work."

Although Oxford was demanding, one could set aside time for fun. Ogilvy wrote book reviews, went to Blenheim on the Duke of Marlborough's birthday, tutored the son of an American millionaire until the man's French mistress tried to seduce him, took advantage of a tip from a spiritualist to win at the Derby, heard Lady Astor preaching against drinking and was converted (for three weeks), partied, and made lifelong friends.

The problem was that he did not complete his required assignments during the six-week breaks. These were not vacations. Students were expected to read voluminously, write papers, and come back and hand them in. Ogilvy did not do that, says Wilkie. "He was sociable. He didn't work. He was young, and full of blood and guts and stuff, and I think he was restless. He was brilliant but confused, and couldn't use his brilliance in a conventional way." After two years, Ogilvy left Oxford in 1931—in the depths of the depression—without a degree, describing himself as "unteachable in any subject. Perhaps it was impatience with academe and the itch to start earning a living. Perhaps I was intellectually out of my depth. Whatever the reason, I failed every examination."

Ogilvy says he was "sent down"—expelled—and calls this the real failure of his life. "I was supposed to be a star at Oxford. And instead of that, I was thrown out." The records do not explicitly state that he was expelled or even that he failed all his exams. The picture is rather one of an uncertain young man changing directions, beset by financial and health problems, and yearning for something more invigorating and eventful. A better way to put it might be that he dropped out.

"Do you know what sent down means?" Ogilvy said later. "I seemed to reach a period when I couldn't understand anymore, where nothing made very much sense. And I didn't really seem to care. It was very bad, you know. I had always thought of becoming a don—I don't know why I should have thought of myself as a don, but I did. I studied modern history. Here I had gotten myself a scholarship at Oxford and then I was sent down. It was a great disappointment to my family. But at least I can say I went there."

What is clear is that, like Albert Einstein, Benjamin Franklin, Bill Gates, and other brilliant people who never finish school, Ogilvy was restless and ready to move on. The experience subdued him, for a time. A local innkeeper and friend commented on the change from "a boisterous, handsome and almost idiotic great lad" at Oxford to, just 18 months later, "a very quiet, thoughtful fellow."

For the rest of his life, he kept his school report cards as a reminder to do better. He respected academic achievers, especially Baker Scholars at Harvard. And he was proud of his honorary Doctor of Letters from Adelphi College. But whatever Ogilvy achieved in his career does not appear to be a product of formal schooling. He felt his life at school had been a failure and wanted to start fresh. His education was about to begin.

THREE

THE MAKING
OF A SALESMAN

When Ogilvy left Oxford in 1931, Britain was mired in a deep depression. In just one year, 1930, unemployment had nearly doubled. Millions were on the dole. A very bad time for the world, Ogilvy recalled. "Things were very grim. Very difficult to get a job."

He was ready for change, even if he had picked the worst possible time. He felt he had to get away and wanted nothing more to do with higher education, with philosophers, with *educated* people. He decided he wanted to live with artisans—people who use their hands—and found employment as a cook in Paris. Of all the artisan-type enterprises, why a *kitchen?*

A chef always has enough to eat, Ogilvy reasoned to a friend, telling others that he learned about good food from his mother. "When she wanted to know if her children were clean, she *sniffed* us. When dishes were handed to her at dinner, she picked them up and smelled them. I have inherited her nose, and I have a good palate."

In fact, food had nothing to do with it. He needed a job, and his father gave him a letter of introduction to an old flame, Mrs. Will Gordon, who occupied seven rooms in the Hotel Majestic in Paris. Or so he said. Another story is that the introduction came through the parents of some pretty young girls he met at Oxford. Either way, he so charmed the elderly woman that she almost adopted him. Mrs. Gordon was the restaurant's biggest customer, and was able to coerce the head chef—"who wanted a Scotsman like a hole in the head"— to hire Ogilvy.

Many people who succeed in advertising lack college degrees. Instead of conventional credentials, they learn from one or more eclectic life experiences. That would be the pattern of Ogilvy's education, starting with a seminal experience in a French kitchen, where he observed and was taught high standards and leadership.

The Majestic, then at 19 Avenue Kléber, a huge luxury hotel built in 1907 not far from the Arc de Triomphe, was the site of historic diplomatic meetings after World War I. It became a state-owned international conference center and was seized by Hitler for one of the headquarters of the Wehrmacht in occupied France during World War II. After the war, the French foreign ministry took it over. The Majestic is where Le Duc Tho and Henry Kissinger thought they had ended the Vietnam War. It closed as a hotel in 1937 and did not reopen until 1960, two blocks away.

The hotel's restaurant was the best in Paris at the time, commanding the highest rating in the Michelin Guide all through the early 1930s. Ogilvy said Henri Soulé of Le Pavillion in New York told him the Majestic in those years, with its Rabelaisian brigade of 35 cooks, was probably the best kitchen there ever has been. Monsieur Pitard, the imperious head chef, a "terrifying martinet" to Ogilvy, shocked him by firing one chef because he could not get his brioches to rise straight. But the apprentice sous-chef came to realize that such extravagant standards made the other chefs feel they were working for the best kitchen in the world. Working in a great French kitchen was a first step in Ogilvy's postgraduate (or, more precisely, nongraduate) education; Pitard's management style became his model for hard work, discipline, and excellence.

> The Majestic was probably the last hotel in the world to have a kitchen in the grand old manner. I remember my first day there. I was peeling potatoes. And I was standing there like this [lounging against the wall]. Then this chap came by and told me, "Stand up straight: Everything you do here is important—be proud of everything you have to do." It made an impression.

Ogilvy later likened becoming the head of a big French kitchen to becoming the chief of surgery in a teaching hospital—or, by implication, the head of a large advertising agency.

> You have to know a vast repertoire of dishes. You have to be able to discipline a brigade of hot-tempered lunatics. And, rare among chefs, you need sufficient education to cope with the paper work of ordering supplies and planning menus.

Ogilvy started at the bottom, preparing hot bones for a customer's two poodles, but worked hard enough to earn two promotions. He moved up to whisking egg whites for the chef pâtissier, then to preparing hors d'oeuvres, 26 varieties for each meal. Working in underground kitchens ten hours a day, six days a week, by early morning Ogilvy would be soaking wet from head to foot. Entire walls were lined with huge ovens. People ran around excitedly, yelling and using language he found "vile." An angry chef once threw eggs at him; if he stood still for a few minutes, the others called out, "*Quoi donc, rien a faire? Rien a faire?*" (Nothing to do?)

It was exhausting work, for which young Ogilvy was paid seven dollars a week, but it got him out of academia, taught some lasting lessons, and provided him with stories he never tired of relating. And Paris was not the worst place to be. He romanced one of the salad girls, played court tennis, spent free time in Montparnasse, and on a free night would climb up Montmartre to take in the lights of Paris.

Hopeless at the beginning, Ogilvy claimed he found a way to take special care of his patron. Mrs. Gordon loved baked apples. Ogilvy developed a technique in which he baked *two* apples, then carefully scraped out everything with a small spoon and put the insides of both apples into one shell. Mrs. Gordon had never tasted an apple like this. "If I can't have the boy doing those apples, I move out." With Mrs. Gordon standing behind him, Pitard kept him on, and he learned how to cook well enough in about three months.

Ogilvy said that after a year, he got to be good enough that the head chef didn't want him to leave. He retold innumerable times the story of his assignment to decorate the thighs of cold frogs with chervil leaves: "this was not cooking, it was jewelry, requiring good eyesight, a steady hand, and a sense of design." One time he became aware that Pitard was watching intently. An important occasion: the president of France was coming to dinner. After five minutes of ominous silence, suddenly Pitard signaled for the entire brigade to gather around to observe. "That cow," Ogilvy thought nervously, "he is going to fire me, and he is going to do it in front of an audience, like a public hanging." Ogilvy kept working, his knees knocking together like castanets. When he was done, Pitard pointed to his frog's legs and said to the other chefs: "*That is the way to do it.*" Ogilvy called it the proudest moment of his life.

Ogilvy said that he saw Paul Doumer, the president of the republic, eating his frog's legs a few hours later. Then, in a startling non-sequitur, he recounts: "The following week he died." Sometimes Ogilvy would explain that Doumer was shot by a mad Russian. Years later, Ogilvy took a French colleague to the former Majestic building and emotionally pulled him in front of a small window overlooking the basement restaurant, showing him the place where he cooked for the president of the republic. As he told the story, his eyes were wet.

⁓

Although he passed the test as a chef, Ogilvy saw little potential in working long kitchen hours. After a year and a half in Paris, he turned to his brother, Francis, who by this time had an important job with Mather & Crowther, a major London advertising agency. Francis had a good grasp of his younger brother's talents and, not for the last time, steered him in a good direction.

Mather & Crowther had launched the Aga Cooker, a unique and expensive stove found in better kitchens throughout England and on the Continent, and Aga had become one of the agency's largest accounts. Since the initial advertising budget was small, Francis came up with the notion that the best prospects were schools, and the only ones he really knew were the better public schools. He personally composed a sales letter to headmasters of these schools—in classical Greek—that produced dozens of replies, some apologetic they had no master who could read Greek. To these and to others who had not responded, he sent a follow-up letter—in classical Latin.

Francis introduced David to W. T. "Freckles" Wren, then sales manager (and later chairman) of Allied Ironfounders Ltd., the stove's manufacturer. Wren was looking for someone to sell his stoves to restaurants and hotels in England, and needed a man who could speak French to the chefs—kitchen French, just what Ogilvy had mastered in Paris. Wren hired him as a sales representative.

The Aga Cooker ("as British as roast beef and Yorkshire pud" in one description) has an almost mythical standing in many English homes. It was created in 1922 by Gustaf Dalén, a Swedish physicist who felt his wife needed a kitchen range that required less attention and less fuel. Blinded by an experiment that misfired, Dalén was still able to come up with a brilliantly simple cooker: an insulated iron box with compartments that vary in temperature according to their distance from the heat source (initially, coke or coal). No dials or gauges were required. The name came from the last three of his company's initials: Svenska Aktiebolaget Gas Accumulator. The first ads promoted its phenomenal fuel economy, cleanliness ("no fumes, dust or dirt"), and what came to be its defining feature: The Aga was always on ("always ready for immediate use"). It won quick acceptance, even affection, in homes, clubs, schools, and with the British Royal Family.

Ogilvy's first assignment was to save an Aga customer. A club in London had installed the cookers but couldn't figure out how to use them and was ready to throw them out. Ogilvy put on his Parisian chef's uniform—to talk chef to chef, not as a salesman—and went down into the kitchen. Told the Aga could not cook pancakes, Ogilvy poured batter in a frying pan and cooked one side. When it came time to turn the pancake over, he threw it high in the air, the kitchen brigade of 18 chefs watching, put the frying pan behind his back, caught it flat in the pan, and fell on the floor. *And saved the sale.* That is his story, and it might even be true.

He was promoted to become the company's first sales representative in Scotland, selling stoves door to door. The Aga was the most expensive stove on the market. Making cold calls on canny Scots in the depths of the depression could not have been easy, but Ogilvy made sales by showing cooks how to use the Aga, doing the cooking himself if necessary. He offered to give free cooking lessons with each stove, and found plenty of takers.

Ogilvy revealed his sales approach on a BBC television program, circa 1989. In it he describes how he would always go around to the back of the house ("below-stairs") to talk to the cook about the Aga, because if she was not on his side, he would never sell the lady of the house. When he sold more by offering six cooking lessons for three guineas (but free if you bought the stove), Ogilvy learned something about the power of the word "free."

A breakthrough came when he sold an Aga to the Roman Catholic Archbishop of St. Andrews and Edinburgh ("a very sweet old man, the nearest thing to an angel I've ever known"). The bishop asked if it would help if he wrote letters of introduction to all the institutions in his archdiocese. Ogilvy agreed that it would.

> For about four months, I just drove around Scotland, ringing bells at convents and monasteries and schools and hospitals. A nun would come to the door. I'd say, "My name is Ogilvy. May I see the Mother Superior?" "She's waiting for you." I went in and there she was, pen in hand, and signed the order. My sales just shot up. It wasn't always as easy as that—there weren't many Archbishops around.

After a day of selling cookers to nuns, Ogilvy often spent evenings at a boys club in Edinburgh, where he made friends with the probation officer, whose job was to keep delinquent boys out of prison. Ogilvy's assignment was to coach the boys in dramatics. When three of his productions won gold medals in a drama festival, the judge pronounced the director of the plays as "the greatest hope for the national theatre movement in Scotland." Other nights he played cards with a widow 40 years his senior (she fell in love with him, he says) at the boardinghouse where they lodged. Weekends were often at the Dumfries house of his friend Mrs. Murray of Murraythwaite, who impressed him by employing 16 maids.

The experience of door-to-door selling turned Ogilvy into a salesman. "Otherwise, I might have been something quite different. It made me think always in terms of selling things—and nothing else." That "nothing else" is a characteristic exaggeration, but the focus on sales remained dominant throughout his career. Just as many of his views about how to lead an organization were formed in a Parisian kitchen, his beliefs about the purpose of advertising were shaped by his reception at the doors of Scottish households. "No sale, no commission. No commission, no eat. That left a mark on me."

Ogilvy figured it took about a half hour to properly describe the features of the Aga, a lesson he transmuted into a lifelong belief in "long copy"—ads with several hundred words of text presenting informative explanations of a product's virtues. But the larger mark of the experience was a mistrust of flashy advertising and creative awards that have no clear relevance to selling a client's product or service. It led to his embrace of direct mail, with its counting of coupons to verify results. Sales became his measure of "good" advertising, an obsession that only grew over time in reaction to what he saw as ever-greater excesses in the name of "creativity."

So effective was Ogilvy at selling stoves that the company (not knowing of the secret help from his Archbishop friend) asked him to write a guide for the enlightenment of his fellow salesmen. Published in 1935, when he was 24 years old, "The Theory and Practice of Selling the Aga Cooker" became the company's sales bible. In an article about him 30 years later, *Fortune* magazine called it "probably the best sales manual ever written." Not only an amusing classic of its kind, it displays Ogilvy's capacity to draw lessons from experience and the eagerness to teach what he had learned, traits he was later to apply to the theory and practice of advertising.

The 32-page all-text booklet contains advice that can be applied to selling any product. Implicit throughout is the view that the worst fault a salesman can commit is to be a bore. Aga's star salesman cast up tips in memorable images:

> Heat storage is the oldest form of cooking. Aborigines bake their hedgehogs in the ashes of a dying fire.

Although the initial cost for an Aga was high, using it didn't cost much:

> Stress the fact that no cook can make her Aga burn more fuel than £4 a year, however stupid, extravagant or careless she may be, or however much she may cook. If more fuel is being consumed, it is being stolen, and the police should be called in immediately.

Its portrayal of a good salesman may derive from Ogilvy's view of himself:

> The good salesman combines the tenacity of a bulldog with the manners of a spaniel. If you have any charm, ooze it.

In the booklet, the benefits of the product come alive:

> ALWAYS READY. You cannot surprise an Aga. It is always on its toes, ready for immediate use at any time of the day or night. It is difficult for a cook or housewife who has not known an Aga to realize exactly what this will mean to her. Tell her she can come down in the middle of the night and roast a goose, or even refill her hot water bottle. . . . Hot breakfast may be given to the wretched visitor who has to start back to London at zero hour on Monday morning.

Aga salesmen are urged to learn about cooking as well as stoves:

> It is hopeless to try to sell a single Aga unless you know something about cookery and appear to know more than you actually do. It is not simply a question of knowing which part of the Aga boils and which simmers. You must be able to talk to cooks and housewives on their own ground. . . .

The manual suggests using different approaches, from cooks, to men, to children making toffee. It proposes responses to anticipated objections and encourages jokes:

> Above all, laugh till you cry every time the prospect makes a joke about the Aga Khan.

In a BBC documentary just before his death, Ogilvy talked about how the Aga had become part of upper-crust life in England:

> You have to have a shooting stick, you have a spaniel, you send your children to some ghastly boarding school, and you have an Aga.
>   We started selling from the top down; sort of a snob status symbol. I will never forget old Queen Mary coming to have a look at it and someone telling her that one of the royal aunts had been given one free because she had been so kind to us. Queen Mary was furious that this royal aunt had gotten one free because her second son—the Duke of York, later George VI, Bertie—had to pay for his.

Ogilvy was to use snob appeal effectively in advertisements in years to come. He became personal friends with "Freckles" Wren, his Aga boss, and he remained a fan of the stove: "No lousy fancy-pants industrial designer ever worked his will on it; it remains an honest-to-God functional thing."

Most significantly, through his work selling the Aga stove, Ogilvy became a confirmed salesman. He appears to have been something of a natural. Selling door to door taught him how to talk to people without talking down to them. He would later become famous for his admonition: "The consumer is not a moron. She is your wife. Don't lie to her, and don't insult her intelligence." The Aga experience taught him the importance of not being a bore but keeping a prospect interested with anecdotes and jokes as well as facts about the product and its benefits. He took these lessons into advertising—without the jokes.

Whatever Ogilvy learned in the kitchens of the Hotel Majestic or in demonstrating the proper use of luxury cooking stoves, it was not a personal appreciation of great food. The former sous-chef was less interested in haute cuisine than in putting on a show. He might order a plate of ketchup—nothing but ketchup—as his main course, just to make a dramatic effect on the people watching. If service in a restaurant was not instant, he would get up and leave or, childishly, bang his knife and fork on the table and announce loudly, "I want my food. I want my food." A former colleague concurs: "David had little interest in fine dining and viewed food as fuel rather than as a ritual or as the highlight of the day; he would eat whatever was handy as long as it was basic and especially if it was one of his Favorite Four—mayonnaise (from a jar), Grape-Nuts, bacon, and chocolate. He wanted to eat when he was hungry, and he grew quickly irritable if he was kept waiting for a meal."

Dining at Ogilvy's New York home could be equally eccentric if his wife was out. Guests might be served oysters—nothing but oysters—for dinner. Or lobster bisque from a can, followed by cheese and ice cream. "We'll dispense with the main course if that's all right with you." An agency executive took to bringing a sandwich in a brown bag when invited to dine Chez Ogilvy, to be sure of getting something he liked to eat. After working in a great kitchen and selling to good cooks, Ogilvy seldom cooked a meal again or even showed much interest in food. He was interested in *people*—people who had accomplished remarkable things. He consumed facts rather than food, gossip if there were no facts.

Ogilvy confessed to gilding the lily in his account of having been a chef in Paris. Whether or not he was a real chef, he did know the difference between good food and bad. And he knew how to prepare dishes like carbonade flamende (beef cooked in Guinness) and queues de boeuf (oxtail) simmered in red wine.

What he learned about haute cuisine is less relevant than the standards he digested. Pitard once confronted him: "My dear David. What is not perfect is bad."

In the official history of the Aga stove, Ogilvy is cited as "a pivotal figure" in its success. Years later, trying to comfort a man who had been fired, he made the implausible assertion that Aga had "axed" him. "It hurt me something cruel. But thank God it happened—I might still be peddling cookers."

There is no evidence that he was fired, but there was also no chance Ogilvy was going to be a stove salesman all his life. He sent the manual to his brother at Mather & Crowther as evidence of his aptitude for advertising and was hired as a trainee in London. The Aga experience provided a foundation for his beliefs about advertising and instilled in the young man the habit of hard work. And, as he would later recall, when Mather & Crowther doubled his salary, "I tasted blood."

FOUR

WHO WAS MATHER?

*A*dvertising has always been a young man's business. The roots of the advertising agency that became Ogilvy & Mather (pronounced MAY-ther) go back to a British agency founded in the mid-nineteenth century. Edmund Charles Mather was just 27 years old when he started his agency in London at 71 Fleet Street in 1850, soon becoming known as the best-dressed man on Fleet Street. Two years after his death, his son Harley joined with Herbert Oakes Crowther to form Mather and Crowther in 1888.

The advertising agency business was born in this era.[*] Newspapers had carried advertising for 200 years, but its growth had been restricted by taxes: on paper, on each newspaper sold, on each advertisement. As these burdens were removed, suddenly more advertising space became available, and newspapers hired companies to sell it. These companies—agents of the newspapers[**]—were the first advertising agencies, and Mather & Crowther was prominent among them.

In those early days, manufacturers had to be persuaded that advertising would pay *and* that it was socially acceptable, tasks Mather

---

[*] The first U.S. space broker, Volney Palmer, was founded in Philadelphia in 1841. Palmer coined the term "advertising agency" in 1850.

[**] Agents were paid by the newspapers, not the advertiser—the start of the commission system.

& Crowther undertook in a series of promotional brochures mailed to prospects. "Is it 'Infra-Dig' (undignified) to advertise?" rhetorically asked one. NO, it answered: "firms manufacturing articles of ordinary use *cannot afford* in these days of keen competition *not* to advertise . . . otherwise their advertising rivals will outdistance them." NO, witness the success of others. NO, advertising will not compromise their social position: "There are numerous members of the House of Commons, and not a few members of the House of Lords, who are partners in firms manufacturing articles that are largely advertised."

One brochure cautioned against "Wasteful Advertising"— buying space in the wrong publications, failing to capture the reader's attention, including too little or too much information about the product, or using methods not in good taste. In an early nod to consumerism, another brochure observed that women are likely to be consulted on most purchases of advertised goods, and sharp buyers are not likely to be fooled.

Mather & Crowther rode the boom of England's imperial prosperity with clients that were ready for a new way to do business.

> Venus Soap: "Does the work for you. Not a rub in the tub"
> Mellin's Food: "For infants, for invalids"
> Stower's Lime Juice: "As supplied to Her Majesty. No musty flavour"
> Royal Worcester American Corsets: "Ease. Comfort. Elegance"
> H. Samuel's World Famed Watches: "Promptness and Punctuality Pave the way to Prosperity"
> Mother Siegel's Syrup: "I keep my bowels open, and my blood pure, by a daily dose"

Another London agency comes into the picture with S. H. Benson, which later joined Mather & Crowther in funding David Ogilvy's start-up venture in New York. In 1893, Samuel Herbert Benson, then 39, was asked to set up an agency to advertise Bovril, a thick, salty beef extract popular in England. Benson's agency rode its Bovril relationship successfully, even exploring that era's version of new media: "electric advertising"—throwing "luminous" advertisements on public buildings, monuments, even clouds—with short messages like "Cold Night Drink Bovril." Ivory Soap and other clients would follow Bovril into the agency.

Rowntree's Elect Cocoa: "It's different"
Caley's Milk Chocolate: "Delicious and Absolutely Pure"
Virol: "Try it if your child seems to be wasting away"
Coleman's Starch: "The secret of good ironing"

It was not long before there were efforts to professionalize the business with a spate of "how-to" books. In 1895, Mather & Crowther published *Practical Advertising,* and Benson followed with *Wisdom in Advertising* (1901) and *Force in Advertising* (1904). J. Walter Thompson, already established on both sides of the Atlantic, came in with its *Blue Book on Advertising* in 1906.

What Samuel Benson in particular saw was that advertising had no criteria except *sales*. A showman as well as a salesman, Benson deployed promotions that sold goods by making news. Bus drivers gave away free samples of Rowntree's cocoa, for example, and the event was featured in newspapers as "The Cocoa War." In an early gesture to sponsorship, Benson persuaded Bovril to launch a national sand-castle competition for children with prizes presented by mayors of seaside resorts. During the Boer War, grocers posted news from the front in "Bovril War Cables."

Over time, the founders of these agencies passed on and were succeeded by the next generation of management. There was no one in the Benson family to succeed Samuel Herbert. At Mather & Crowther, Edmund Lawrence ("Laurie") Mather, the founder's grandson, succeeded his father Harley as chairman in 1935. A benevolent figure, he presided in Pickwickian style, going around and patting people on the head and asking "What do you do, my boy?" He resembled a quiet, well-to-do English farmer who had come up for a day or two to London to stay at his club.

Both Mathers and Bensons—as the agencies were known in London—had distinguished themselves in the period between the wars. Guinness became the identifying campaign for Bensons— "Guinness is Good for You," "Guinness for Strength," "Guinness Time," and "My Goodness, My Guinness." For Colman's Mustard,

Bensons created the Mustard Club. "Has Father joined the Mustard Club?" caught the imagination, and the joke caught on—music hall comedians had fun with Father's new excuse for being kept away from home. Amazingly, the advertising got people talking about mustard.

In the 1920s, Mathers pioneered generic (non-branded) advertising with its "Eat More Fruit" campaign and its enduring slogan "An apple a day keeps the doctor away." During World War II, when many food products were not available or were rationed, Mathers created ads to tell housewives what food was available and how to make the most of it, helping it win more advertising for basic foods after the war—for bananas, fish, and milk ("Drinka Pinta Milka Day.")

One of the most famous slogans, "Go to Work on an Egg," is credited to the novelist and short story writer Fay Weldon, who started in advertising to support herself and young son after a divorce. Rising at 5 A.M. to write for three hours before going to work at Mather & Crowther, she went on to write more than 50 scripts for theater and television, including the first episode of the landmark TV series *Upstairs, Downstairs,* for which she won a Writers Guild award.

Another who bridged the worlds of writing and advertising was the mystery writer Dorothy L. Sayers. A copywriter at S. H. Benson in the 1920s, Sayers loved working in both worlds and took advertising very seriously. "Nothing in the commercial world could have suited her better than the work she was doings at Bensons," writes a biographer. "She was earning her living by performing her favorite activity, playing with words. Whether she was composing an advertisement for stockings or writing a sonnet or villanelle, ideas still had to be fitted into a neat, predetermined form and expressed with the maximum possible impact." In her 1933 novel *Murder Must Advertise,* Sayers portrays the Bensons agency of her time.

Agencies were becoming known for their creative talents, not just their ability to peddle space in newspapers.

$\sim$

Enter Francis Ogilvy, David's elder brother by eight years and the great influence in his life. More than anyone else, Francis would play a defining role in the incubation of his brother's advertising agency in the United States.

When he answered a Mather & Crowther advertisement for a copywriter in 1921, Francis did not know what a copywriter was, he later wrote, "but I was just the chap they were looking for. So Mather & Crowther took me on at 5 pounds a week." His grandmother learned that Francis was going into advertising and remarked: "Oh well, the boy always wanted to write."

Francis had read classics and law as a scholar at Magdalene, Cambridge, after glories at the Fettes school in Edinburgh. Between Cambridge and copywriting, he had tried schoolmastering ("Discovered I hated little boys and poverty"), the oil business in Calcutta ("Discovered I hated India after having malaria, dysentery, sunstroke and middle-ear disease simultaneously"), and, although he was an amateur actor and had married an actress and his son, Ian, became an actor[*]: "Discovered I hated actors and actresses and continuing poverty."

At Mathers, Francis quickly moved up the ranks, becoming managing director at 34 and then the first chairman who was not a member of the founding family. He remarked: "I discovered that I adored advertising and advertising people and still do. Accepting that life is 'nasty, brutish and short,' I find advertising as good a way of spending that life as any I have come across."

As recent as the 1950s, London agencies were regarded as gentlemen's clubs, and Mathers was still an agency known for its formality, even though "swinging London" was about to burst on the scene. For board meetings, directors wore pinstriped trousers, black tailless jackets, and stiff collars. When a director rang a bell on his desk, a messenger would come scuttling in. There was a waiting room for chauffeurs, who wore uniforms and caps. Francis sat behind a plain desk, with no visible paper or pencils. He had two buttons under the desk; one brought his secretary with a pad and pencil; the other summoned a man with matches and a package of cigarettes, which he would open and put in front of Francis.

---

[*] Ian Ogilvy appeared in over 60 British TV shows, including *The Return of the Saint*, which made him a contender to play the James Bond role at one point.

Office hours were 9:30 A.M. to 5:30 P.M., except in the summer, when they were 9 to 5, so people could get away to play tennis. (Recruits were told they would be expected to work extra hours without pay when the occasion demanded.) Since Francis was seen as stern and standoffish, fellow directors suggested he walk around the agency a bit and talk to people. The next Monday, he got in the elevator, and a young woman got in with him. "Good morning, my dear," he said, apparently with a leer, since such camaraderie was new to him. "Dirty old man," she retorted.

As chairman, Laurie Mather had inherited a firm that was not merely old but ancient in its thinking. He made the right first move to rejuvenate the agency in picking Francis as managing director to replace the man who had been in the job for 33 years. A bigger version of his brother David, Francis was a burly, powerful-looking man, over six feet tall, with a rounder, reddish face and wavy auburn hair. He walked with a strange gait, holding his arms rigidly by his side. A bon vivant, he enjoyed food, drink, and women. Responding to a comment about the many attractive women in the office, he explained that women who care for their appearance are more careful about other things as well. It was rationalization, said David. "That's just Francis's excuse for hiring pretty girls." Francis liked to show off his intellect. For an advertisement aimed at schoolteachers, he wrote a headline in Latin; he also warned writers, "I know we're all very proud of our classical educations, but I won't tolerate *per capita.* It should either be *per caput* or *a head.*"

Francis launched a youth movement that took Mather almost overnight from respectable dullness into a new era, building it into one of the leading agencies in London while also writing some of its most successful advertising. He also created public relations campaigns, once mounting an exhibition on a commuter train to show architects and local authorities the kind of appliances they could get in the brave new world. He applied advertising techniques to labor relations in dealing with the Labour Party in Wales, to convey the economic facts of life to the working people. Tall, dignified, and immaculate, he presented an impressive if odd figure in union meetings, steelworks, and beer clubs but was accepted by the toughest of shop stewards and left-wing politicians.

He was particularly noted for his ability to write clearly and articulately on many subjects, including advertising.

> Many people come into advertising because they want to write for their own satisfaction. Do so. For heaven's sake do so. But don't do it in office hours. Make a synopsis of what you must say and what you need not say. Build the advertisement to the simplest possible structure with the fewest possible bricks. And only when you have done that start writing. The austerity you impose upon yourselves will produce taut, clear, intelligible writing. You will save other people's tempers and your clients will grin like Cheshire cats.

Someone once came upon David reading a letter from his brother. "Francis tells me he has just finished writing 22 advertisements in a morning," he said ruefully. "Lord, it's all I can do to write one advertisement in three days." When it was pointed out that many of his brother's clients were government agencies, he brightened. "You're right. All you have to say, really, is Drink Milk, Eat Fish." He paused dreamily, then added: "Make Love."

Francis tended to blurt out whatever came to his mind and act on impulse. At a performance of the Rodgers & Hammerstein musical *The Sound of Music,* sitting with colleagues and clients, he took one look when the curtain went up. "Christ! Nuns and children. I'm off," he muttered as he walked out of the theater, leaving others to explain his actions to the clients. He listed his recreations as travel, books, the countryside, and international politics, and followed that with a list of abominations: "London, noise, music and my fellow man." He belonged to the Conservative Club.

He was a paternal figure, ran a paternalistic agency, and was adored by the staff. "Part of the problem that David had with us in London," says a Mathers man, "was that he lost out by comparison with Francis." But Francis was irresponsible and drank too much, say his former partners. He was expansive and optimistic, and saw no connection between income and expenses; someone would wait until he went to lunch, gather bills from his bottom drawer, and pay them. He was known to have one or more mistresses, possibly several at the same time, while maintaining two roller-coaster marriages.

Although the brothers were similar in many respects, David, eight years his junior, was in Francis's shadow at the start. Francis had a brilliant school and university career, graduating from Cambridge with honors in classics and law. David did not graduate from Oxford. Francis was already running a big agency when David was still finding his way. Both were clever and witty. Both were snobs and could be prickly at times. They were insatiable questioners, both incessantly asking *why*. They were persistent and driven, working long hours. Francis worked most Saturdays and some Sundays, even if the staff observed more conventional hours. People would come in on Monday morning and find "From F.O." notes on their desk: "You promised in a note on. . . . Pray expedite." Or "I asked for . . . Pray explain why you have not yet. . . ."

Francis was known for his ability to dictate with no notes. His secretary said that to take dictation from him was to be spoiled forever. He rarely hesitated or changed his mind, but if he did and had to ask for something to be retyped, he would apologize as if he had let his secretary down. His standards were high, his pronouncements Victorian. "I don't know how a man of such talent can have the handwriting of a housemaid," he sniffed to one staffer.

Both brothers were good businessmen, with very different styles. Francis held to the English belief that leadership should be gentlemanly and withdrawn, and (the polar opposite of his brother) resisted personal publicity. A shy man who hated public speaking, he had to be bullied by his partners to publish his speech on leadership, "The Seven Pillars of Survival." "I don't want that sort of thing. I don't need my name mixed up with that. Let's just run a successful agency." To Francis, playing the game was more important than winning, advertising was inherently a fascinating job and should be done to the best of everyone's ability, but money and growth were not terribly important—not exactly his brother's attitude.

An instinctive teacher like David, Francis set down principles for others to follow. His "Creed for Copywriters" could have been written by either man.

> Learn your craft, master the grammar. My guess is that before Sheraton and Chippendale started designing furniture, they became master carpenters. Before designing a chair for an old lady, they made quite sure she would never puncture her bottom on the end of a nail.
>
> If you're a writer, pretend you are talking to your wife. Then you won't dare talk nonsense.

> Read ten pages of the Bible or Robert Louis Stevenson every morning before you get up. And thank God on your knees every night that you are not a Frenchman with the thinnest vocabulary in the world.

The brothers had a close but complicated relationship, which David mostly concealed. Ogilvy barely mentions Francis in his autobiography, instead talking about his affection for their unsuccessful father. Some think David was jealous and did not want to admit to any dominant influences. Francis was everything David wanted to be, says someone who worked with both brothers: "He was older and more successful. David came to the U.S. in part to find new ground away from Francis."

By the 1980s, when memories of the founding agencies were but a distant memory, and David's agency was well established as Ogilvy & Mather, people would ask: "Who was Mather?" It became something of a standing joke. The possibility of changing the parent company's name had been discussed from time to time—even David had raised it—but it became more of an issue as other agencies with different names were acquired. When the subject arose again at an executive committee meeting, Ogilvy was ready: "It is a terrible mistake to change a company's name." Slamming his fist on the conference table, "I will fight it with every ounce of my breath." Pause. "But if you do change it, you don't need Mather."

FIVE

LUCRE IN AMERICA

*I*n 1935, David Ogilvy started as a nine-dollar-a-week trainee in London at Mather & Crowther, the agency run by his brother. He was 24. It was his first experience in advertising, and he spent time in every department. One of his first assignments was a marketing presentation to his former employer, Allied Ironfounders, makers of the Aga Cooker. His analysis, presented in a hardbound, gold-blocked book, recommended that the company downsize its large line of cookers and boilers and focus on a limited number of products.

He was less sure-footed with his first advertisement, also for Aga. The illustration, one in the agency's "Old Masters in Advertising" series, was a reproduction of Manet's controversial painting *Le Déjeuner Sur l'Herbe,* depicting a nude woman and two fully clothed men picnicking on the grass. The point Ogilvy was trying to make was that just as the painting shocked people at the time because it broke new ground, so too was the Aga Cooker "revolutionary." While the company refers to the advertisement as "seminal," Ogilvy was soon embarrassed by the amateur analogy and seldom mentioned it.

In London, he shared an apartment in Soho with his sister Christina, went to concerts and balls that lasted until dawn, "skylarked" with girls, attended debates in the House of Commons, and toyed with the idea of running for a seat in Parliament. He cut a dashing figure, going to work in a morning coat with a flower in his buttonhole, like some senior executives of the agency. An American who met him thus dressed was not impressed: "My God, aren't I glad I don't work in an office and have to wear a morning coat every day."

Finally, Ogilvy was ready to start his career—and *work*. He subscribed to a Chicago clipping service so he could get all the new advertising campaigns from America, and copied the best for his British clients. He studied the business feverishly, reading everything he could find. After just one year, the young man had learned enough to write a marketing plan, which he described many years later to his partners in New York.

> In the section on Advertising there is a passage which proves two things:
> A. At 25 I was brilliantly clever.
> B. I have learned nothing new in the subsequent twenty-seven years.

One of Ogilvy's strengths was that he played the same tune all his life. Among his marketing plan prescriptives was this directive from the former door-to-door salesman:

> Facetiousness in advertising is a device dear to the amateur but anathema to the advertising agent, who knows that permanent success has rarely been built on frivolity and that people do not buy from clowns.

～

By 1938, although not yet considered a huge success, Ogilvy nevertheless did well enough to be promoted to account executive and persuade his brother to send him to the United States to study American advertising techniques.

During this sabbatical and subsequent stints abroad, the brothers stayed in touch with a staggering volume of correspondence. They wrote each other several times a week, sometimes twice a day—single-spaced typewritten[*] letters, two to three pages long, occasionally as many as seven pages. On at least one occasion, Francis

---

[*] Transcribed to a typewriter from their handwritten notes.

wrote David a 14-page single-spaced typewritten letter, on many subjects but largely about advertising.

In Ogilvy's mind and plans, London was a way point en route to his ultimate destination: America. He first visited in 1934, at 23, vacationing on a ranch in Montana. Over the years, he professed a grab bag of reasons for his interest in going to the United States: adventure, an admiration for the Roosevelt New Deal, and what he called a "passionate" interest in North America fueled by reading Willa Cather, Edith Wharton, and Sinclair Lewis. He said (with characteristic hyperbole) that he read *Huck Finn* every year and longed to float down the Mississippi River on a raft.

Those were not his only reasons, of course. He wanted to prove himself on his own, away from the shadow of his brother. And *money*. "I figured that the same effort would produce three times as much lucre in America as in little England." Whether due to childhood poverty or other reasons, money was never far from the surface with Ogilvy. And he could be startlingly direct. His first question to the head of a major advertising group was "How much do you make? How much are you worth?" He probed the senior partner of a prestigious law firm: "Do you make a good buck?" He was genuinely curious how an Oxford classmate could raise a family on a professor's salary.

Ogilvy dramatized the poor-me theme on a 1963 interview program. "I have been poor most of my life. I was poor as a child. My parents had five children and their income was less than $1,000 a year." His former colleague, David McCall, on the same program, challenged that characterization. "My impression is that he was a boy from a good family who were in reduced circumstances, which is a far cry from being poor." However one looks at it, it is clear that compared to his peers in early life, Ogilvy was less well off. Notwithstanding that he eventually made enough to buy and maintain a nice château, money was a constant theme. Yet, like royalty, he seldom carried cash, expecting others to handle such mundane matters.

Although he entered advertising to make money, Ogilvy had become interested—*obsessively* interested—in the business itself. He said he had read every book that had been written on the subject, and, as a young man, had reason to believe he would be good at it and would enjoy it. Since American advertising was years ahead of advertising anywhere else, he decided to study the trade where it was done best.

~

Arriving in the United States (in steerage) in 1938, Ogilvy said he wept with exultation when he saw the Manhattan skyline. He came with several useful introductions but no money. NBC gave him the run of its facilities, and he made the rounds of Madison Avenue. "When I looked at Young & Rubicam ads, or heard them on radio, I sat in awe. Those Sanka coffee ads! I was completely swept away by it all."

An introduction from his cousin Rebecca West got him invited to weekends at Alexander Woollcott's island retreat on Lake Bomoseen in Vermont, where his wit and striking good looks made him welcome. The most influential drama critic in New York and a leader of the Algonquin Round Table, Woollcott was the model for the acid-tongued Sheridan Whiteside in the 1930s Broadway hit *The Man Who Came to Dinner.* Woollcott enjoyed inviting people to a place where he could direct the action. Ogilvy's arrival at the island was described by actress Ruth Gordon:

> Bull's motorboat hit the dock and a tall young man with flaming red hair got out and followed his luggage up the path to the breakfast table.
>
> "Livingstone, I presume," said Woollcott and turned to the table. "This is David Ogilvy. David, these are the spongers."
>
> "Good morning," said the new guest, "is there a writing table?"
>
> "What kind of goddam unnatural question is *that?*" asked Woollcott. "Sit down and drink some coffee, better than you or any subject of your government deserves."
>
> "Thanks, but first I must write the President of the Central of Vermont Railroad about that *disgraceful* trip."
>
> Woollcott's interest was caught. "What disgraceful trip was that?"
>
> "This country must *do* something about that roadbed. May I have a sheet of paper? I wish to register my complaint."
>
> "Do you write letters about everything that annoys you? If you're going to spend time in this country, you'll need more pens than the late James Boswell."

The "spongers" included, at various times, actress Ethel Barrymore, playwrights Robert Sherwood and George S. Kaufman, comic actor Harpo Marx, *The New Yorker* owner Raoul Fleischmann, and other literary and entertainment luminaries of the day. Bantering was the island sport. During a lull in the conversation at dinner, Woollcott said in a loud voice, "Ogilvy, you are a middle-class Scotsman with no talent." It was a show; Woollcott became a friend, and Ogilvy saw a lot of him until his death. Ethel Barrymore was one of Ogilvy's favorites; he rowed her on the lake one evening. In New York, he was introduced to the colorful mayor Fiorello La Guardia. He was in heady company.

One crucial introduction was to Rosser Reeves, who became the first of a series of mentors to Ogilvy, a seeker of father figures and a self-acknowledged hero-worshipper. Along with Reeves, Ogilvy later named Claude Hopkins and John Caples as the main influences on his ideas about advertising—views that remained substantially unchanged throughout his career.

More than copywriters, all three men were *theorists* who wrote books expounding on their beliefs. Ogilvy was eventually to write forewords to new editions for two of them and praised the third effusively. When Reeves, who became head of Ted Bates & Company, was inducted into the Advertising Hall of Fame in 1993, Ogilvy talked about their complicated relationship.

> When I came to work in the United States 58 years ago, I was a typical British advertising man of my generation—a pretentious highbrow. A few days after leaving Ellis Island, I met Rosser Reeves. We acquired the habit of lunching together once a week. During those lunches, Rosser talked without stopping and I listened. What Rosser said changed my life. He taught me that the purpose of advertising is to sell the product. And he taught me how to sell. Some people will tell you that Rosser and I were rivals—even enemies. I was his disciple. Bless you, dear Rosser. You taught me my trade.

"This beautiful boy appeared," recalled Reeves, then a copywriter at the Ted Bates agency, of their first meeting. "In those days,

David looked just like Lord Byron. Since he didn't represent any competition, we all opened our doors to him and told him what we knew." ("Rosser's wrong," Ogilvy corrected later. "I looked like Rupert Brooke.")

Ogilvy would go on to credit more than one person with changing the course of his life. There was no overstatement as to Reeves, who reinforced his natural predilection toward selling and introduced him to the thinking of Claude Hopkins, lending him the manuscript of Hopkins's *Scientific Advertising,* which had not then been published.

Hopkins, Ogilvy later proclaimed, is to advertising what Escoffier is to cooking. The most successful copywriter of his time, Hopkins was so valued for his ability to build sales for clients of Lord & Thomas that the agency's owner, Albert Lasker, paid him a salary (in today's dollars) of $4 million. Lasker considered *Scientific Advertising* too valuable to publish, and locked the manuscript in a safe for 20 years. Ogilvy's introduction to the 1966 reissued edition (long since released from the safe) made clear his debt.

> Nobody, at any level, should be allowed to have anything to do with advertising until he has read this book seven times. Every time I see a bad advertisement, I say to myself, "The man who wrote this copy has never read Claude Hopkins." If you read this book of his, you will never write another bad advertisement—and never approve one either.

What Ogilvy so admired was clear in Hopkins's opening paragraph:

> To properly understand advertising or to learn even its rudiments one must start with the right conception. Advertising is salesmanship. Its principles are the principles of salesmanship. Successes and failures in both lines are due to like causes. Thus every advertising question should be answered by the salesman's standards.

In these words, one can see the Aga Cooker salesman ringing the doorbell. Hopkins writes about the importance of offering service in ads, headlines that sell, being specific, telling the full story, and especially lessons from mail order advertising where "false theories melt away like snowflakes in the sun."

John Caples, the preeminent mail-order writer of his day, was described by Ogilvy as knowing more about the *realities* of advertising than anyone else. In his foreword to a new edition of Caples's *Tested Advertising Methods*, Ogilvy wrote:

> Experience has convinced me that the factors that work in mail-order advertising work equally well in all advertising. But the vast majority of people who work in agencies, and almost all their clients, have never heard of these factors. That is why they skid hopelessly about on the greasy surface of irrelevant brilliance. They waste millions on bad advertising, when good advertising could be selling 19½ times as much.*

What Hopkins, Reeves, and Caples were saying only reinforced what Ogilvy had learned selling door to door: Advertising had to be judged on its ability to sell rather than entertain. It should be based on research about what consumers want. In print, it should lead with a headline that offers a consumer benefit. Often it should rely on long text packed with facts ("The more you tell, the more you sell," as he would later preach.).

~

Returning to London after just one year in the United States, Ogilvy was ready to reveal what he had learned about the differences between American and British advertising at the time and to tell his elders precisely what they were doing wrong. "I launched an attack on Sir Francis Meynell, who was then Creative Director of Mather & Crowther," he recalled. "While I admired him as a typographer and as a poet, I thought his advertising campaigns were pretentious nonsense. I was 27, and had yet to write my first advertisement."

Meynell challenged him to a debate. "With some generosity, and even condescension, I arranged that this bright spark (my junior by

---

* Caples had written "I have seen one mail-order advertisement actually sell, not twice as much, not three times as much, but 19½ times as much merchandise as another ad for the same product."

20 years) should meet me in formal debate before the whole staff."
Ogilvy's presentation, remembered as a tour de force, started.

> My ideas about advertising have been completely reoriented during
> the past year. I have experienced the biggest personal revolution of my
> life. I know now that aesthetics have nothing to do with advertising.
> The most important job of an ad is to center all the attention on the
> merchandise and none on the technique of presenting it. Advertising
> has got to sell. And the worst thing about your advertising is that it
> lacks sales punch.
>
> In writing ads, act as you would if you met the individual buyer
> face to face. Don't show off. Don't try to be funny. Don't try to be
> clever. Don't behave eccentrically. Measure ads by salesmen's stan-
> dards, not by amusement standards.

Ogilvy went on to enumerate 32 "basic rules of good advertising," starting with "The proved principles of mail-order advertising
should be applied to all campaigns." He lauded the ability of direct
mail to measure results with coupon returns, and described the benefits of long copy and offering service and the effectiveness of photographs over drawings. "In mail-order advertising there is no palaver.
There is no fine writing. There is no attempt at entertainment."
Ogilvy outlined formulas for writing successful headlines, sales promotion tactics, "rules for injecting readership into your advertising,"
and "stopper" ideas for illustrations: the clinch picture, bridegroom
carrying bride ("and all sex pictures"), famous people, babies, dogs,
and other animals.

"What I have brought back is not just a collection of tricks,"
he concluded, "but a fundamental New Deal. Everything I have
said tonight is elementary, simple and childish. There is nothing
clever about good advertising. It is a question of common sense
and obeying certain proved principles. Tonight I have given you
the principles."

Meynell conceded defeat. Ogilvy "overwhelmed me," he wrote
in his autobiography. "He had the findings of research. I had only
opinions." Ogilvy was sure he was on the right track. "Anyway,
Mather & Crowther—and particularly my brother Francis—
thought so. That afternoon I lit a candle which is still burning 40
years later."

∽

With this triumph, Ogilvy was ready to return quickly to New York to seek his fortune. Since he had little money—he said he arrived with ten dollars, although he checked in at the tony St. Regis Hotel in New York—he had to get a job in a hurry. He seemed always to have connections whenever he traveled; this time it was an introduction to the public opinion pollster George Gallup from an Englishman who started the Gallup Poll in England.

Gallup had made headlines in 1936 by challenging the prediction of the reigning political poll, the *Literary Digest,* that Alfred E. Landon would defeat Franklin Roosevelt in the presidential election. The *Literary Digest* polled by telephone; its circulation was rapidly growing but still not in every home, and the poll results thus favored upper-income households. Gallup used a more representative sample and correctly predicted that Roosevelt would be reelected. The dramatic win made Gallup's name and galvanized interest among politicians and business executives.

Gallup had conducted some of the first advertising research at Young & Rubicam. A lot of his work involved what he called factor analysis, identifying those factors shared by successful advertisements and by those that failed. It was not easy, said one of Gallup's Y&R disciples—they had a hard time convincing people in their own agency to pay attention, let alone clients. By the time that Ogilvy showed up, Gallup had moved to Princeton, New Jersey, to set up his opinion research firm, Audience Research Institute (ARI). Gallup was impressed by his interview with Ogilvy and hired him as associate director, at 40 dollars a week.

Ogilvy came up with an idea to approach the motion picture industry, and wrote his brother that he would like to apply Gallup's methods to measure the popularity of movie stars and pretest stories: "The motion-picture industry is thrashing about in ignorance of what the public really likes. I swear it is possible to eliminate the blind ignorance and false statistics which are throttling this giant industry."

Coincidentally, Gallup had come to the same conclusion, so they went together to scout the terrain, taking the train cross-country, with Ogilvy providing the entertainment. He was one of the best raconteurs, said Gallup. "He could tell stories from the time we got on the train until we got off, and never repeated one." When they arrived, Ogilvy called studios from the Beverly Hills Hotel and said he was Dr. Gallup's secretary. Gallup once asked him why he did that. Ogilvy explained these people were impressed by any man who has a male secretary. "And they are doubly impressed with an Oxonian accent."

Ogilvy arrived with Gallup and, yet again, an introduction, this time from someone he had met in New York: Henry Sell, an advertising man (and the inventor of Sell's Liver Pate). "A very beautiful and rich young Englishman is on his way to Hollywood," Sell wrote the actress Constance Bennett. "He would make a perfect extra man in case you were looking for one. He's definitely not the regular run of Englishman but more the Evelyn Waugh type. Very modern ideas. Unusual and bright. His name is David Ogilvy." "Rich?" corrected Ogilvy. "I had $400."

The team made their first sale to RKO. The Gallup team would measure the popularity of movie stars in terms of their power to sell tickets, pretest film ideas and titles, and find out how many moviegoers had heard of a movie before it was released. Ogilvy, who would be doing the work, discovered that some stars had a *negative* effect at the box office—their names on the marquee repelled more ticket buyers than they attracted. "Their personalities dazzled the producers but left the public cold." He called this top-secret list "box-office poison" and claimed that he had ruined the careers of some of the most famous names in the business. Hollywood script writers started calling him the "Gallup Gestapo."

As time went on, other producers showed interest—"high muck-a-mucks, who were more interesting than the movie stars," said Ogilvy. And it was he, not Gallup, who was dealing with them. "There was I, going to Hollywood all the time, and dealing with big shots like David Selznick and Sam Goldwyn. I was *dealing* with them. I had meetings with them, alone! I was on the telephone with them all the time. For that Gallup was paying me 40 bucks a week!"

Ogilvy saw himself as a champion of viewers he felt were overlooked. The motion picture audience is *broader-based* than the legitimate theater audience, he wrote in one report. "A play can succeed on Broadway or [London's] Shaftsbury Avenue provided it appeals to the upper income levels, but the present organization of motion picture distribution demands that any story which is to succeed on the screen must appeal to *all* income levels." To keep abreast of the market, Ogilvy had to go to the movies three to four times a week, an experience that had such an effect that he almost never went again.

Although Gallup got much of the credit for a book they co-authored on their movie studies, it was Ogilvy who did most of the work. For three years, from 1939 to 1942, he was the contact between the Gallup organization and Hollywood, writing the reports on 467 nationwide surveys. He interpreted ARI's methods and data to the film industry and relished the opportunity to make sweeping generalizations about American filmgoers, although, as Susan Ohmer notes in *George Gallup in Hollywood,* Ogilvy himself was a recent immigrant to the United States.

He reminded studio executives that most Americans could not afford the moguls' favorite pastimes. "When RKO proposed setting a film at a racetrack," writes Ohmer, "Ogilvy chided executives that while going to the races may be one of their favorite activities, most Americans preferred football or baseball games." That does not mean that he had the common touch. In a report about *The Corn Is Green,* he sniffed: "We can only report the comments recorded by our interviewers, without attempting to justify their tastes." He referred to the "nether segments" that liked Abbott and Costello and the "proletarian admirers" of George Raft.

Ogilvy predicted the importance of the teen market for movies and felt that one of ARI's most important discoveries was that people under 30 bought 65 percent of all tickets, and people under 20 accounted for half of that number. Until that time, there had been a tendency to dismiss the adolescent market. ARI's research helped the careers of younger performers, but it often demeaned older ones. Noting that Irene Dunne was older than 76 percent of all filmgoers, Ogilvy wrote that watching her in a drama of emotional development is "approximately equivalent to watching the emotional development of one's aunt. The aunt can be very funny or amusing in a comedy situation, but it is embarrassing to observe her in a serious clinch." Whether Ogilvy found the embarrassment in the research or in himself is not clear.

Reports drew analogies designed to flatter clients. In a 1942 letter to Selznick, Ogilvy wrote: "Our function in the Hollywood setup should be the same as that of the Intelligence Department in the Army set-up. Just as Intelligence keeps a stream of facts flowing across the desks of General Marshall and his staff, so we must strive to keep a stream of facts flowing to our clients in the motion picture industry."

Ogilvy developed a theory of self-identification, arguing that "boys want to see boy stars, old women want to see old women stars, sophisticated people want to see Katherine Hepburn and Laurence Olivier." Wisely or not, he cautioned against foreign accents and foreign backgrounds, and urged RKO to make a film based on the best seller *An American Doctor's Odyssey,* because the protagonist "is an *American* doctor." His conviction that U.S. filmgoers wanted to see native-born stars in familiar U.S. settings led him to underestimate the appeal of performers who did not fit into these categories, such as Ingrid Bergman and Charles Boyer. ARI's research also underestimated the significance of female filmgoers and damaged its reputation by predicting that *Kitty Foyle,* which became RKO's biggest moneymaker, would be a flop.

On top of its mixed results with movie predictions, ARI fell into the trap of being linked more closely with New York executives than with Hollywood and its stars, scripts, and actual production. But, through his research and surveys—and evidence that many of his findings were correct—Ogilvy had altered the thinking of the motion picture business.

During his Gallup years, Ogilvy split his time between Los Angeles and his office in Princeton, where he was seen as flamboyant and "purposely eccentric," according to George Gallup Jr. "He made sure everyone knew when he sneezed. He always acted differently from others; he rode his bike to work when others drove." Although he complained about his pay, somehow he lived in a beautiful eighteenth-century house called Mansgrove in a leafy academic neighborhood. His neighbor, Gerard B. Lambert, became a close friend. Lambert had made a fortune inventing a disease called "halitosis" (otherwise known as bad breath) and promoting Listerine as its cure. Ogilvy enjoyed cruises on one of the several yachts owned by Lambert, an ocean sailor.

Ogilvy forever described his work with Gallup as the luckiest break of his life.

> If you ever decide to seek your fortune in a foreign country, the best thing you can do is to get a job with the local Gallup Poll. It will teach you what the natives want out of life, what they think about the main issues of the day. You will quickly get to know more about the country of your adoption than most of its inhabitants.

"David was my strong right arm for years," said Gallup, calling him one of the most talented persons he had ever known. Ogilvy acknowledged his debt, saying Gallup gave him more insights into the habits and mentality of the American consumer than most native copywriters had.

What his Gallup experience did was to make Ogilvy a *researcher*—or, more accurately, someone who *believed* in research. He knew what kind of research he wanted and became a vocal advocate of the necessity and virtues of creating advertising based on quantifiable consumer opinion. "Probably the only other man I would put in the same category as Ogilvy," said Gallup, "was Raymond Rubicam [founder of Young & Rubicam]. These two people made better use of research than any other people I've known. The research gave them a lot of ideas." Ogilvy would later ask Gallup to join him in starting a new advertising agency. Gallup considered it for about a month, then declined and started his own copy testing service.

∾

Landing the job with Gallup gave Ogilvy a new life and the feeling that he could marry and have a child.

When Ogilvy met Melinda Street, he was totally smitten with the 18-year-old student at the Juilliard School of Music. She was tall, slender, and attractive, and dressed in preppy Greenwich, Connecticut, style. No makeup, dark hair, comfortable with herself. She hated him on sight, finding him pompous and stuck up. The next day there were so many roses in her room she could barely open the door. Finally he prevailed on her to have another date. A week later, after just four dates, they were engaged. A very good salesman, observes their son.

Melinda Graeme Street came from one of the first families of Virginia. Her sister had married Rosser Reeves, so Ogilvy and Reeves were now brothers-in-law. A friend was surprised at the match, expecting Ogilvy to marry someone more flamboyant. Melinda was quiet, gracious, and, said one person, "the nicest person on the planet." She had a wonderful sense of humor, and people would cluster around her at parties while Ogilvy sulked in the corner, looking at some prints, because he was not the center of attention.

If Ogilvy came to America for lucre, he found other things, including a family and a fully formed view of advertising. But if advertising and the money it might provide were his goals in moving to America, he would only get there after a couple of detours that sent him far from Madison Avenue for some years.

SIX

THE FARMER
AND THE SPY

*O*gilvy had been moonlighting since 1939 as an advisor to the British government on American public opinion, at the same time he was working at Gallup. In 1942, with the United States now embroiled in World War II, Ogilvy resigned from the Audience Research Institute and went to work full time in British military intelligence, initially in New York. He called it the "Hitler War" and was prescient in recognizing what was at stake. His first client at Mather & Crowther in 1937, the Council of German Jewry, raised money for refugees from Hitler. Ogilvy claimed his threat to resign from the agency stopped it from accepting Hitler's ambassador as a client. He and Melinda supported four refugee children from England while they were living in Princeton.

His new boss in the spy business, Sir William Stephenson, was the head of British Security Coordination (BSC) and the central figure in covert operations involving Britain and the United States in the years leading up to World War II. BSC was to represent all British intelligence services in the Western Hemisphere.

A compelling personality, Stephenson became a model for Ian Fleming's famous secret agent 007. "People often ask me how closely the 'hero' of my thrillers, James Bond, resembles a true, live secret agent," wrote Fleming, who was working in British Naval Intelligence and was fascinated by the cloak-and-dagger world. Bond is not in fact a hero, he explained, but a highly romanticized version of the true spy—and not in a class with Stephenson, a man of "super-qualities," a super-spy and a hero "by any standard."

Fleming drew on Stephenson's intelligence operations for several Bond stories. The giant fish tank at the Hamilton Princess hotel in Bermuda, a BSC station, became the glass wall that separated Bond from Dr. No's sharks. A plan concocted by BSC to rob Martinique of gold, to keep it out of German hands after the Nazis conquered France, led to the novel *Goldfinger*. Bond earns his double-O classification by shooting a Japanese cipher agent in Rockefeller Center, where the BSC's code-breaking operations were based in New York. Stephenson was the source of Bond's martini recipe, according to British Special Operations secret agent Vera Atkins : "Billy mixed the deadliest martinis. Booths gin, high and dry, easy on the vermouth, twist of lemon peel, shaken not stirred." Fleming respected Stephenson's martinis, served in quart glasses.

The full story of how the United States entered World War II is still not widely known. The Japanese attack on Pearl Harbor was of course the ultimate provocation, followed by Germany's declaration of war. Yet America's involvement started earlier, in 1940, on two floors of the International Building at Rockefeller Center in New York, in Stephenson's secret intelligence operation. Nazi Germany had invaded Czechoslovakia and Poland and was moving through the rest of Europe, but President Roosevelt's search for a U.S. role was constrained by a powerful isolationist bloc, popular resistance to foreign entanglements, and the American Neutrality Act.

In Britain, short of arms and supplies and facing certain invasion, a desperate Winston Churchill told his son Randolph there was only one possible solution: "I shall drag the United States in." In the years leading up to Pearl Harbor in 1941, Stephenson led Britain's covert operations in the United States as Churchill's secret weapon. A successful Canadian businessman and inventor, Stephenson was alarmed to discover on one of his buying trips during the 1930s that virtually all German steel production was being diverted to armaments, a serious and worrying violation of the Treaty of Versailles. Churchill, the only one to listen to his solitary campaign to alert the British government, gave Stephenson the job of coordinating an unofficial prewar relationship between British and American intelligence, under the standard diplomatic cover of "British Passport Control."

A small man with piercing blue eyes, the strong-willed Stephenson—Ogilvy described him as "quiet, ruthless, and loyal"—took on the difficult task of combining propaganda for the British cause with intelligence work and counterespionage and, far more hazardous, carving out a working arrangement with American intelligence within the limits of the Neutrality Act. All communication had to be kept secret, even from the U.S. State Department. "If the isolationists had known the full extent of the secret alliance between the United States and Britain," FDR's speechwriter (and playwright) Robert Sherwood commented later, "their demands for the President's impeachment would have rumbled like thunder through the land."

Churchill, a believer in apt code names, knew that the man to bring the Americans into the war must be fearless. "Dauntless?" he considered. Then, to Stephenson, "You must be—*intrepid.*" Intrepid became his code name and cable address as head of British Security Coordination. Stephenson was not a professional spy, nor were many of the people he recruited. His unlikely team was largely comprised of enthusiastic amateurs whose names and faces were not known to enemy intelligence agencies; it included actors Leslie Howard, David Niven, and Cary Grant, director Alexander Korda, author Roald Dahl (who would later assist on a history of BSC), and Noel Coward, whose disguise was to be . . . Noel Coward. "Celebrity was wonderful cover," said Coward. Ogilvy served in the Secret Intelligence Division; his friend and former Aga boss "Freckles" Wren headed BSC's Security Branch in London.

"Ogilvy was perhaps the most remarkable of the younger men to join Stephenson's BSC," wrote Harford Montgomery Hyde in his insider's book *Room 3603*. Recruited by Hyde in 1941, shortly after his thirtieth birthday, Ogilvy said later that Stephenson (like several others he named before and later) had changed his life. He considered Stephenson a man of "extraordinary fertility. . . . It took eleven secretaries to keep up with him."

Ogilvy's history of fragile health had prevented him from serving in the armed forces like his brother, who enlisted in the Royal Air

Force at the beginning of the war but was too old to fly and was working for bomber command intelligence. Later, when David was criticized for not serving, Francis came to his defense: "Despite his robust appearance and rampageous behaviour, David is physically C–3, or lower. He has been a chronic invalid since babyhood, suffering particularly from asthma. He has also a double mastoid on the same ear, which has left him about 85% deaf in that ear. There could never have been any question of his joining any fighting service." Asthma, which started when he was nine, afflicted him for the rest of his life.

At the same time that David was working for BSC, Francis was working in British intelligence. He made a memorable impression on one assignment in Scotland. Hyde talks about Francis arriving "complete with black hat and striped trousers, in a remote Scottish village, and, on asking the post-master if he would accept two parcels of stores, was promptly handed over to the police." Safely extricated from police custody, he went on to serve in a less conspicuous but more influential role. When Churchill became prime minister in 1940, he defined one of the requirements for his staff as the ability to write well, listing among several candidates a professor of English at Oxford and "that man who's writing the bombing reports." It was Francis's reports that Churchill had been reading.

For most of World War II, Squadron Leader F. F. Ogilvy lived in the underground Cabinet War Rooms, not far from 10 Downing Street in London, where he was on watch every night. As he described it, you'd get to sleep at some unearthly hour, the Old Man would come down, shake you and dictate—not verbatim as one would to a secretary, but in broad general terms, outlining what he wanted to say, leaving it to the transcriber to do the actual writing, in Churchillian style. I want a cable to Roosevelt, Churchill might say. Copy to Stalin, copy to the Joint Chiefs of Staff. Then he would outline his ideas. "And have it ready for me at breakfast." Francis said that, when he started this job, he had thought he could write well, and everybody else thought so too. "I realized I couldn't. But by the time he finished shouting at me and educating me, by the end I thought perhaps I could."

David started his new job by attending a course for spies and saboteurs at Camp X, officially Special Training School 103, a top-secret British training school on the north shore of Lake Ontario in Canada. There he said he was taught the tricks of the trade: how to follow people without being observed, how to blow up bridges, how to kill a man with his bare hands. People who knew him to be something of a physical coward were amused by this and by his claim that he learned how to cripple police dogs by grabbing their front legs and tearing their chests apart. Confronted by a police dog, says a former colleague, Ogilvy would be gone in a flash. He would employ other talents.

Like his brother, David also learned something about writing from his time in the intelligence service. Stephenson was a master of the terse note. Memos to him were returned swiftly to the sender with one of three words written at the top of the page: YES, NO, or SPEAK, meaning to come see him. Asked to identify his source for a report that a Japanese attack was expected on Pearl Harbor, Stephenson responded: "The President of the United States," a still controversial allegation. Ogilvy later directed his agency's newsletter to publish Churchill's 1941 memo to the First Lord of the Admiralty: "Pray state this day, on one side of a sheet of paper, how the Royal Navy is being adapted to meet the conditions of modern warfare." It was Ogilvy's model of clarity and brevity.

Instead of being parachuted behind enemy lines, as he expected (or, more likely, feared), Ogilvy was placed in charge of collecting economic information from Latin America, to assist BSC agents in foiling businessmen known to be working against the Allies by supplying Hitler with strategic materials. He helped develop "black lists" of profitable German and Italian businesses that could provide money, help, or information, possibly even spying. In every Latin American country, there were prosperous Germans who went to dinner parties and saluted "Heil, Hitler" when they came in. The Mexicans thought Hitler was *fantastico*. "Heil, Hitler. *Fantastico*."

Ogilvy's experience with Gallup was particularly valuable to Stephenson, who commissioned a series of polls to analyze U.S. public opinion toward Britain. The results countered isolationist doubts of British ability and will to win the war. Ogilvy's report, with its cumbersome title, "A Plan for Predetermining the Results of Plebescites, Predicting the Reactions of People to the Impact of Projected Events, and Applying the Gallup Technique to Other Fields of

Secret Intelligence," showed how polls could assess the true strength of political movements in different countries and guide British policy. Although neither the British embassy in Washington nor the London Secret Intelligence Service (SIS) went along with the report's recommendations, General Eisenhower's staff later did pay attention and successfully carried out polls in Europe as Ogilvy had advised.

Ogilvy's basic job, says intelligence expert Richard Spence, was to spin or spike polling information considered harmful (or helpful) to British interests. BSC wanted results that would steer opinion toward support of Britain and the war—front-page stories that showed people were more interested in defeating Hitler than staying out of war—and make sure the polls told people what they wanted them to hear. Espionage work sounds more romantic than it was, Ogilvy conceded later in life, although it did have its cloak and dagger side. He sometimes came home from work with a briefcase handcuffed to his wrist.

His effectiveness in targeting pro-Axis operators led to him join the BSC team that helped the United States set up a foreign intelligence service—it had none—that became the Office of Strategic Services and today's Central Intelligence Agency. "At one point, I was giving OSS about 80 reports a day from my sources," said Ogilvy.

But professional spies in MI6 felt threatened by street-smart "amateurs" like Ogilvy. There were efforts to debunk Stephenson, even questioning whether Intrepid was his code name. Ogilvy remained Stephenson's admirer, although he deplored those who exaggerated his boss's real accomplishments. Noel Coward agreed. "On one hand, [Stephenson] was certainly a James Bond-like 'M,' a puppet master cannily twitching the strings, as his 'boys' went about his business. But his real contribution was to lie in his domain of information—information on what the Germans intended to do next, so it could be thwarted." General Bill Donovan of OSS ("Big Bill," as distinguished from "Little Bill" Stephenson), confirmed his contributions: "Bill Stephenson taught us everything we ever knew about foreign intelligence operations,"

Before long, German aggression started to edge American public opinion away from isolationism toward aiding another democracy, with an assist from BSC. Some called it "gentlemen's espionage," and Ogilvy recognized his own wartime service as tangential to the main action. But BSC had helped bring the two countries together—this was the start of the "special relationship" between the United States and Britain—and supported the war effort, as well as helping America build its own intelligence service.

~

Ogilvy's work on economic issues continued when he was named second secretary at the British embassy in 1943. Although he was meeting top figures in and out of government, much of his work was ordinary business intelligence—compiling statistics on U.S. production and writing brochures—and Ogilvy soon had his fill of bureaucratic infighting. He had reveled in dealing with secret documents and personalities on the world scene but bridled at his mundane duties and the politics of diplomacy, and resigned from the staff of the embassy in 1945. He turned down the offer of a permanent job in the commercial department of the SIS foreign office, but continued to be regularly consulted as an advisor. By that time Francis was out of the RAF and back at Mather & Crowther, and the brothers were ready to return to private business.

Unlike other parts of his life, Ogilvy seldom talked or wrote about this glamorous period, practicing what is known as "diplomatic amnesia." He was proud of his wartime work, but he was still under the Official Secrets Act and respected the rule that spies do not talk. He criticized a report that would expose a colleague for his secret polling: "SIS does not make a practice of compromising its friends." He considered Hyde's book "blazingly indiscreet." Keeping notes, diaries, or copies or papers was strictly forbidden; Ogilvy left all his embassy papers in Washington. Names do not appear in the published history of BSC, which avoids identifying individual officers. All the archives were destroyed in a bonfire; only 20 copies of an official history existed. Stephenson kept two, which were later destroyed as well. In his biography of Stephenson, Montgomery Hyde acknowledges assistance from Ogilvy as one of several BSC "insiders."

Perhaps another reason for Ogilvy's lifelong silence was that many former BSC people did not want to be too prominently identified with a British espionage organization, fearing that it might blight a postwar business career in the United States. He did talk about people he met, like the writer Roald Dahl, a young RAF pilot posted to the embassy and then BSC; they shared quarters in Washington's Georgetown district, while Ogilvy's family remained in Princeton. The two men became friends—Ogilvy attended Dahl's wedding to actress Patricia Neal—but they later fell out with each other. Ogilvy called him a "stud" (naming Dahl's "victims") and considered him "arrogance personified."

Stephenson put on record his high regard for Ogilvy's abilities— "literary skill, very keen analytical powers, initiative and special aptitude for handling problems of extreme delicacy," adding "David not only made a good intelligence officer, but he was a brilliant one." This—plus the offers to stay on—confirms Francis's assessment: "David played a full part in this war and evidently played it successfully." Ogilvy himself had a less exalted view of his wartime work. "If I give myself Alpha for the work I was to do later on Madison Avenue, I cannot claim more than a Beta-minus for my performance in Washington."

~

Like so many others, after the war Ogilvy did not know what to do. But before the war, while working with Gallup, he had discovered a place in America that would become his home and workplace for the next several years, and one of his great loves.

> On a fine evening in June 1940, George Gallup and I were going to Chicago when we saw from the train window a group of men who looked like Pilgrim Fathers. Gallup said they were Amish. Three weeks later my wife and I took our bicycles to Lancaster, Pennsylvania, and set out in search of them. After riding for two days, we found ourselves on the outskirts of Intercourse, and there on the porch of a spick-and-span farmhouse, we saw a stack of wide-awake hats. It was Sunday morning and the Amish were having church.

A rich agricultural community, Lancaster had more cows than people; its farm buildings are still among the best maintained in the world. Ogilvy paid a second visit in 1943 and was enthralled. He quoted the characterization that visiting the Amish is like visiting a

very large rural monastery. The local postman found an Amish family who would take lodgers. David and Melinda and their baby son,
David Fairfield, spent every weekend that they could there, escaping
from Washington and the embassy.

Their Amish landlady introduced the family to Annie and Levi
Fisher. For six months in 1944, the Ogilvys lived with the Fishers,
and became lifelong friends. The night of their first visit, a storm
came up and blew half the roof off. Everybody was out mopping
water. Undeterred, the Ogilvys returned the next year and, in 1946,
David used a small legacy to buy a farm on Denlinger Road in Gap
for $20,817. The property, on 81 acres, included a redbrick house
with white shutters.

And, astonishingly, Ogilvy became a farmer. Well, not exactly.
He rented the land and the farm buildings to an Amish farmer. To
Gerry Leszt, who interviewed him for the *Lancaster New Era* soon
after he arrived, Ogilvy was not a farmer but a man who lived on a
farm. He was a local mystery, says Leszt, "a man who obviously had
some wherewithal, a gentleman of leisure, a member of the literati,
very urbane. But we had no idea who he was or what he did, or that
out of this cocoon would fly this butterfly." Ogilvy did let on that he
had come in part to recover his health, although he never specified
what he was suffering from.

On the farm, Ogilvy raised cigar leaf tobacco, the leading cash
crop in the area. In keeping with his new life, he wore an Amish
broad-brimmed hat and overalls with shoulder straps, and chewed
Mail Pouch tobacco. And he grew a short Amish-style beard. "What
are you made up for, David?" asked a friend who later spotted the
bearded Ogilvy on Madison Avenue. "He was then thirty-five,"
wrote *Fortune,* "an amiable dilettante—or so he seemed—with no
career and no very clear prospects."

The Ogilvys were welcomed in the Amish community. Melinda
made friends and went to quilting bees. David was fun—people
would beg him to sing the old song "Michael Finnegan-Finnegan-
begin-again." A self-appointed expert on Amish do's and don'ts, he
advised visitors on customs (don't gawk, no photos); recommended a
children's book, *Rosanna of the Amish,* as a guide to the sect's prac-
tices; and consulted on the Broadway Amish-based musical *Plain
and Fancy* ("no hex signs, no arranged marriages"). He was tickled

that at his first Amish party, the conversation turned to the fact that he and his wife had only one child. "This struck them as bizarre, and a venerable great-grandmother suggested my wife should 'get a new rooster.'" His cousin Rebecca West visited when she covered the Republican Convention in Philadelphia in 1948 and impressed the key people in the town with her fiery opinions.

The Amish call everybody who is not Amish "English," whether they are or not; Ogilvy was, and was called "the Englishman." He drove around town in his Model A Ford touring car, wearing a cloth hat. A friend tells of a dinner at his farmhouse, lighted only by candles, with Ogilvy appearing at the top of the stairs in a kilt. He just stood there, so everyone would have the full effect. Another time, dinner guests got one lobster on a plate—nothing else—and left hungry. Years later, a neighbor recalls Ogilvy floating up the driveway of their house in a big Bentley with pennants on the fenders; it seemed as if the Queen were arriving.

The contrast between flamboyant Ogilvy and the understated Amish could not have been much greater. There was a double paradox: his unstinting admiration of the sect and their views on modern living while conducting himself in a style that was anything but plain and simple. Yet despite his behavior, he still managed to ingratiate himself in the community. Ogilvy claimed that he had become disenchanted with city life and preferred the Amish lifestyle: no razors, no telephones, no automobiles, no electric lights. "I love these people and their way of life. Like them, I prefer driving behind a team of horses, reading by candlelight, eating what you grow, communicating by note. I love their combination of seventeenth-century theocracy and Rabelaisian happiness."

Admiration had its limits. The idea of living on a farm appealed to the showman, but farming was something else. He was not about to keep the records of crops and how they did and was no match for the tobacco buyers, who bamboozled him. And the pure physical labor held little allure. Farming is very tedious, he said later. "The years we spent in Lancaster County were the richest of my life. But it became apparent that I could never earn my living as a farmer. I *worried* too much. I was not physically strong enough to do the work. I was not sufficiently mechanical to keep the machinery in repair. I was ignorant of animal husbandry, which cannot be learned out of books."

As Ogilvy's enthusiasm for farming dwindled, advertising again engaged his interest. He studied it night after night. The Lancaster library got him everything that was published on the subject—books, ads, magazines—which he organized to the extent of drawing up a list of potential clients for an agency that existed only in his imagination. "I remember how my grandfather had failed as a farmer and become a successful businessman. Why not follow in his footsteps? Why not start an advertising agency?" He was 38.

~

Ten years earlier, Ogilvy had started to think about a British advertising entry in the United States. In 1938, on his first foray to the country for Mather & Crowther, he reported that it was time to pay preliminary attention to the case for a New York office. His letter to Francis outlined capital requirements, recognition by industry associations, client prospects, and publicity. He proposed staffing the operation not with Brits but first-rate young Americans who are "more ambitious than [their] British confrere[s]" and willing to take risks.

But David was not yet committed on a choice of career, and sought Francis's counsel. Should he join a company to promote trade between North and South America? Should he set up in New York to represent British commercial interests? Should he return to private employment with Gallup or Young & Rubicam, or return to the foreign service, or join an international service organization like UNRRA, the United Nations Relief and Rehabilitation Administration? In 1945, he had started a trading company with John Pepper, his direct boss at BSC, to market British goods in the States. Pepper ("a very able, very cold man") was president; Ogilvy was vice president and director, but quit after three months. Pepper stayed and made money.

Now advertising called again. Observing that no British advertising agency had a branch anywhere in the Western Hemisphere, he proposed that Mather & Crowther consider opening branches in New York, Rio de Janeiro, and Buenos Aires, with him in a dual role: serving in an intelligence capacity in New York (checking advertisements, promotion materials, and techniques that might be of interest to British manufacturers and a source of ideas for Mather & Crowther) and chasing new business for the agency.

For four years, starting in 1945, David conducted an almost weekly correspondence with Francis, via "sea mail," on a range of business and personal issues, with side notes about their family. "I am reading the Forsyte Saga for the first time. It must have influenced our mother profoundly—she came to think of all Ogilvys as Forsytes." Much of the brothers' correspondence dealt with the prospects for a New York agency.

By 1946, David had made a sale. Mather & Crowther appointed him its paid representative in the United States—with its eyes wide open as to his credentials. As Francis acknowledged to the board, "New York is a city of freaks; there is always room for one of everything."

From a tiny two-room office (for David and his secretary) erupted a blizzard of memos and papers, including a manifesto for the Mather & Crowther London creative department. Ogilvy proposed "Thirty-Nine Rules" for headlines, body copy, illustrations, layouts, and the use of humor. His paper noted that in the *Punch* summer issue, 41 percent of the ads were "headless wonders—no headlines whatsoever." His first rule made the case that "the heart and guts of every ad is its B.S.P. [basic selling proposition]. Everything else is mere technique." Anticipating resistance to "rules," Ogilvy reasons:

> Even the copywriter and the layout man who regard their work as art rather than as a science can take comfort from the fact that obedience to sonata and sonnet form did not noticeably cramp the styles of Mozart and Shakespeare.

Surprisingly and graciously, the agency's London board endorsed the recommendations of this newly emerged authority and credited Ogilvy with having "devoted three years and an incredible amount of ingenuity" to dig through evidence on both sides of the Atlantic as to the factors that determine the effectiveness of advertisements. With his paper, Ogilvy took credit for reorienting Francis's agency away from "poetry, typography and nonsense" and "an opportunity to patronize fine writers, modern writers and typographers." He sent a copy to Reeves, expressing his gratitude to his "kindergarten instructor."

Ogilvy sold the farm in 1948 for $35,000, a $14,000 gain after two years, and bought a house in Old Greenwich, Connecticut. By the end of his sojourn, the fresh air—with "a touch of horse manure," adds Gerry Leszt—had worked and he had regained his health. Why did he return to the city? *Lucre,* he replied, sighing.

∾

By the fall of 1947, nine years after his initial proposal, plans for a U.S. agency were being actively discussed, with Ogilvy putting forth the unlikely notion that he might prefer *not* to be a part but would perhaps remain independent or join an American agency. But he was confident the new agency would succeed:

> To those of you who are scared by the idea of a New York agency: England must export or starve. If England can export textiles and cars and whisky and chartered accountants, why not also advertising agents? It is, of course, ridiculous to maintain that the tin-pot American agencies which are now handling most of the British advertising in the United States are superior to S. H. Benson Ltd. or Mather & Crowther Ltd.; they are not in the same street.

By early 1948, Ogilvy had ceased being coy about joining the venture, known in its formative stage as "Benson & Mather," representing the two sponsoring English agencies. He had met S. H. Benson's chairman Bobby Bevan while Beven was attached to the Royal Navy and both men were serving at the embassy in Washington. Now Bensons (the largest British agency) was ready to consider a joint venture with Mather & Crowther (number five in the United Kingdom) with the former pollster-spy-farmer as their point man in the colonies.

The driving force in its creation, Ogilvy would not be its leader. Whatever he had learned in diligent self-education was seen as largely theoretical by the British partners, who insisted that he hire an experienced American to be his boss as a condition of backing the plan. Ogilvy had "no clue" about the agency business, said one of his early associates. His brother put it more gently: "If David had more experience in a really responsible position in an agency, I would have no hesitation in going ahead, since I have great confidence in his ability. But I do feel that at his age, and with his experience, he is more properly cast for the role of No. 2."

In 1939, during his Gallup research years, Ogilvy had written an article for *The Nielsen Researcher,* naming 11 men to his "All-Time All-American Agency Team," with Raymond Rubicam as chairman. As twelfth man, he nominated Rosser Reeves. "He is going places, or my name is not David Ogilvy." Now Reeves, a rising star at Ted Bates & Company (and his brother-in-law), was his first choice for president for his new agency. "I question whether you could find any American advertising executive with a more coherent concept of his business or a more profound conviction of its inevitable success," David wrote to Francis. "Let him write the ticket." To Reeves he wrote: "We want you BAD."

When Reeves declined, after meetings in London and New York, Ogilvy found Anderson F. Hewitt, a seasoned account supervisor with J. Walter Thompson in Chicago. A Navy veteran and Princeton graduate, Andy Hewitt was a typical sociable advertising man of the period. Highly charged and unpredictable, he was considered a "likeable nut." Some remember him as the first man who wore tas-seled loafers, others that he dictated letters while having his hair cut. But he "knew everybody" and knew the business, and his top-drawer social connections went down well with Ogilvy.

Ogilvy would be number two and the representative of the English interests, at a salary of $12,000—as soon as the operation could afford it. Until then, he was asked to make do on his $6,000 salary from Mathers for serving as its U.S. representative. A retainer to "run errands," in his words.

D-Day for the British invasion of the United States was set for the following year. With Wing Commander Francis Ogilvy (he had been promoted from Squadron Leader) and Royal Navy Captain Bobby Bevan directing the action, it is hardly surprising they sought a military style code name for their beachhead in America. So confi-dent were they of success that they chose the name Churchill had designated for the Allied landing at Normandy: Operation Overlord.

SEVEN

BIG IDEAS

*I*n the post-World II period, national advertising reached Americans through a handful of radio networks and four major magazines: *Life, Look, The Saturday Evening Post,* and *Reader's Digest.* Television was in its infancy; just one in ten Americans owned a TV set. With several strong newspapers in every major city, it was still largely a print world. The economy was booming, with a flood of new products coming onto the market.

Advertising had settled into a predictable pattern. The novelist and lawyer Louis Auchincloss recalls this exchange with Ogilvy in the bar of the Knickerbocker Club in New York.

> Tell me, are there any statutes or laws in this country that require advertising to be boring?
> I assured him that there weren't, although I asserted it was one of our oldest and proudest traditions.
> It could be changed, then?

"I was in at the birth of a new age," Auchincloss remembers concluding.

∽

Operation Overlord established its beachhead in America on September 1, 1948, as Hewitt, Ogilvy, Benson & Mather, Inc. The British sponsors, Mather & Crowther and S. H. Benson, each put in

$40,000 as preferred stock and held control. Anderson Hewitt, the new agency's president, mortgaged his home and put in $14,000. Ogilvy came up with $6,000, for a total of $100,000. He would be secretary, treasurer, and research director.

Since it was obvious that neither of the principals had the qualifications to run the creative end of things—the actual copy and art—that kind of talent would have to be hired. The agency's charter was to assist British clients in the United States. The London partners disagreed about whether the new agency could hope to flourish exclusively on British clients. It was decided that the new company would devote itself to British interests but not refuse any American account offered.

HOBM opened for business at 345 Madison Avenue, across from Brooks Brothers, Madison Avenue's outfitter. *The Man in the Gray Flannel Suit,* a 1950s novel (and movie) about a public relations man, reflected the style of the period. The most striking furnishing of Ogilvy's office was not the two large Audubon prints but a set of green and red lights outside his office door indicating either it was OK to walk in or Do Not Enter, if he did not wish to be disturbed.

It was David against Goliath: a start-up British outpost against dozens of major agencies with established pedigrees. A handful of tiny overseas accounts with unfamiliar names. Minimal funding, an unproven president, and a brash research director with lots of theories but no practical experience in advertising. Not exactly a sure bet. Ogilvy understood it would be a tough struggle to carve out a niche in the United States, but he put up a brave front and, on the day the agency opened, outlined his goals in a bold memo.

> This is a new agency, struggling for its life. For some time, we shall all be overworked and underpaid.
>
> Our main object is to provide a pleasant living for the people who work with us. Next comes profit.
>
> In hiring, the emphasis will be on youth. We are looking for young Turks. I have no use for toadies or hacks. I seek gentlemen with brains.
>
> Agencies are as big as they deserve to be. We are starting this one on a shoestring, but we are going to make it a great agency before 1960.

Ogilvy often talked about a list he set down at the outset, of the five clients he wanted most: Shell, Lever Brothers, Campbell Soup, General Foods, and Bristol-Myers. A wildly ambitious roster. The only list found in his files names 23 prospects. General Foods, Shell, and Bristol-Myers were on it, at #3, #9, and #17. Not the other two, although he eventually won all five. The name at the top was Cunard, which he also won.

The four starter accounts the British partners sent across the Atlantic spent only $250,000 a year on advertising.* Fifteen percent of that, the standard agency commission, is $37,500. How could the agency survive? Wedgwood China and British South African Airways would never be mass-market goods. Guinness and Bovril were household words in the United Kingdom but unknown in the States with unknowable potential. The advertising would be created by a copywriter and an art director hired for their big-agency experience, but neither was a star or a budding genius. Ogilvy was later to proclaim the preeminence of creative ideas: "Unless your advertising is based on a BIG IDEA it will pass like a ship in the night." In the beginning, the agency's promotion materials said the heart of the operation was copy research.

Ogilvy the research director was taking the train home to Connecticut one evening in 1950 when an idea for Guinness popped into his head. He got off at the next stop and called his office: "You won't believe this, I've had an idea." (He said his family was equally astounded with this first evidence that he could be creative.)

The idea was to borrow interest for Guinness from the fascinating foods you drink it with. Immersing himself in a Yale biologist's book on shellfish, Ogilvy conceived "The Guinness Guide to Oysters," a guide to nine varieties of oysters. The text was by copywriter Peter Geer; the concept was pure Ogilvy.

OYSTER BAYS. Oyster Bays are mild and heavy-shelled. It is said that oysters yawn at night. Monkeys arm themselves with small stones. They watch for an oyster to yawn and

---

* About $3 million in current dollars.

then pop the stone in between the shells. "Thus the oyster is exposed to the greed of the monkeys."

BLUEPOINTS. These delicious little oysters from Great South Bay somewhat resemble the famous English "natives" of which Disraeli wrote: "I dined or rather supped at the Carlton . . . off oysters, Guinness and broiled bones, and got to bed at half past twelve. Thus ended the most remarkable day hitherto of my life."

An instant success, the oyster guide was followed by guides to game birds, cheeses, and other foods that go well with Guinness. More accounts came across the Atlantic: Viyella fabric, the Scottish Council, HP Sauce, *Punch* magazine, and Macintosh raincoats. They were small accounts, but labor intensive. By 1950, the staff had grown to 41.

One of the first and best hires was a treasurer who knew *nothing* about accounting or advertising. Shelby Page had been working at the Metropolitan Life Insurance Company and was introduced to Ogilvy by Hewitt, who had married Page's cousin. Ogilvy did not want to hire Page at the start but was impressed that his grandfather, Walter Hines Page, had been U.S. Ambassador to England during World War I. Page cheerfully agreed to learn something about finance, picked up a book on advertising agency accounting, and took a correspondence course.

What Page brought to the agency was common sense. "I figured my job was to try to keep no more money going out than came in. Sometimes that was difficult with David. The minute we had any profits, David would say he needed a new creative genius." A self-described "skinflint," Page kept the agency out of financial trouble. One of his several duties was doing things Ogilvy avoided, such as firing anyone. Before Ogilvy left for his long summer vacation, he would tell Page who had to go. By the time he returned, the body had disappeared as surely as if a Mafia contract had been put out on it, said one who observed the ritual.

If Ogilvy shied away from firing people, he had no qualms about imposing his standards. "You had to have the hide of a rhinoceros to survive a meeting with Ogilvy, or have done your homework in depth and executed your strategy impeccably," said David McCall, a copywriter in the 1950s and early 1960s. "He was not above the ad hominem method or any other attack that he felt would get through to the sinner. And, like De Gaulle, he felt that praise should be a rare commodity lest you devalue the currency." Ogilvy's insistence on high standards—and his own hard work—inspired a feeling of working in a great place. He was usually the last to leave the office, and people worked weekends without a murmur. It was Camelot, says an account manager of the period

The payoff from installing Hewitt as president came when he delivered two accounts: Sun Oil (Sunoco), then a major company with thousands of gas stations, and, through his father-in-law, Chase National Bank. To get Sun, the agency had to discount the 15 percent commission. Since that was verboten—the full 15 percent was then mandated by the American Association of Advertising Agencies, known as the 4As—money was surreptitiously kicked back to Sun. Ogilvy would later take the lead in changing the 4As from a club to a professional organization. In the meantime, he chose to circumvent the rules.

Even with the Sun account, the agency was running out of money. Page and Hewitt went to Walter Page (another relative) at Morgan Guaranty, who took a chance and lent $50,000 to help them through a shaky time. It was a matter of survival, says Page. "We didn't have money to pay the payroll. The initial $100,000 was gone. It was the difference between life and death for the agency."

~

Ogilvy's first win on his own was the cosmetics queen Helena Rubinstein, to whom he had been introduced by "her crazy son" Horace Titus. It was "Madame Rubinstein" by day, "Princess Gourielli" in the evening, from her second marriage to a purported Russian prince (a marketing ploy, some thought). A tyrant who fired her agencies every year or so, Madame was regarded by Ogilvy as "a fascinating witch." He charmed her and flattered her, crowning her "the first lady of beauty science" in his ads. She was a diminutive woman, only four feet ten inches tall, with black hair in a tight chignon, and looked old but well preserved, like a mummy. With a prominent nose, a commanding manner, and a hard middle-European accent, Madame did much of her business from a Salvador Dalí–designed bed in her three-story house on Park Avenue, its walls covered with portraits of her by different artists.

With a personal fortune of over $100 million, Madame could indulge her passion for jewels. Gazing into a Tiffany's window, she explained: "I just *luff* looking at jewels. They rest my eyes." Her assistant, who did not know jewels, was said to sort them by color: whites, reds, and blues. Ogilvy said she filed them alphabetically: diamonds under D, emeralds under E, and so on. A tough lady who fled Poland carrying her secret formulas, Madame nonplussed burglars who got into her apartment and demanded the jewels in her safe. "I'm almost 90. They're not here and if they were, I wouldn't give them to you. I'm a very old lady. If you want to kill me, go ahead."

"Your ads are too big," she told Ogilvy at lunch, folding a large napkin in half, then half again, then again. "That big. That's how big they should be," also insisting that 12 different face creams be shown in a single ad. Ogilvy overrode the first stipulation and met the second with a headline: "Now Helena Rubinstein solves 12 Beauty Problems." Faced with a parade of creative alternatives before seeing the agency's recommendation, Madame snapped at Ogilvy: "Enough of that crap. Let's see the one you like the best." When she wanted to add points to a 60-second commercial and was told they would make the commercial too long, she had the answer: "Buy 10 more seconds."

She berated Ogilvy for not paying enough attention to her. "You're getting all these new accounts. We're not important any more." He went back to the agency, gathered all the people who worked on her account—writers, art directors, account executives, financial types, secretaries, mailroom people, about 30 in all—and marched them back to her bedroom. "I want to show you how important your account is. All these people work on your business." Madame took in the scene. "They must be very stupid people, because they do bad work."

The work could not have been that bad. A Rubinstein "Hair Cosmetics" ad revolutionized the company's advertising approach, replacing small units with a "news" approach in large newspaper ads.

Within three weeks, a single advertisement brought in orders equal to sales estimates for the next 12 months. No more could run until the factory increased its production. When Ogilvy resigned the Rubinstein business in 1963, the press noted that it was the first agency that had kept the account for more than a year; he held it for 15.

~

Over the next decade, Ogilvy would produce a striking succession of advertising campaigns that put him on the map as a creative force and built his agency into a powerhouse that attracted the biggest advertisers in America. Several of those campaigns would take their place in advertising history. He called them his Big Ideas.

The first involved a small shirt company in Waterville, Maine. In 1951, C. F. Hathaway was not widely known and had never advertised. It was proposing to spend just $30,000 to compete against far bigger campaigns behind well-known shirts like Arrow. "I almost burst into tears," said Ogilvy. Hathaway's president, Ellerton Jette, candidly admitted it would never be a large account and the agency would never get rich handling it, but promised he would never fire the agency and never change a word of copy, promises he honored.

The story of "The Man in the Hathaway Shirt"—with his black eye patch—has been told many times, with slight variations. There is no dispute that Ogilvy, purportedly still the agency's research director at the time, was the sole creator of one of the most famous campaigns in advertising history. He knew he had to do something unorthodox. At some point he mused, "I wouldn't mind an elegant black patch over one eye." But it was far from a "Eureka!" moment. On his lists of photo ideas, it was #9 in one, #18 in another, and he bought several eye patches almost as an afterthought for 50 cents each at a drugstore en route to the photo session. "Just shoot a couple of these to humor me," he remembered telling the photographer, "then I'll go away and you can do the serious job. As soon as we saw the photographs, we knew we'd got something."

The model was George Wrangel, a middle-aged mustached man resembling the author William Faulkner. In one version of his background, Wrangel was a displaced White Russian baron; in another, a noble Spaniard from Málaga. There was nothing wrong with his eye.

The patch was there to imbue the advertisement with what Ogilvy called "story appeal." The reader wonders how the arrogant aristocrat lost his eye. Ogilvy said he discovered the concept of story appeal in a book by Harold Rudolph, a former agency research director who had analyzed attention and readership factors of illustrations. It was the first time shirt advertising focused as much on *the man wearing the shirt* as on the shirt itself.

The first insertion, in *The New Yorker,* cost only $3,176. Within a week, every Hathaway shirt in stock was sold out. The advertisement caused such a stir that it was reprinted alongside articles in *Life, Time,* and *Fortune.* It was imitated around the world. Other companies ran ads featuring eye patches on dogs, cows, and babies. Men and women wearing eye patches turned up at fancy-dress balls. The eye patch became a stock gag on Broadway, on TV, even in cartoons in *The New Yorker.* One showed three men looking at a store window display of shirts; in a second panel, they walk out of the store all wearing eye patches. "For some reason I've never known," said Ogilvy, the eye patch "made Hathaway instantly famous. Perhaps more to the point it made *me* instantly famous too."

The idea was prompted by a photograph of Ambassador Lewis Douglas, who had injured his eye while fly fishing in England. The Man in the Hathaway shirt—always the same man—became so recognizable it once ran with only the photograph—no headline, no copy, no mention of the brand—and was instantly identified by readers as a Hathaway ad. Wrangel, until then a fur salesman, married an heiress and moved to a castle in Spain. Later on, negotiating a model fee, he told Ogilvy, "My dear old boy, it's not the money, you know—that doesn't mean a thing to me. I'm glad to help you out, old fellow. This thing is bigger than both of us."

The copy "tells the truth and makes the truth interesting," said Ogilvy, who poured himself into its writing and described it as "a silk glove with a brick inside it." David McCall called it the clearest, most amusing copy in history. "He wrote it for himself. Who else would have started a piece of shirt copy with this sentence: 'The melancholy disciples of Thorstein Veblen would have despised this shirt.' Ogilvy didn't give a damn whether his audience knew who Veblen was, much less what he thought. It just felt good to him."

Whatever his reasoning, the copy was hard sell, the down-to-earth virtues of fabrics, cut, stitching, even buttons, all sewed up with a veneer of sophistication and wit.

Ogilvy admitted that Hathaway's aristocratic aura reflected the Secret Life of David Ogilvy, a fantasy derived from the classic James Thurber short story, "The Secret Life of Walter Mitty." Ogilvy/Mitty was shown in evocative settings—in a vintage Rolls-Royce, with his collection of butterflies, playing an oboe, conducting in Carnegie Hall, leaving $5 million (and all his Hathaway shirts) to his son, copying a Goya at the Metropolitan Museum, contemplating a $2,000 Purdy shotgun, or playing the organ.

The Hathaway magic started a blazing-hot streak in new business. The agency was creating the "sockiest" copy in America, commented a 1951 industry newsletter. "By now there can be no fluke. It's happened too often."

~

When his London partners first offered him Schweppes, then an upper-crust British soft drink and mixer, Ogilvy tried to turn it down. Its budget was only $15,000, which would produce just $2,250 in commissions, and he was fed up with "shop window" accounts, he told Francis. "The problem is to avoid getting bogged down in trivia." Pressured into accepting the business, Ogilvy's initial creative approach almost lost him the account at the start. He proposed announcing Schweppes as now available in the United States at 15 cents; the client had a different plan for their high-class prestige line: "Plush it up."

The idea of putting Schweppes's bearded U.S. president in the ads came from the U.K. management, says Stephen Fox in *The Mirror Makers*. Ogilvy says explicitly it was his. The true story may never be known. What is known is that Commander Edward ("Teddy") Whitehead was an impressively handsome man, a physical fitness buff with a magnificent dark red, luxuriously thick beard—a quintessentially perfect photographic subject. After what Ogilvy called "a token show of diffidence, which lasted only five minutes," Whitehead backed off his view that it was undignified and "un-English" for the head of a company to appear in advertising and agreed to become the embodiment of Schweppes in the United States and the spokesman for "Schweppervescence."

The first ad showed Whitehead alighting from a British airliner in New York, with bowler and furled umbrella, carrying a dispatch case said to hold the secrets of the Schweppes "elixir," looking more distinguished than any diplomat. "My bathing suit," said Whitehead. "That was what was in there."

"Whitehead's bearded mug has captured the imagination of the American public," marveled Ogilvy, reporting the campaign was an instant hit. Whitehead stopped traffic on Park Avenue. Cab drivers turned and asked, "Are you that Schweppes guy?" People passing on the street pointed out "Mr. Schweppes." In Hollywood, Gary Cooper asked for his autograph. But initial sales were disappointing, and the head office started to get cold feet. After only one month, Ogilvy was told to develop a completely different style of advertising, more hard-hitting, with more price emphasis. He fought back, saying he had come to the conclusion that "Teddy's hairy kisser is a far more important property than any of us realized." He prevailed; the Schweppesman stayed.

Ogilvy personally vetted every detail of the advertising. The ads portrayed the Commander as a distinguished presence, turning up at polo matches, backstage at the theater, with jockeys at a racetrack. He asked Ogilvy of one scene: "Do you think this makes me look like a rabbi?" "You might be mistaken for a rabbi," Ogilvy agreed, "by somebody who saw only the photograph. But there's a headline under it—and who ever heard of a rabbi named Commander Whitehead?" In one ad, a motherly looking type gazes at the Commander and exclaims in the headline: "Bless me, Teddy, you've grown a beard!"

Sales leapt 600 percent in the first six months. Hotels and bars started stocking Schweppes. In many, Schweppes was the only choice if you asked for a gin and tonic. It was, wrote the *Financial Times,* "one of the most successful campaigns for a British product ever waged anywhere at any time—and this in the land of promotion." The agency was doing well enough to run an ad in the *London Times:* "Success of British Agency in America." There was a bit of magic about the upstart; it was winning almost every new account it sought, although Ogilvy admitted that he competed for only those accounts he felt certain he could win.

1952 was a presidential election year in which Rosser Reeves made advertising history with 20-second TV commercials featuring General Dwight Eisenhower as "a man of peace." One of the few on Madison Avenue who supported Adlai Stevenson, Ogilvy told his brother-in-law, "Rosser, I hope for your sake it all goes well and for the country's sake it goes terribly." It went well for Rosser. The articulate Stevenson lost to a war hero. "Can you imagine Winston Churchill allowing himself to be made into television commercials the way poor Eisenhower did?" Ogilvy sourly observed.

Impatient with trying to convey to writers and art directors what he wanted, more and more Ogilvy was *showing* them how to do it, writing the advertising and directing its look—big beautiful photographs (never artwork), usually a one-line headline beneath the photo serving as a caption, plus three blocks of readable text in a simple classic typeface. Ogilvy moved the names of products, usually relegated to logos at the bottom of ads, to the headline at the top.

Clients got "a first class ticket." The advertising reeked of quality: the products advertised, the tone of the writing, the uncluttered layouts, and where they appeared. The tiny start-up bought more pages in *The New Yorker* than all but one other agency.[*] Though the ads ran in *The New Yorker*, their design derived from *Holiday*, an upscale travel magazine Ogilvy admired for the way the magazine was laid out. He reasoned that as people read a magazine, wouldn't they prefer to read an advertisement in the same spirit, without logotypes or copy set in (his main hobgoblin) reverse white type on a solid background. Unreadable, he argued. It never seemed to occur to him that the editorial style of *The New Yorker*, at that time entirely devoid of photographs, bore little resemblance to that of *Holiday*.

Ogilvy was blessed in finding Ingeborg Baton, a Danish typographer. For a small agency, employing a full-time typographer was

---

[*] During one stretch in the 1950s, Ogilvy's ads plus editorial contributions from his cousin Rebecca West and her son Anthony West accounted for an impressive number of *The New Yorker*'s total pages.

extraordinary. Ogilvy was very concerned about the appearance of advertisements, and Borgie was key to this endeavor.* She would never comment on the typography until she had read every word of the copy and understood what the writer was trying to say, no matter how long it took. Although he was not a fan of creative awards, Ogilvy did not mind recognition for excellence in layout, art, and typography, boasting that in 1950, the agency ranked behind only the much larger N.W. Ayer and Young & Rubicam, producing six advertisements judged by *Advertising Agency* among their "50 Best."

$\sim$

Poverty-stricken Puerto Rico, then a territory administered by the United States, presented the next opportunity for the agency to shine. Luis Muñoz-Marín, the governor of Puerto Rico, and his economic ally Teodoro "Teddy" Moscoso told him that unemployment and poverty in their country were appalling, and they desperately needed industry. They had been working to improve conditions in the country; it was Ogilvy's task to relay that news accurately to the American public, especially for manufacturers. Viewing the mission as a higher calling, Ogilvy threw himself into portraying Puerto Rico as "an island in renaissance."

He complained he never got credit for what he considered the best advertisement he ever wrote, an all-text, full page (with a coupon) signed by economist Beardsley Ruml outlining the tax advantages of establishing a plant in Puerto Rico. Fourteen thousand potential employers cut out the coupon and mailed it in; many established factories on the island and brought jobs.

One day Ogilvy observed that the program for industrial development was going well, with hundreds of new factories, but if they were not careful, they would turn that lovely island into an industrial park. What do you suggest? asked Moscoso. "Well, my native island Scotland was always regarded as a barbarous place until Rudolph Bing went to Edinburgh and started the Edinburgh Festival. Why don't you

---

* One obituary said that calling Baton a typographer was like calling Chippendale a carpenter.

start a festival?" Moscoso made a note in his little diary. Three months later, he persuaded the cellist Pablo Casals to come to live in Puerto Rico and start the Casals Festival of Music. In one ad, instead of showing Pablo Casals just sitting there, playing the cello, which Ogilvy said would have been a "visual bromide," the photograph showed an empty room, with a cello leaning against a chair. The evocative scene, described by a creative man as "lit by Vermeer," became a classic.

Ogilvy understood from the start that the underlying problem was the country's image. A study that he commissioned found that Americans thought of Puerto Rico as dirty, squalid, and unpleasant. Under the guise of promoting tourism, the agency went to work on a campaign to correct that image. Ogilvy's charge to the creative team was delivered in a telegram, received on location:

> WHAT WE NEED IS ABOUT 12 IMMORTAL PHOTOGRAPHS. THE ADVERTISEMENTS MUST BE BEAUTIFUL, SPIRITUAL, UN-FORGETTABLE.

He also instructed: "Under no circumstances photograph the firehouse at Ponce," a gaudy tourist attraction featured on postcards.

Ogilvy became emotionally involved in Puerto Rico, saying that changing the image of a country was "the most important thing he had ever done." He considered Muñoz-Marín the best client he had ever known and Moscoso an inspiring leader. When their party was returned to power, he wrote: "Dear Governor: Thank God. Yours ever, D.O."

"David Ogilvy's knowledgeable influence has turned HOBM into a conspicuously successful medium-sized agency," reported the trade magazine *Printer's Ink,* saying he had "become at once the conscience and catalytic agent on Madison Avenue, proving that you need not talk down to the consumer. His place among the great advertising writers of all time is practically assured." This about a man who had written his first ad only five years earlier.

～

More paths were leading to Ogilvy's door. Agencies came with proposals to merge or for him to join them as president. Prospective clients called. Ogilvy said he turned down 20 new accounts in 1955 alone, including Edsel—now considered a joke, but then the first new car to be introduced since 1938 and lusted for by every advertising agency without a car account. He declined to compete not because of any prescience but because the account would be so large that, if successful, it could dominate the agency; if a failure, it could take the agency down with it.

Revlon came to him twice. "Not on your tintype," he said. "I won't go near that son of a bitch [Charles Revson]." He turned down "another SOB" (Louis Rosenstiel of Schenley) twice. "He was a real bad egg." Now that he could be choosy, Ogilvy decided he would never take an account if he didn't like the client personally. He told the head of Thom McAn Shoes he was resigning the account because the executive vice president was "a shit" and treating his people atrociously.

Haloid Xerox came to him with the first plain-paper copier. Ogilvy was not interested in an invention he did not understand, even when offered some of its stock. "It's too small for us," he said. "Go see my friend Fred Papert. He's just starting an agency." Xerox was soon spending $10 million through Papert, Koenig, Lois, and Fred Papert became wealthy with Xerox stock. "He ought to share it with me," said Ogilvy. He returned a 50-page questionnaire from the Better Vision Institute with an icy note commenting on the rudeness involved in expecting busy people to fill out lengthy questionnaires, adding: "P.S. What is the Better Vision Institute?" It turned out to be a good client for Doyle Dane Bernbach.

When Hallmark said it was thinking about firing Foote, Cone & Belding and wondered if Ogilvy might be interested. "You must be mad," he told the huge greeting card company. "They're doing a marvelous job for you, and have been for years. If there's anything wrong with the relationship, tell Fax Cone. He'll put it right." Hallmark stayed with FCB, except for a brief fling with Ogilvy's agency many years later.

~

Lever Brothers arrived in 1957 with two assignments. It was the agency's first packaged goods account, a real mass-market consumer product sold in supermarkets. Ogilvy's biggest win so far both in terms of potential and immediate income, the Lever account put the agency into the major leagues.

For Lever's Good Luck margarine, Ogilvy's Big Idea—totally atypical for a packaged goods product generally promoted on television—was a full-page editorial-format print ad with a provocative headline:

> A challenge to women who would never dream of serving margarine—Lever Brothers defy you to tell the difference between GOOD LUCK margarine and you-know-what.

In three long columns of type, the writer talked about trying to persuade his wife to try to tell the difference ("Our consort was *flabbergasted*") and related how they served it at dinner parties in little French crocks. The advertisement explained the product's nutritional and health benefits, argued that 97 percent of its ingredients came from American farms, and closed with the story of a Greenwich child who ate a quarter of a pound *"straight."*

Even more startling was his next effort for Good Luck—persuading the former first lady Eleanor Roosevelt, still widely admired after the death of Franklin Roosevelt, to appear in a television commercial endorsing the product. She donated her $35,000 fee to the United Nations. "I'm rather ashamed of that ad," Ogilvy said later, "because I exploited Mrs. Roosevelt's innocence." She sold a lot of margarine, even though viewers remembered her and not the product.

With Rinso, the second assignment from Lever, Ogilvy stubbed his toe—twice. The first time was with a magazine advertisement showing 16 common stains (one, he claimed, his own blood) and how to take them out. Perhaps stain removal was the wrong strategy; perhaps the ad should have been on TV; perhaps nothing could have saved the tired old brand. Sales didn't move. Then Ogilvy resorted to an embarrassing jingle to introduce a new synthetic detergent under the famous Rinso soap name: "Rinso White or Rinso Blue? Soap or detergent—it's up to you!" The confused consumer went to the store and bought Tide; the agency lost the Rinso account, its most profitable one.

Ogilvy had a chance to redeem himself with a third assignment from Lever. When he met Dove, it had not been launched. This product is unique, the client told him. It is not soap. It is a *detergent*. It is the first "beauty bar" that is neutral—neither acid nor alkaline; that is big news. That is how I want you to advertise it. That evening Ogilvy had some housewives interviewed and exposed the "neutral" promise to them. It left them cold, as he had expected. He informed the client of the results and asked to see the product's formula. One of the chemists began a long dissertation on the properties of the ingredients, which included stearic acid, the chief ingredient in cold cream.

So was born Ogilvy's biggest sales idea:

DOVE IS ONE-QUARTER CLEANSING CREAM—IT CREAMS YOUR SKIN WHILE YOU WASH.

The first magazine ad was hardly sophisticated—a woman in a bathtub talking on the telephone, using an embarrassing pun to deliver her message: "Darling, I'm having the most extraordinary experience. . . . I'm head over heels in Dove." But the basic idea of one-quarter cleansing cream resulting in softer, less dry skin than washing with soap was insightful and effective beyond anyone's imagination. Side-by-side face tests demonstrated the difference in magazines. On television, cleansing cream was poured into a plastic Dove-shaped mold. Over the years, the campaign helped grow Dove into the number-one cleansing brand in the world.

When Lever bought time on the most popular TV show of the day, *Have Gun, Will Travel* and the program was recommended (appropriately) for Dove, Ogilvy rejected it out of hand. "You can't sell Dove on horseback."

~

By 1953, the agency had 18 accounts and ranked 58th among U.S. advertising agencies. Among the new accounts were Tetley Tea and Pepperidge Farm breads and cookies, both of which were served at afternoon tea in Ogilvy's office. Tetley ads were built around the actual Tetley tea taster, Albert Dimes. If the actual head of Schweppes could establish authenticity, why couldn't its taster do the same for Tetley? The Pepperidge Farm campaign grew from an idea Ogilvy said came to him in a dream—a grocer delivering baked goods in a horse-drawn wagon, a throwback to his Amish days. Other writers turned "Titus Moody," a New England Yankee character from the Fred Allen radio show, into the Pepperidge spokesman. Titus, "Howdy, Ma'am," and old-fashioned goodness went on for years.

Taking on Rolls-Royce in 1960—"over the dead bodies of most of my then partners, who thought that would just fix forever our reputation as being a fancy carriage-trade agency"—was an astute decision. Ogilvy saw it as an opportunity to do remarkable advertising and further burnish the agency's reputation, doing "something better than Detroit had ever done."

Ogilvy spent three weeks talking with engineers and reading everything about the car. He said he wrote over 100 headlines and freely admitted that he did not invent his eventual choice but pulled it out of an article that had appeared 20 years earlier: "At 60 Miles an Hour the Loudest Noise in This New Rolls-Royce Comes from the Electric Clock."* The headline provoked an austere British engineer to note: "We really must do something about our clock." (Later Ogilvy was told that the same headline had been used in a 1933 ad for the Pierce Arrow, and reported this discovery to Rolls-Royce.)

His long, meticulous text was packed with facts: "The coach is given five coats of primer paint, and hand-rubbed between each coat, before nine coats of finish paint go on." The Bentley, made by Rolls-Royce but with a different grille, is bestowed with a famously startling adjective: "diffident." The copy describes the small but important difference: "Except for the radiators, they are identical motor cars, manufactured by the same engineers in the same works. People who feel *diffident* about driving a Rolls-Royce can buy a Bentley." The ad ran in just two newspapers and two magazines but stimulated more praise than anything the agency had produced. Agency leader Leo Burnett judged it to be not only the best automobile ad but perhaps the best ad of all time. People in the business could recite whole paragraphs verbatim. More important to Ogilvy: "It sold so many cars we dare not run it again. Our client's production isn't

---

* The headline now represents Ogilvy in the *Oxford Book of Quotations*.

big enough. Just think what would happen if Ford, Chrysler or General Motors hired Ogilvy, Benson & Mather."

The former Amish farmer now wanted a Rolls-Royce for himself. Page told him, "We just can't afford a damn Rolls-Royce, and who's going to drive it? We'd have to pay a chauffeur." Page prevailed until he took a vacation. "When I got back, there was a Rolls sitting in front of the office with a chauffeur. It was second-hand, 1932 or 1933. A beautiful car." The license was OBM–2, to suggest there was another. Author Peter Mayle, then a copywriter at the agency, remembers trudging down Fifth Avenue on his way to the office on a hot and humid summer day. A Rolls-Royce pulled up next to him, and Ogilvy put his head out the window. "If you work very hard and are very successful, one day you'll be able to go to work in a car like this. Don't be late." With that, he drove off.

Years later, Ogilvy resigned the account and gave as his reasons pressure from dealers to advertise like Buick, the company's "scandalous" service, and its tendency to make "lemons." He reminded the company he had been a miracle worker with a microscopic budget . . . and told them he would continue to drive his "magnificent" Silver Wraith.

~

Growing fame and the agency's success emboldened Ogilvy to do what he had long wanted to do: force a confrontation with Hewitt. When they started out, Ogilvy called Hewitt a genius, and Hewitt thought the world of Ogilvy. Now the two were fighting the whole time. Ogilvy complained Hewitt was not working as hard as he was and came to realize they were hopelessly mismatched in style and temperament. Hewitt spent his time drinking martinis with clients. Ogilvy had a more professional view of the nature of the business. He threatened to resign several times, asking other executives whom they would support in a showdown. Finally, he just walked out in frustration and left others to sort things out. Complicating life was the fact that all the profit came from Hewitt's clients and all the glory and hope of the agency came from Ogilvy's.

The British partners flew over to patch up the rift but soon concluded they would have to make a choice. In spite of his ingratiating good nature, Hewitt never had a chance. At the end of the week, the majority owners placed their bets on Ogilvy. Hewitt gave an emotion-packed speech and departed, soon to join Kenyon & Eckhardt. Hewitt's departure clarified the leadership, but he took several people with him and, as expected, the Sunoco and Chase Bank accounts. The split caused a financial and a PR hit. "It was touch and go whether we would survive," said Ogilvy. "I didn't know if the whole thing would go up in smoke." The company remained standing, as Ogilvy, Benson & Mather.

Faced with lingering insecurities about himself and prospects for his agency, Ogilvy started two years of Freudian psychoanalysis, a fashionable thing to do in the 1950s. "Every day for years I thought [the agency] was going to fail. I was always scared sick. I remember saying one day: if this is success, God deliver me from failure." When the psychiatrist told him he had an anal complex and suggested after a number of sessions that it may be time to talk about his attitude toward sex, Ogilvy exclaimed, "You don't expect me to talk about that, do you?" got up, and stalked out.

The cure was found not on a psychiatrist's couch but in *work*. Ogilvy redoubled his efforts, working deep into the night and virtually full time on weekends. Creating campaigns. Hunting new business. And it was all work. He seldom entertained clients, telling them he "worked his guts out" trying to produce good advertising and couldn't do that and take them to the theater as well.

He walked the halls at night, leaving notes telling people to turn out lights and keep the office tidy. ("I feel a little bit like a slum clearance crusader who builds a new development, only to find the tenants keep coal in their new bathtubs.") Confronted by a comment on his own desk piled high with papers, "Tidy desk, tidy mind?" Ogilvy considered the rebuke and responded: "Sterile desk, sterile mind." He exhorted his staff in memos: "Raise your sights. Compete with the Immortals. Blaze new trails. Soak yourself in research. And never stop selling."

He was everywhere, giving interviews and speeches—proposing a National College of Advertising and Marketing, lobbying against billboards, inveighing against "weasel merchants and purveyors of poor taste." His most important speech, to the 4As in Chicago in 1955, injected the concept of brand image into the marketing world.

"I didn't invent brand image. I pinched it," Ogilvy volunteered. He took the idea from an article in the *Harvard Business Review* by Burleigh Gardner and Sidney Levy and put it into his own sweeping terms: *Every advertisement is part of the long-term investment in the personality of the brand.* The concept was not entirely new in advertising circles, but after putting the spotlight on it, Ogilvy was dubbed the "apostle of the brand image." Brands took on greater importance as products themselves became increasingly similar, and branding became central in advertising discussions, eventually entering the language in worlds far removed from marketing.

Ogilvy was becoming something of a cheerleader for a business that had been seen by some as not altogether respectable. "When Ogilvy talks about advertising, he gives it a dignity it has rarely had in this country," commented the trade magazine *Madison Avenue.* "He strips it of the phony, shell-game, patent-medicine-spieler aura. 'Tell the truth,' he says over and over again." The agency was winning so much new business, Ogilvy could afford to be selective; he turned down 50 clients in 1957.

In 1957, Vance Packard's book *The Hidden Persuaders* delved into the ways that advertising bypasses consumers' rational minds. Ogilvy, said Packard, created "a highly successful nonrational symbol for an obscure brand of shirt—a mustached man with a black eye patch." The book became notorious for its view that "many of us are being influenced and manipulated—far more than we realize."

Surprisingly, Ogilvy seemed to jump on the bandwagon with a piece for *Harper's Magazine,* "A Hidden Persuader Confesses." His confession, however, contained little that he had ever hidden. In the article, Ogilvy "confessed" that he learned that selling is a *serious* business from his days selling door to door.

> You push the door-bell. The housewife opens up—not very wide. You stick your foot in the door and start selling. You don't stand there and sing at her; she would think you were a lunatic. You don't stand there and clown. So today I eschew singing commercials on TV. So today I never write humorous copy in advertisements. You talk to the housewife personally, as a human being, and you tell her what your product would do for her. So too in advertising.

Harper's turned down his article; clients bought his pitch.

~

Despite his reputation for creative brilliance, some feel that the best ad Ogilvy ever wrote was not the Hathaway eye patch but an agency "house" ad under the headline "How to run an advertising agency," propounding leadership principles that apply to almost any business. People were still requesting reprints ten years after it ran. Never content with just writing ads, Ogilvy's larger goal was to create an enduring institution. Although he said he had studied every book on advertising, that wasn't the way he would learn management. He would go to the smartest people and pick their brains.

"In the 1950s, four men were independently trying to build professional service firms linking theory with practicality—Marvin Bower of McKinsey, David Ogilvy, Leonard Spacek of Arthur Andersen, and Gus Levy of Goldman Sachs," writes Elizabeth Edersheim Haas in her biography of Bower. "They would frequently lunch at The University Club and compare notes on their common ambition." Bower and Ogilvy were particularly close. They shared philosophies, spoke of each other as role models, encouraged each other in breaking new ground, and shared an "unremitting drive to achieve excellence," says Haas. "Inside both McKinsey and Ogilvy & Mather, everybody from the boardroom to the mailroom knew and understood what the firms' values were, what the mission was, and 'the way things are done here.'"

Ogilvy studied management at Bower's feet, even admiring his attention to writing. "It is said that if you send an engraved wedding invitation to my friend Marvin Bower, the great man of McKinsey, he will return it to you—with revisions." One such opportunity arose when Ogilvy drafted his statement of purposes for the agency, starting with "earn an increased profit every year," and sent it to Bower for comment. "Marvin gave me holy hell. He said that any service business that gave higher priority to profits than serving its clients deserved to fail." Years later, Ogilvy was thrilled to be invited to address the McKinsey partners, and opened his talk by relating a ditty from his youth:

Who takes care of the caretaker's daughter
When the caretaker's busy taking care?

> I have always wondered who management consultants consult. Now I know. You consult *me*, that's who.

Ogilvy was serious in taking principles of how to run a professional services organization directly from Bower. McKinsey in turn devoted several Saturday training sessions to talking about Ogilvy's philosophy and how it compared to McKinsey's.

By the end of the decade, Ogilvy was starting to build a corporate culture, although that term had not yet come into vogue. Dazzled as a youth by the red of his rich aunt's chic household, Ogilvy adopted the color for the agency, first in his own office and then throughout the office halls. "It felt like the House of Lords after the dingy precincts of other agencies I'd inhabited," says a former copywriter. The culture was communicated in many small signals, some captured in a Welcome booklet for new employees. There were sections on tidiness (nothing on tops of file cabinets), customs (writing the word "percent" rather than using the % sign), and courtesy (answer your own phone.) Also, "Paper clips are dangerous. When they are used to fasten papers together they frequently pick up papers which don't belong. Staples or bulldog clips are much safer and more efficient."

Ogilvy was building the culture as much by personal example as by philosophy. In 1959, the *Play of the Week,* a cultural icon on television, was at risk of being canceled. Broadcast on Channel 13, New York's public television station, the show offered high-quality theater week after week—plays by O'Neill, Steinbeck, Sartre, with top talent. But the ratings were predictably low, and sponsors were dropping out.

Ogilvy was looking for a television opportunity for his client Standard Oil (New Jersey), the second biggest industrial company in the world, doubly attractive because it was headed by Monroe (Mike) Rathbone, a friend. They worked well together. Now they had a chance to do a good thing together. Rathbone wanted a program that would reflect Jersey's own high standards and was not about to share the stage with TV spots for yogurts, bras, and denture cleansers. Ogilvy agreed and told the producers at Channel 13 he thought he could find a single company to underwrite the whole program—but *only* the whole program.

People at the agency and at Channel 13 went to work to persuade the few remaining underwriters to swap their spots for another program or simply cancel, so the show could go on. Company after company and agency after agency responded favorably—with one exception. Lennen & Newell had bought one or two spots for the P. Lorillard Tobacco Company and balked, arguing that they had made a good buy, their sole responsibility was to their client, and they would hold Channel 13 to its contract.

Ogilvy stepped in, calling a Lennen & Newell executive he knew. He went through the history of the project and launched every argument he could think of, including an appeal to public spirit: It was "in the national interest" that *Play of the Week* should survive. The executive said he could not interfere and hung up. The program appeared to be doomed. Ogilvy sat for a moment, picked up the phone, and got the Lennen & Newell man back on the line.

"Go to your chairman immediately. Tell him that our agency will pay Lennen & Newell all the commission that will accrue from *Play of the Week* sponsorship over the next two years. I will wait for your answer."

Within five minutes, the executive was back. "You've got a deal."

Gone were protestations of representing Lennen & Newell's client interests. Gone were arguments about the value of the spots. Gone was any semblance of honor for their agency. But *Play of the Week* survived, its rescue front-page news in *The New York Times*. *Life* magazine said if there were a Congressional Medal for business, it should go to Standard Oil. The *New York Post* credited the decisive role to Ogilvy, saying his heroic save would "enshrine him in the hearts of the literate public at which he has often aimed his commercial arrows." The tone was set at the top.

Ogilvy developed such a reputation for personal integrity that the industry newsletter *The Gallagher Report,* which made a practice of assigning nicknames to agency leaders who appeared regularly in its columns, crowned him "Honest David."

Ogilvy's exposure to Bower and McKinsey reinforced his concept of making advertising a *profession,* with principles and a "corpus of knowledge." Principles were communicated in speeches and memos, institutionalized in presentations, stressed in training, and dramatized in quirky flourishes like the Russian matryoshka dolls, which directors found at their places at a board meeting. Opening the painted, nesting dolls, each smaller than the one before, every director found the same message typed on a piece of paper inside the tiniest doll:

> If you hire people who are smaller than you are, we shall become a company of dwarfs.
> If you hire people who are bigger than you are, we shall become a company of giants.

Hire Big People, people who are better than you, Ogilvy demanded. "Pay them more than you pay yourself if necessary." Russian dolls became part of the culture.

So did Ogilvy's penchant for eccentric terminology. Region directors were "Barons." Group creative directors were "Syndicate Heads." Bright stars with management potential were "Crown Princes" whose careers should be developed. At the other end of the spectrum were "barnacles," who were not contributing or were past their prime and had to be scraped to keep the ship moving. Scraped by others, not by Ogilvy, who was better in principle than in practice when it came to scraping any individual barnacle. When one such barnacle was named to the board (at Ogilvy's insistence), a director commented, "At Ogilvy, when the music stops, we add chairs."

He issued a directive to recruit "high-flyers." "Hot creative people don't come around looking for jobs; they have to be rooted out like truffles, by trained pigs. Do our trained pigs do any rooting? I don't think so." To further the image of professionalism, Ogilvy referred to his executives as "partners."

Following McKinsey's commitment to training its people, he used the metaphor of a "teaching hospital."

> Great hospitals do two things: They look after patients, and they teach young doctors.
> Ogilvy & Mather does two things: We look after clients, and we teach young advertising people.
> Ogilvy & Mather is the teaching hospital of the advertising world. And, as such, to be respected above all other agencies.

Training was made important, to indoctrinate *everyone* in what the agency believed about creating advertising and treating people. Programs were created at every level and every discipline—new employees, mid-level, heads of offices, creative, media, and so on. After the entry level, training was positioned as a *privilege* rather than a duty—one had to get good evaluations to be admitted. Ogilvy personally attended every training program he could—if he didn't have to fly. He toyed with the idea of starting a school of advertising at the postgraduate level and proposed paying the tuition of employees who took courses in advertising at places like Harvard Business School.

On the advice of his banker grandfather, he adopted J. P. Morgan's policies of only "first class business, and that in a first class way" and "gentlemen with brains" as guiding principles for his agency.

~

Ogilvy was also honing his advertising philosophy.

Content is more important than technique: "What you say is more important than how you say it." Remember the image of the brand. Offer the reader some reward in return for her time and attention. Include the brand name in the headline. No "blind and dumb" headlines that require reading the body copy to be comprehensible. Words that "sell." "What you show [in TV] is more important than what you say." Most important: "Unless your campaign is built around a BIG IDEA, it will be second rate. Once you decide on the direction of your campaign, play it loud and clear. Don't compromise. Be strong. Don't beat about the bush. GO THE WHOLE HOG."

Ogilvy had built a strong team of talented writers and art directors, attracted by the agency's sparkling work and his winning personality. By the late 1950s, he was writing very little advertising himself. "For a short period in my life, maybe ten years at the outside, I was close to being a genius. Then it ran out."

His energy was going into the pursuit of new business. He saw his employees as hungry little birds in a nest, waiting beaks open for him to drop a worm down.

At a presentation for KLM, in front of eight people from each side, Ogilvy said, "My people, go home," made the case himself, and won the account. With the Rayon Manufacturers Association, which

had given each agency exactly 15 minutes to make its case before ringing a bell, he asked how many of the 12 people present would be involved in the agency decision. "Why, all of us." And how many will be
involved in approving the advertising?" The 12 members of Committee, representing 12 manufacturers. "Ring the bell," said Ogilvy, and
walked out. To make presentations for the Greyhound Bus account, he
and Herb Strauss of Grey took the train to San Francisco—why they
didn't take the bus is another question. By the second day, they could-
n't stand the suspense and agreed to show each other their campaigns.
Before the presentation, Ogilvy called the Greyhound advertising
manager. "I've seen Herb's work. I know mine. He deserves to get your
account," he stated. With that, he went back to New York.

Nothing was left to chance. "Don't lean back. Lean in," Ogilvy
counseled people on how they should sit while he was presenting.
"Because your body is coming in, you're interested. Whether you've
heard this presentation twice is immaterial." He made lists of targets,
sent mailings, cultivated leads, investigated prospects, tailored presentations, worried over details, humanized introductions of his executives, and presented his agency's work as the actor he was, using
every ounce of his charm.

To win an assignment from Armstrong Cork, the Scotsman
wangled an invitation from the Donegal Society to speak from the
pulpit of an old Presbyterian church near the Armstrong factory,
knowing its chairman, Hening Prentice, would be in the congrega-
tion. Ogilvy sang the praises of "Scotland, my native country" and
recognized the Scottish Prentice, "an industrialist who has contributed so much to the prosperity and culture of Lancaster
County." The agency won the ceiling tile account but lost it a few
years later. "You've come to fire us," said Ogilvy when the bearer of
bad news came. "You're right. We didn't do a good job for you."

As in the early days, not every client had to be a moneymaker.
He took on the $60,000 Steuben Glass account, knowing it would
lose money, offering five reasons: It was a leader in its industry, it
would do no harm for the agency to build "a portfolio of thorough-
breds," the advertising would be read by heads of corporations who
bought Steuben products for their own personal use, Steuben was a
subsidiary of Corning Glass (a target), and "the Steuben office is
only one block away from ours."

As it grew, the agency moved twice to larger quarters—first up Madison Avenue near Fifty-seventh Street, then in 1954, to 589 Fifth Avenue (known by the side-street address of its entrance, 2 East Forty-eighth Street).* Ogilvy's spacious ninth-floor office had windows and an outside terrace along one wall, a counter and corkboard (to display ads) on the opposite side, with a private bathroom off to the side. He sat behind a large, traditional desk at the far end. Visitors had to cross an expanse of red carpet to reach him At the near end, above a red leather couch, was an Act of Parliament clock. Ogilvy liked telling how it got its name: When Parliament voted a tax on watches, the canny Scots retaliated by not carrying watches, and obliging innkeepers installed large, tax-free clocks on pub walls. "My biggest problem is finding time to do everything," he said. "The clock is to remind visitors that time is passing and they must pass along too."

~

One weekend in 1957, Ogilvy went to a house party with Melinda and, in a characteristically impulsive, romantic, exciting, thoughtless act, left on Sunday with another man's wife. His 18-year marriage had been coming apart, and now he was smitten again. A friend commented that David and Rosser Reeves married two of the great Southern ladies, and treated them both badly. Ogilvy divorced Melinda and married Anne Cabot that same year. Melinda, who always adored him, never remarried.

Anne Flint Cabot was beautiful and intelligent; some remember her glamorous photograph in *Life* magazine. Ogilvy described her as a real all-American girl. Telling people he had married Anne Cabot was not exactly accurate, said a friend. "He married Anne Flint, who happened to marry Tom Cabot. But he liked everybody to feel he had married a Cabot from Boston."

The newly married Ogilvys moved to New York City with Anne's three young children, buying a remodeled brownstone at 521 East Eighty-fourth Street, near Gracie Square, a few steps from the Chapin School, where her daughters would be enrolled. The three-story

---

* Where it remained until 1989.

house was furnished with English and Portuguese antiques. Anne was a very good cook, and the Ogilvys entertained in a large eat-in French-type kitchen (there was no dining room) that led out to a small backyard. Beautiful copper pans lined the stripped-down brick walls. "You let your wife do the cooking?" his client Helena Rubinstein asked in astonishment when she came to dinner.

After dinner, guests moved to the living room, some sitting on the staircase, to watch Ogilvy's favorite film, *The 20th Century*—a documentary narrated by his neighbor Walter Cronkite, with documentary footage of Sarah Bernhardt, Emperor Franz Joseph, Rodin, and Renoir. Ogilvy showed it so often the film finally wore out.

Living next door, Cronkite said he often heard noises in the adjoining wall as he tried to read. Little bumps, like a small animal, but he couldn't determine the source and never saw a mouse. The first night he and his wife were invited to dinner, Ogilvy knocked his pipe on the mantel to get the ashes out. "It was a revelation," said Cronkite. "I realized the noise was not an animal—unless you consider him one."

Ogilvy said he walked to work every day, 36 blocks, partly through Central Park. Well, maybe not every day. Cronkite would stand at the window with the curtains drawn. When he saw Ogilvy come out, he would emerge and hope to be offered a ride in the Rolls-Royce. "It didn't work all the time, and I think he caught on after a while, but I did get to ride in that magnificent car. I was pretty impressed."

After his early rush of creativity, Ogilvy took to referring to himself as an "extinct volcano." He may not have been erupting, but he still gave off plenty of heat. He continued to work very hard, taking home two stuffed briefcases. He often left the theater between acts and returned to the office, leaving Anne to get home on her own. "It used to boil Anne," recalls one colleague. Says another, "He was very short-tempered, very focused and totally obsessed with one thing—this advertising agency."

Was he doing it for recognition, fame, a sense of accomplishment? "Many of the greatest creations of man have been inspired by the desire to make money," Ogilvy said. "If Oxford undergraduates were paid for their work, I would have performed miracles of scholarship. It wasn't until I tasted lucre on Madison Avenue that I began to work in earnest." He was administering a staff of 120, going to six meetings a day, occasionally writing copy ("a slow, laborious job"), and at the beck and call of 18 "hydra-headed" clients. "I work from nine in the morning until midnight, seven days a week," he wrote. "I have no time or strength for any private activity. I haven't read a book, gone to a concert, been to a party, or written to a relation for five years."

By the late 1950s, when he was in his late 40s, Ogilvy had come up with most of what he would later count as his Big Ideas, which he defined as campaigns that ran for 20 or more years, like Hathaway, Pepperidge Farm, and Dove. One of his favorites ran just once: "LOST—MY DOG TEDDY. Looks like Lassie." The publicity—it attracted newspapers as far away as Latin America—was amazing. He called it a Big Idea as it got his dog back.

Of all his ideas, the biggest—or at least the most preposterous— was the notion that he could run an advertising agency in America. Here Ogilvy describes himself as of the day he started the agency:

> He is 38 and unemployed. He dropped out of college. He has been a cook, a salesman and a diplomatist. He knows nothing about marketing and has never written any copy. He professes to be interested in advertising as a career and is ready to go to work for $5,000 a year. I doubt if any American agency will hire him.
>
> The moral: "It sometimes pays an agency to be imaginative and unorthodox in hiring."

EIGHT

THE PHILOSOPHER KINGS

*O*nly a handful of advertising leaders have had a view of their business broad enough and articulated vividly enough to be called a philosophy. By the early 1960s, Ogilvy was already on the fringes of this small group, which then included Rosser Reeves, Leo Burnett, and Bill Bernbach. Soon he would become their full-fledged peer.

In the spring of 1962, Ogilvy told his staff that he planned to spend much of his summer at a cottage he had rented in Ipswich, on the north shore of Massachusetts. He said the "hurly-burly" of his daily routine in New York left him too little time to reflect on the future development of the agency. What Ogilvy did not at first reveal was that he had decided to write a book. He would use this sabbatical to put down on paper everything he had learned about advertising: "a textbook, sugar-coated with anecdotes." He was not starting from scratch. For some time, he had been expounding on his thinking in staff memos, speeches, and presentations. This volume would be a full exposition of his philosophy of advertising.

Although 12 publishers to whom he had broached the idea had expressed interest, Ogilvy guessed that the book might sell only 4,000 copies. Seeing it more as a way to attract new business than as a moneymaker on its own, he assigned the royalties to his son for his twenty-first birthday. For six weeks that summer, Ogilvy spent days at the beach, returning home at 4 P.M. and writing until bedtime. The chapter drafts were sent to colleagues in New York to critique.

The agency had prospered during the previous several years, while Ogilvy's reputation had soared. He became a director of the New York Philharmonic, where Leonard Bernstein was riding high. John D. Rockefeller III asked him to head the Public Participation Committee of Lincoln Center, then under construction. He added the Brook to The Century as his clubs in New York. His ads for Rolls-Royce and Hathaway made *The 100 Greatest Advertisements 1852–1958,* Julian Watkins's compilation of advertising classics during the past century. Ogilvy was listed among ten "super-salesmen," along with Albert Fuller of brush fame, Thomas Watson of IBM, and Charles Revson of Revlon. The Rubinstein account had been resigned, but was more than replaced by International Paper, Standard Oil of New Jersey, Sears Roebuck, KLM Royal Dutch Airlines, and three accounts that would change the agency: General Foods, Shell, and American Express.

The publication in 1963 of *Confessions of an Advertising Man* added a new dimension to Ogilvy's success. Sales propelled six printings in six months and put the book on *Time*'s best-seller list. A highly readable mélange of personal history, advertising philosophy, and management principles, the book portrayed a civilized business that was at the same time both colorful and professional.

When asked by an executive at his agency why he had never written a book, Raymond Rubicam replied, "David Ogilvy took it all and put it in his book." Rubicam contributed a promotional blurb ("You will be both inspired and exasperated by it, but you won't be bored") and told Ogilvy: "You are Claude Hopkins enriched with an intellect and an Oxford education and you should knock Claude off the shelf as the classic 'how to' author in the field." (He also chided Ogilvy for not acknowledging Y&R's pioneering work with Gallup, which "you appropriate so freely.")

After describing Ogilvy as hitting Madison Avenue "like a regiment of Royal Hussars," the trade magazine *Printer's Ink* said with *Confessions,* he still fell short of other authors: "With this book, David Ogilvy contributes about as much to advertising as Elizabeth Taylor contributes to London. This attempt to sit in hard covers

alongside Albert Lasker and James Webb Young doesn't make it."
Young, himself a veteran copywriter at J. Walter Thompson, dis-
sented to Ogilvy: "I cheered everything you said, except about
agency compensation. I could name a score of the points you made
at which I cheered." In one review, Ogilvy emerges as "one of the
most lovable rascals in literature."

Leo Burnett called the book "stimulating, rewarding, brilliant,
enjoyable . . . in its way, a great one." Reeves called it "highly literate,
colorful and ripe with advertising wisdom." According to Gallup, it
was "the best ever to be written about advertising and the advertising
profession." PR man Ben Sonnenberg found it "rich in insights and
anecdotage, with many a delicious tale told out of school." Ogilvy's
cousin Rebecca West mysteriously compared it to the joy of "swimming prodigiously in the Hellespont." The director of the U.S.
Travel Service (a client) sent his copy to President John F. Kennedy.
Charlie Brower, head of BBDO, gave it his characteristic spin: "You
help to give advertising the illusion of maturity."

Despite the title, the volume contains few actual confessions, in
contrast to earlier published Confessions—from St. Augustine's in
the fourth century to Thomas De Quincy's nineteenth-century *Confessions of an English Opium-Eater.* But there were enough juicy tid-
bits that few readers felt misled. Amazon now lists 145,000
"Confessions" titles, including *Confessions of an Economic Hit Man,
Confessions of an Ugly Stepsister,* and *Confessions of a Shopaholic.*
Ogilvy told one would-be title imitator, "Dear girl, in the world of
advertising, the word confessions belongs to me." An associate told
Ogilvy he found the title in a Paris bookstore, in the erotica section,
next to *The Story of O.* "There is much to be gained from a headline," replied the author.

There are chapters on managing an agency, getting clients,
building campaigns, even how to rise to the top of the tree. Many
of the lessons are drawn from Ogilvy's personal experience; he
writes that managing an advertising agency is "like managing any
other creative organization—a research laboratory, a magazine, an
architect's office, a great kitchen," referring to his time at the Hotel
Majestic.

If some of the advertising examples are a bit dated, little else feels
old. What makes the book endure (it is still selling) is Ogilvy's ability

to distill experience into principles and state these in pungent and memorable aphorisms.

> You cannot bore people into buying.
> Committees can criticize advertisements, but they cannot create them.
> Compromise has no place in advertising. Whatever you do, go the whole hog.

And the most quoted of all:

> The consumer is not a moron. She is your wife. Don't insult her intelligence.

The final chapter takes its lead from "my Socialist elder sister [Kythé]," who invites Ogilvy to agree that advertising should be abolished. Ogilvy defends his profession but does agree that much advertising, particularly on television, is a vulgar bore—this is its great offense in his eyes. He concludes: "No, my darling sister, advertising should not be abolished. But it must be reformed."

Confessions made Ogilvy a *public* figure, lifting him beyond the advertising community to the general reader. The best-selling advertising book of all time, having sold over 1.5 million copies, it remains the only book on advertising many people have ever read. It became a standard text in business schools, forming the views of thousands of students and luring some to advertising careers. And it led to a lot of new business for the agency.

The triumph of *Confessions* lifted Ogilvy above most of his peers into the company of the small group of thought leaders in advertising, somewhat like the philosopher kings described by Plato: thinkers as well as practitioners, who led with their vision and insights. These leaders contributed to the knowledge of the business, articulated how it should be conducted—and attracted followers.

The four contemporaries who fit this mold—Rosser Reeves, Leo Burnett, Bill Bernbach, and Ogilvy—were all copywriters. Each had his own philosophy of what constitutes good advertising. Their philosophies, distinct from each other in many ways, overlapped in others, and governed the output of their respective agencies, which all prospered on the principles of their leader.

～

Rosser Reeves was known for keeping a message running long after most people would consider it "worn out." A favorite Madison Avenue story tells of a client who remarked that the agency had not changed his commercial in five years, and wondered what the 120 people working on the account were doing. "Keeping you from changing your ad," answered Reeves. Reeves's most notorious campaign was described in the opening of a 23-page profile in *The New Yorker.*

> Hammers pounding horribly within the cerebrum, jagged bolts of lightning striking right to the midbrain—these were the nightmare images that flashed before the eyes of anybody who watched television in the nineteen-fifties and the early nineteen-sixties. The apparitions were imprinted into the minds of millions of viewers on behalf of the manufacturers of Anacin during the heyday of the hard-sell commercial, an art form once all-powerful in television.

It was said that Anacin commercials were so strident and so endlessly repeated that just seeing them was likely to make the viewer's head ache. "And any commercial that had the ability to bring on the very distress that the product it advertises is alleged to relieve is about as hard as a hard sell can get," concluded the article's author, Thomas Whiteside, who told of being regaled by Reeves with other "evocations of successful assaults against the central nervous systems of consumers."

Two years before *Confessions,* Reeves had published *Reality in Advertising.* The book became famous in advertising circles for its advocacy of U.S.P.—the unique selling proposition: "Each advertisement must make a proposition to the consumer. It must be one the competition either cannot, or does not, offer. It must be so strong it can move the mass millions to your product." The advertising that came out of Bates could be abrasive; seeing it over and over made it more so. Reeves was known for explaining his philosophy in the form of a question to his clients: "Do you want to be rich, or do you want to be liked?" He unabashedly described the Anacin commercials as the most hated in the history of advertising.

Reeves was "the most influential theoretician of how advertising worked in the fifties," writes Stephen Fox in *The Mirror Makers.*

Reeves joined Bates as a copywriter and rose to chairman, building the agency into the fourth largest in the world. He hit his peak in 1948, the same year Ogilvy started his agency. Recognizing that TV, poised to become the dominant advertising medium, could do what radio could not, Reeves *showed* stomach acid burning holes in handkerchiefs for Rolaids, threw baseballs against a clear shield for Colgate Dental Cream with Gardol, shot ballpoint pens from crossbows for Bic pens, and trapped tars and nicotine in the Viceroy cigarette filter. He used the new medium in a new way. In the first years of commercial television, advertisers sponsored entire programs like *The Jack Benny Show,* as they had on radio. Bates pioneered the 30-second and 60-second commercial ("spots" in the lingo of the trade) in the intervals *between* programs, and became known as "the spot agency."

Ogilvy and Reeves had a complex relationship. They were at various times student and mentor, competitors, friends, and, if not enemies, at least estranged when Ogilvy divorced Reeves's sister-in-law. Some theorized that Ogilvy wrote *Confessions* to compete with *Reality in Advertising.* Their rivalry was on public display at an awards dinner. Telling people he was going to upstage Ogilvy, Reeves went to the Half Moon resort in Jamaica for a week and returned with a deep bronze tan, which he set off with a white dinner jacket. Asked the next morning how the dinner went, "You know what that Scottish son of a bitch did," Reeves spit out. "He wore a kilt."

Ogilvy always acknowledged his debt to Reeves, in one testimonial placing him in the "direct line of Apostolic succession" from Claude Hopkins: "In 1938 you gave me a typed copy of the Hopkins book. It changed my life. I know it by heart. Every year I give away twenty copies, to wordsmiths. They never comprehend." He commented that he and Reeves had the same patron saint (Hopkins), the same bible (Hopkins's *Scientific Advertising*), and belonged to "the same true church, even if his advertising manners leave something to be desired." Ogilvy rejected an invitation to debate Reeves on "Hard Sell vs. Product Image," saying they did not disagree on the fundamentals of advertising. "We do not often employ the same graphic techniques, but the differences in that marginal area are not important when it comes to measuring sales."

Their respective client lists had a profound influence on the advertising they created. In the 1950s, Bates principally worked for consumer packaged goods products, such as Anacin and Colgate; Ogilvy initially built a roster of image-based clients, including Hathaway, Schweppes, British Travel, and Puerto Rico. Reeves "taught me more about advertising than anybody I've ever known," said Ogilvy. "The pity of it is that I couldn't teach him anything." Reeves retorted, "If we ever get out of packaged goods and into luxury items, I'll be glad to go sit at David's feet and listen." When a trade paper quoted Ogilvy as saying that humor could sell, Reeves sent him a telegram: "ARE YOU GAGA?"

"If the Rosser Reeves model of how advertising works is true," believes Jeremy Bullmore, who headed J. Walter Thompson in the United Kingdom, "Hathaway wouldn't have sold a single shirt. Because there are no claims, nothing repeated." A copywriter who worked with both men says the fundamental difference between them was philosophical. "Ogilvy believed that the consumer is not a moron, she's your wife. Reeves believed she's not your wife, she's an idiot."

Ogilvy himself made no such artificial distinctions. In a taped testimonial when Reeves was elected to the Advertising Hall of Fame in 1993, he gave due credit to his first mentor:

> Rosser taught me that the purpose of advertising is to sell the product. And he taught me how to sell. Some people will tell you that Rosser and I were rivals—even enemies. I was his disciple. Bless you, dear Rosser. You taught me my trade.

~

In the 1950s, when cigarette smoking and cigarette advertising were acceptable, Leo Burnett created what some creative people consider the greatest advertising campaign of the twentieth century. When Burnett got the assignment from Philip Morris to broaden the appeal for Marlboro cigarettes, they had been marketed only to women, even to its red filter (so as not to show lipstick). Burnett crammed the research into his briefcase and came back with a startling conclusion: Turn this ladies' cigarette into a masculine brand. The first expression of this strategy was a series of "real men" with tattooed forearms. This masculine image was soon replaced by the ultimate macho symbol, the cowboy of the western plains.

By the time the "Marlboro Man" went national in 1955, sales had increased 3,000 percent to $5 billion. By 1957, sales were $20 billion, even though the first article on the link to lung cancer had already appeared in *Reader's Digest*. In 1964, the cowboy moved to a mythical "Marlboro Country." After cigarette ads were banned from TV in 1971, the print campaign showing cowboys enjoying a smoke on horseback helped make Marlboro the number-one brand in the world.

Burnett, the head of the biggest agency west of the Hudson River, was proud to call himself a "rube" and boasted he was not city-bred. He had worked as a reporter in Peoria and as advertising manager for Cadillac in Detroit before opening his agency in Chicago in the midst of the 1930s depression. His views about the business were collected in several privately printed books, one titled *Communications of an Advertising Man.*

Burnett and his agency were of the heart of America. Chicago *is* the Midwest, Burnett wrote. "Its ad-making ranks are filled with folks whose heads are stocked with prairie-town views and values . . . our sod-busting delivery, our loose-limbed stand and our wide-eyed perspective [makes] it easier for us to create ads that talk turkey to the majority of Americans. . . . I like to imagine that Chicago copywriters spit on their hands before picking up the big, black pencils." A former employee called it "tugboat copywriting," tugging on consumers' heartstrings.

Burnett was totally involved with his agency's advertising, vetting every piece of copy. He frequently rose at 5 A.M. and worked for two hours before breakfast. The lore was that he worked 20 hours a day, seven days a week, 365 days a year: "He takes Christmas morning off." He was an absolute gatekeeper of quality. Reviewing a new campaign for Joy Light Duty Detergent that showed a burly man with his hands on a jackhammer, Burnett rejected "that goddamn jackhammer" as irrelevant borrowed interest. "None of this advertising will ever leave the agency." When the account man pointed out the ads were overdue and the agency might lose the business, Burnett said, "Fine. I'd rather lose the account than send out this advertising."

He was a most unprepossessing man—short, rumpled, usually with a cigarette hanging out of his mouth, ashes spilling on his shirt.

Some thought he looked like a fireplug. A protruding lower lip on his rubbery face visibly expressed his feelings about an issue; his people referred to the LPI, or lip protrusion index.

One alumnus says working at Burnett was like joining the Northwestern University Alumni Association—all the guys were from Chicago. Leo was not above taking a jocular shot at New Yorkers or "the search for the unique selling proposition, or whatever you want to call it." The agency's down-to-earth personality was captured in bowls of apples placed on all Burnett reception desks as a sign of hospitality and friendliness.

Burnett liked to give products a personality and a character—in many cases, animal characters ("critters," as they came to be known in the trade). Tony the Tiger roared that Kellogg's Frosted Flakes were "GR-R-R-E-A-T." Charlie the Tuna hoped to be caught but was "not good enough" for Star-Kist. The Pillsbury Dough-Boy was soft, cuddly, and fresh. The Jolly Green Giant sold canned peas and corn so successfully that the company changed its name from the Minnesota Canning Company to the Green Giant Company. Travelers flew the "Friendly Skies" of United Airlines.

Burnett made the way he felt about the business clear in a legendary talk at a staff meeting. "When to Take My Name off the Door" began:

> Somewhere along the line, after I'm finally off the premises, you—or your successors—may want to take my *name* off the premises, too. . . . That will certainly be okay with me—if it's good for you. But let me tell you when I might *demand* that you take my name off the door. That will be the day when you spend more time trying to make money and *less* time making advertising—our kind of advertising.

His talk celebrated the fun of making advertising, the passion to do it well, the virtues of "good, hard, wonderful work," then warned against growth "just to be big." If this came to pass, he said, he would *insist* they take his name off the door, and would "throw every goddamned apple down the elevator shafts."

The physical contrast between the rumpled Burnett and the elegant Ogilvy could not have been greater—or less important. Their professional rapport was enormous. The two men formed a mutual admiration society, exchanging compliments and sending each other statements of their principles. In 1954, just six years after Ogilvy went into business, Burnett proposed an amalgamation with Ogilvy's young agency at a secret meeting in New York. Ogilvy considered it the best possible merger, telling his London partners that Burnett's creative work was in a class by itself. Because of client conflicts and problems with the English stock setup, the union did not go through, but the two men stayed in touch.

They spoke the same language, with different accents. Both focused on sales rather than industry creative awards. Burnett had its own Black Pencil Award for sales, deriving from his thick pencils with black lead. In the late 1960s, Ogilvy instituted a cash award for the campaign that did the most to increase a client's sales. Both men were intensely loyal to clients, insisting that everyone in their agencies use their clients' products. At one meeting outside the agency, the hypoglycemic Burnett went into shock and desperately needed an infusion of sugar. Someone mentioned a candy vending machine down the hall. Burnett roused himself: "Make sure it's Nestlé."

For the hundredth anniversary of Burnett's birthday, in 1991, Ogilvy sent an all-out accolade for a commemorative book: "The two agencies which I most admired are Young & Rubicam and Leo Burnett. Leo died twenty years ago but has not yet retired. His influence on the agency he founded is still pervasive." Then he added, "That's why it is now the best agency," overlooking the potential of the last sentence to be used competitively against his own company. Burnett management, in a classy gesture, deleted that line but was happy to retain Ogilvy's explanation for why he turned down the earlier invitation to merge: He felt he could never live up to the founder's standards of hard work. Also left in was Ogilvy's recollection of his pleasure when hearing that Burnett told the *Chicago Tribune* that "we were the only agency which belonged to 'the Chicago school'—which was the greatest compliment he could pay."

~

In 1957, Bill Bernbach launched an audacious new advertisement for Ohrbach's department store in New York. The ad ran only once, but it was so startling in its freshness that people in the business pinned it on their walls. A full page in newspapers, the illustration showed a cat wearing a woman's hat with a bow on top, cigarette holder in her mouth, looking smugly at the reader, and purring cattily in the headline: "I found out about Joan." The copy exposed Joan's secret: "The way she talks, you'd think she was in Who's Who. Well! I found out what's what with *her*." What the reader learns is that Joan dresses in mink and Paris dresses she bought for impressively low prices at Ohrbach's.

Much as Ogilvy focused attention on the man wearing the Hathaway shirt more than the shirt itself, Bernbach focused on the Ohrbach's customer instead of the store. The image of a smart, sophisticated shopper, not just the store's low prices, set it apart from Macy's "It's smart to be thrifty." Another ad showed a man carrying a woman under his arm, with the headline: "LIBERAL TRADE-IN. Bring in your wife and just a few dollars . . . we will give you a new woman." With a budget one-thirtieth of Macy's, Ohrbach's seemed its equal in visibility and impact. "Properly practiced," Bernbach preached, "creativity can make one ad do the work of ten."

Bernbach had been working at Grey, a midsize New York agency, when it was fired by Ohrbach's. With Ohrbach's as his first account, he opened his own agency in 1949 with Ned Doyle (responsible for clients) and Maxwell Dane (administration). Founded about the same time as Ogilvy's firm, Doyle Dane Bernbach became a beacon of creativity in the era's advertising, producing engaging work often described as soft sell. "Forget words like 'hard sell' and 'soft sell,'" said Bernbach, the agency's president and creative director. "That will only confuse you. Hard-sell isn't the way an ad looks or how loud it shouts. It's how many sales it makes. Just be sure your advertising is saying something with substance, something that will serve and inform the consumer, and be sure you're saying it like it's never been said before."

The advertising from Doyle Dane Bernbach seemed to be more pleasing, more entertaining, always surprising, and often more amusing than anyone had seen before. The ads for Ohrbach's attracted Volkswagen, a German car trying to enter the U.S. market fewer than 15 years after World War II. After visiting the factory in Germany, the agency team decided to show how the cheap and, to some eyes ugly, Beetle was honest, simple, reliable, and sensibly different. VW advertising was like the car in the simplicity of its unadorned layouts. The car was the hero, always in surprising contexts.

The headline "Lemon" with a bare photograph of the car made quality inspection memorable, telling of a VW inspector who rejected one car because a chrome strip on the glove compartment was blemished. The headline "Think small" made the small car chic—at a time Detroit could only think about big cars.

Bernbach thought visually and approached creative work with a graphic orientation. His art directors favored stripped-down, minimalist layouts and modern sans serif typefaces. The simple graphic approach worked in TV—a Volkswagen making its way through snowdrifts, with the announcer asking: "Have you ever wondered how the man who drives the snowplow drives TO the snowplow?"

Brooklyn-born, Bernbach made a virtue of living there, in contrast to the Connecticut or Manhattan East Side addresses of most agency executives. A counterpoint to flamboyant agency types, he was quiet and soft-spoken, so much so that people often had to crane their necks to hear him. Physically, he was plain and unprepossessing—quite short, with small hands, tiny feet, thin white hair, and a pink complexion. Neatly dressed, he wore only blue button-down shirts, conservative ties, and always a suit.

Bernbach's unassuming appearance was deceptive, says Mary Wells Lawrence, a copywriter at DDB before she founded her own agency. "He communicated such a powerful inner presence that he mowed everyone around him down and out of sight. There was something volcanic; something unsettling going on. . . . In his peak years many people were afraid of him."

Bernbach became the idol of most creative people, the hero who sparked the creative revolution of the 1960s. He was "the Picasso of our business" says Alan Rosenshine, a copywriter who became head of BBDO. "He changed forever the direction of all advertising by destroying old conventions and hoary restrictions and rethinking how advertising works." A Jew in what had been a largely WASP preserve, Bernbach recruited people who had been less welcome at other agencies—Jews, Italians, and other minorities, many from the outer boroughs of Brooklyn, Queens, and the Bronx—and mirrored urban society in his agency's advertising.

He made his philosophy of advertising known in memos and speeches and by talking about ads he liked; he wouldn't mention those he didn't like. What Bernbach was looking for was work that was original. His constant plea: "Please show me something *fresh*." He believed persuasion is an art, not a science. Saying he was not in the communications business but in the persuasion business, he quoted Aristotle to make his case that people are persuaded not by appeals to their intellect but by appeals to their emotions and desires.

Bernbach was highly aware of the need for *impact*—getting people to pay attention. Formulaic approaches worked against that, in his view. "Rules are what artists break; the memorable never emerged from a formula." If you keep doing the same thing over and over, consumers grow bored and the advertising loses impact. "If your advertising goes unnoticed, everything else is academic." (Ogilvy agreed: "You can't save souls in an empty church.")

The success of Volkswagen attracted other "challenger" brands to the agency—small companies with relatively small budgets. VW spent only $28 million in the United States in its early years compared to hundreds of millions spent by GM, Ford, and Chrysler. For the car rental company Avis, Doyle Dane Bernbach made a predicament a virtue: "We're only Number 2. We try harder." Bernbach tasted packaged bread from a small bakery in Brooklyn and said: "No Jew is ever going to eat this." From that came ethnic portraits of Asians, blacks, and Indians with the headline: "You don't have to be Jewish to love Levy's." The headline under a stunning photo of a Goodman's matzo: "Kosher for Passover"—in Hebrew. For El Al Israel Airlines, the headline almost wrote itself: "We don't take off until everything is kosher."

Creative awards rained on the agency and were welcomed as a sign it was doing well—and a lure for new clients. In the 1960s, the agency had no new business presentation. Instead, prospects were shown the agency's reel of commercials and listened to Bernbach talking about the agency's philosophy.

London advertising man David Abbott, who worked at both agencies, compared Ogilvy and Bernbach. "My first hero was David Ogilvy, when I first worked at Mather & Crowther. Everyone received his list of rules about how to do ads, which after 40 years, I still find difficult to ignore." Abbott describes seeing a Bernbach ad and realizing there was another way of doing things:

> I bought in pretty completely to DDB's philosophy. In a way, it wasn't that different from the Ogilvy discipline, but it added something on top of that: the need to be noticed. It also had a more folksy, more witty, charm to it. What David did was to give me the grammar. What Bill added on was the extra need to get noticed, but still with the discipline.

Both men were inspirational leaders and evangelists, Abbott continues, as well as superb salesmen. "Certainty flowed out of them, and in this industry, where there are very few certainties, what makes one campaign take off is often a leap of faith. But you didn't think it was a leap of faith with Bill or David. You think that if you gave them the business, not only would you get great work, but it would be a commercial success."

Although Ogilvy and Bernbach shared a common commitment to getting results for clients, the two men and their agencies represented two quite different philosophies. Bernbach started with a predilection for using emotion: "You can say the right thing about a product and nobody will listen. You've got to say it in such a way that people will feel it in their gut. Because if they don't feel it, nothing will happen." He placed less emphasis on research: "Facts are not enough. Finding out *what* to say is the beginning of the advertising process. *How* you say it makes people look and listen and if you are not successful at that, you have wasted all the work and intelligence and skills that went into discovering *what* to say." Bernbach also aimed more at the heart than the head: "I warn you against believing that advertising is a science." Imagination and ideas were his touchstone: "rules are prison."

Bernbach's roster of entrepreneurial clients accepted that he didn't allow them much room to comment on the work. A copywriter who worked at the agency describes the way it worked. "His idea basically was, 'You make the bread and I'll do the ads.' Bernbach could yell at the guy who made Levy's bread, and the guy yelled back at Bernbach. Then they sat down and worked it out." That approach worked less well with big packaged goods clients, when assistant account executives were sent to fight with assistant brand managers. The target group for the agency's advertising was themselves, says Jeremy Bullmore of J. Walter Thompson.

> Middle class, comfortably rich, probably East Coast, male. They were writing with wit and style in a way they themselves would appreciate.

But when Lever Brothers went to them at the height of their fame and asked them to do a laundry detergent, they had no idea, because they didn't know what it was like to be at home with three kids and not much money and trying to get your clothes clean.

Ogilvy went after big companies from the start, using his success with prestige products as the bait. His principles for creating advertising provided a sense of discipline and certainty in a business where the stakes were too large to use judgment alone. Although Ogilvy was not blind to the role of emotion and used it in the advertising he created himself, he was a researcher at heart and a disciple of direct mail and its rational appeals.

Winning packaged goods companies had an impact on the advertising produced by Ogilvy's agency. At the time, many of these clients tended to rely on a research method called "day-after recall." A research firm calls people the day after a commercial runs, determines if the person on the phone had been watching TV at the time it aired, then asks questions about the commercial and what it said. The technique places a premium on the viewer's ability to memorize and verbalize a rational argument and favors executions such as "slice of life," product demonstrations, and testimonials. What could emerge from the process was a commercial like the one for Imperial Margarine, with crowns popping on the heads of family members to the sound of trumpets as they taste the product. The Imperial "crowns" campaign sold a lot of margarine, but compromised the agency's creative reputation. Although Ogilvy's agency could and did turn out other kinds of commercials—for American Express, for example—much so-called lifestyle advertising for other clients just did not make it through the screen of recall testing.

Ogilvy admired the Volkswagen advertising, telling Bernbach, "Never in all recorded history has an agency sustained such a high level of advertising for any client. The VW people should give you a castle on the Rhine, stocked with victuals and servants, in perpetuity." But the men did not have a personal relationship. Bernbach considered Ogilvy a "showman" and something of a craftsman who had views about the *techniques* of advertising. Ogilvy felt Bernbach's followers misunderstood what he was saying. Ironically, the common touch Bernbach agency had more successes with sophisticated campaigns for Volkswagen, Avis, Levy's, Goodman's matzos, and El Al airlines, while the supposedly elitist Ogilvy agency grew with broad appeal mass-market products.

~

Ogilvy quickly grasped the implications of working for packaged goods clients. In 1961, he wrote to a fellow executive: "It seems we must choose between irrational genius and sterile rationalists." In 1964, he wrote Leo Burnett: "In 1938 I fell in love with two schools of advertising. They were diametrically opposed to each other." One he described as the elegant and entertaining school, led by Young & Rubicam. The other was drawn from Lord & Thomas (Claude Hopkins) and Ruthrauff & Ryan (mail order) and relied on coupon returns to validate its work. "My admiration for these two opposite schools tore me apart. But I have spent sixteen years trying to prove that you can combine the best of both. At the moment I find myself veering toward the entertainment end of the spectrum—at least in television." In 1964, he went on, Bernbach had replaced Young & Rubicam as leader of the entertainment school and Bates had "inherited the mantle of Hopkins."

Some agencies, Ogilvy once told an interviewer, are "like churches where there is no dogma, where they make up their own prayers. Ours is like the Catholic Church." *Time* commented: "For a man who is reputed to be one of Madison Avenue's boldest commandment breakers, his theology is surprisingly orthodox. Celebrated for his audacity and British charm, he prefers to stress basic, old-fashioned disciplines." At the start, Ogilvy was seen as a revolutionary. "Ogilvy's ads have wrought great changes in American advertising," wrote *Printer's Ink*. Leo Burnett agreed: "I regard David Ogilvy's copy as the most significant of our times, proving that hard sell can also be very palatable." For many, Ogilvy brought salesmanship and good taste together for the first time in American advertising.

More of the roots of today's advertising can be traced to Bernbach than to Ogilvy. The most influential creative man of his time, Bernbach inspired the leaders of many successful agencies, among them Jack Tinker, Mary Wells Lawrence, George Lois, Jay Chiat, Jerry Della Femina, and Carl Ally. The low-key, endearing advertising style pioneered by Bernbach and his disciples, and in turn by *their* disciples, became the dominant mode in American advertising.

~

Ogilvy reached out to the major figures of his day. He saw modern advertising as beginning with Rubicam and approached him even before he had started his own agency, saying later he felt so unqualified that he did not apply for a job at Young & Rubicam, the agency he admired the most. Ogilvy sought Rubicam's views and reported on his progress. "Alas, I was never in your agency, so I have little to guide me today. But I aspire to build another first-class agency."

He flattered the older man, writing in 1954: "It is a remarkable fact that the best copywriter in America should have gone on to become the greatest administrator and leader in agency history." Rubicam returned the compliment, calling Ogilvy "a star of the all-American team of any advertising generation." Several years after he retired in 1944, Rubicam volunteered to become chairman of Ogilvy's agency, but that did not come about.

Ogilvy also had a great deal of respect for Stanley Resor, who ran J. Walter Thompson for 50 years and built it into the world's largest agency. He admired Thompson's aim to be a "university of advertising." The *Thompson Blue Book on Advertising*, published in 1906, is wholly about the efficacy of advertising, notes Jeremy Bullmore, who ran J. Walter Thompson in the United Kingdom, and suggests that much of it could have been written by Ogilvy 50 years later.

Ogilvy had two dealings with the brilliant Oklahoma-born Marion Harper, who like him had been a door-to-door salesman and a student of advertising research. Harper rose from the mailroom at McCann-Erickson to become research director and then president of the agency in 1948. Viewing advertising as only one part of the marketing process, Harper pioneered the concept of joining several agencies with related services, such as public relations and sales promotion, to form a conglomerate, thus creating the first holding company in marketing communications, The Interpublic Group.

At one point in the 1950s, Harper wooed Ogilvy and tried to buy his agency for $500,000. One story is that he played on their shared background in research, inviting Ogilvy to watch commercials while a camera focused on his eyes, measuring whether the pupils expanded or contracted. "It's quite marvelous," Ogilvy is reported as saying, "but what do you do when the eyes are closed?" Years later, Harper called with a different proposal. He asked for a loan of $400,000 to save Interpublic from bankruptcy, a danger brought on by Harper's disastrous financial management, including a corporate fleet with a DC–7 he used like a taxi. Ogilvy passed on both proposals.

Following the success of *Confessions* came dinners at the White House, an honorary degree from Adelphi College in New York, election to the board of Colby College in Maine, and membership in several Halls of Fame. A 1964 poll by *The Gallagher Report,* an industry newsletter, asked agency executives, advertisers, and marketing men to name the outstanding advertising agency executives of that year.

Results:

1. David Ogilvy
2. William Bernbach
3. Norman Strouse (J. Walter Thompson)
4. Robert E. Lusk (Benton & Bowles)
5. Marion Harper

Author Roald Dahl, Ogilvy's sometime friend and former embassy colleague, wrote Ogilvy that *Confessions* entertained and instructed him, adding:

> It is the longest copy you have yet written for any client.
> And the most effective.
> The client will be gratified by the results.
> More people than ever will demand his product.
> But who is the client?
> You know as well as I do.
> Your client is you.

NINE

THE TRUE CHURCH

*A*merica in the 1960s is remembered nostalgically as the perfect time and place to work in advertising. The economy was booming. John F. Kennedy radiated optimism from the White House. Television, the first true mass-market communications medium, was coming into its own, helping consumers select from among 10,000 products in bright new supermarkets. Advertising of the period portrayed family values in an idealized setting, often a preposterous one. The mother, always a housewife, did her chores and cooking in a dress and high heels.

For Ogilvy's young agency, the 1950s had been a golden age. "For seven years we got every account we competed for," Ogilvy claimed. "We never missed once. We were fashionable as hell." By 1960, Ogilvy, Benson & Mather was the twenty-eighth largest agency, with $30 million in billings—up from $3 million in 1950. Ogilvy's personal star continued its rise. In 1962, he was on the cover of *Time,* along with a dozen agency chiefs, as one of the "Visible Persuaders" of advertising—"visible" in contrast to Vance Packard's *The Hidden Persuaders.** *Time's* article noted his "flair for creating ads that are literate and entertaining

---

* Packard, a journalist and social critic, exposed the ostensible manipulation of consumers by Ernest Dichter, Burleigh Gardner, and other practitioners of "motivational research."

while tugging at the purse strings that has made him the most sought-after wizard in today's advertising industry."

Despite the publicity and the winning streak in new business, most of the agency's accounts were small. Ogilvy, Benson & Mather—the name following Hewitt's departure—was what would later be termed a "boutique." The list of top agencies in 1960 was headed by J. Walter Thompson; Batten, Barton, Durstine & Osborn*; McCann-Erickson; Young & Rubicam; and Ted Bates. We are the high-brows' darling, Ogilvy lamented. "Intellectuals come up to us at cocktail parties and tell us that our agency is the only one that doesn't insult their intelligence. I have not found this role a profitable one. It tends to make commercially-minded manufacturers suspicious of us." Often saying that no agency is small by choice, Ogilvy set about growing.

Three events, two with unintended consequences, changed the agency and contributed to its growth in the 1960s: An international merger. A public offering. And most of all, the arrival of big clients.

Four of the companies on Ogilvy's much-discussed target list of five most-wanted clients were consumer packaged goods companies, which he viewed as professional, civilized—and big spenders. He had seen how brilliant creative work attracted certain clients, but understood that to bag big game, he needed big people. "Before I made any key appointment, I used to think, will this impress General Foods? I was always titrating everything against General Foods."

That led Ogilvy to Esty Stowell, who had run the General Foods account at Benton & Bowles. "I titrated Esty against General Foods. I knew what they thought of him. We were sort of a boutique before he came, a bit peculiar and snobby. Esty made us respectable." It took one year for Ogilvy to persuade Stowell, a pipe-smoking graduate of St. Paul's and Harvard, to come in as executive vice president. With his patrician bearing, Stowell looked like a president—and soon would take on that title.

We've got a good creative department, Ogilvy told his new partner. "I'll run that. You take everything else. I don't know anything

---

* Comedian Jack Benny quipped that the agency's name sounded like a trunk bouncing down a flight of stairs.

about media or marketing, and I'm a hopeless manager." Stowell raised hiring standards, brought in smart pros from Benton & Bowles, McCann-Erickson, Colgate, and Procter & Gamble, and replaced "account handlers" with well-grounded marketing men. "The most incorruptible of all God's men," said Ogilvy, relating how Stowell turned down the son of the chairman of General Foods who came in for a job. Although Ogilvy endorsed Stowell as a great partner, some found him aloof, an impression dispelled when he was shown a commercial for approval. The ex-Marine studied the screen, took the pipe out of his mouth, and delivered his verdict: "This may seem like fly-fucking, but it seems to me . . ."

Stowell made it possible for big clients to have both Ogilvy's charms and sophisticated marketing. General Foods soon assigned Maxwell House ground coffee, its biggest brand, to its newest agency, a vote of confidence justified when the agency produced a commercial that ran for six years and became a classic.

> The glass top of a percolator fills the screen for almost the entire 60-second commercial. The camera focuses on the glass top, the coffee starts to "perk" rhythmically against it, music punctuates the rhythm: *bpppa-bpppa-BPPPA, bpppa-bpppa-BPPPA.*[*]

"Perking Pot" demonstrated that the boutique agency was capable of turning out effective packaged goods ads *on television*. Ogilvy's first visit to the coffee roasting plant in Hoboken, New Jersey, prompted the commercial's theme. Struck by the rich coffee aroma, he wondered if it tasted as good as it smelled. "Tastes as good as it smells" joined "Good to the last drop," a slogan born from President Theodore Roosevelt's enthusiastic exclamation when he tasted the first blended coffee during his stay at the Maxwell House Hotel in Nashville, Tennessee.

Success was rewarded with more assignments from General Foods, including its biggest new product, freeze-dried coffee. Dissatisfied with the copywriter's initial creative efforts, Ogilvy sent him back to work with an unusual charge: Write the advertising as

---

[*] The coffee was propelled from under the table by squeezing a rubber bulb.

though Smith Kline were introducing a new ethical drug. The copy-writer knew immediately what Ogilvy wanted and came up with a symbolic depiction of the freeze-drying process, dramatizing how Maxim differed from traditional spray-dried instant coffees. Another winner. By the mid-1960s, GF was on its way to becoming the agency's largest client.

The new client that made the most dramatic and immediate difference was Shell, in 1960. It nearly doubled the size of the agency. Ogilvy had seized the opportunity of a Scottish Council lunch to meet Max Burns, Shell's president, and cultivated him over several years. The opening came when J. Walter Thompson, whose relationship with Shell had been deteriorating, dismissed the idea of a fee instead of the standard 15 percent commission as "unethical." Burns laughed, pointing out that it was not unethical to pay your doctor or your lawyer a fee, or your accountant, while commissions as a percentage of what was spent on advertising made the agency's motives suspect when recommending a budget increase.

"We would actually prefer to work on a fee basis," Ogilvy told Shell. His public position was moral, that the agency-client relationship is most satisfactory when the agency's emoluments are not related to the amount of money it can persuade the client to spend. Privately, there was less enthusiasm. Thompson's president begged Ogilvy not to do it, warning it would destroy the agency business. None of his partners wanted to do it. Clients forced us, says Shelby Page, the agency's longtime financial chief. "The first time was with Sun Oil. Later on, the U.S. government travel office insisted we go on a fee instead of a commission. We did it on Shell to get the account—to give a discounted price via a fee."

Ogilvy bulled ahead, buoyed by support from marketing leaders who applauded his "courage" and "guts." The former marketing chief at Campbell Soup called it a major breakthrough, noting "the fact that it is an agency of your stature and reputation and a sizeable account such as Shell gives it much added significance." His competitors were less happy as the fee system spread and considerable profit went out of the business, even as remuneration became more "professional."

Ogilvy had demurred when Shell asked to see speculative campaigns as evidence it should trust its account to a tiny agency. "We don't make love until we're married," he explained. It didn't hurt that Shell liked Ogilvy's Rolls-Royce work and disliked Thompson's TV cartoon ads showing cars sidling up to its pumps as evidence that "Cars love Shell." Awarded the business, Ogilvy went in the opposite direction, recommending serious advertising that would portray Shell as "a company that derives its distinction from its scientists." He persuaded Shell to abandon its treasured TV franchise positions on every major newscast and place its entire budget in newspapers— full-page, long copy ads, packed with facts about gasoline.

> BULLETIN: Shell discloses the nine ingredients in today's Super Shell and shows how they give your car *top performance*

"I don't *read* the ads," said agency head Jack Tinker, "but I sort of think any gasoline that a copywriter can find that much to say about must be pretty good gasoline." No oil marketer had ever advertised gasoline's ingredients and what each offers the motorist. Newspaper ads gave way to dramatic demonstrations on TV, culminating in cars using "Super Shell with Platformate" breaking through paper barriers as evidence of better mileage. The campaign turned around a decline in Shell's share of U.S. gasoline sales and established it as the industry leader. The advertising director of Shell sang the agency's praise to the advertising director of another large company, citing the creative work, the analytical approach to advertising problems, the research, and continuing search for the facts—"and the results they get."

Responsibility for running the Shell business was the bait that lured John "Jock" Elliott from BBDO, where he headed that agency's big DuPont account and was a rising star. Getting him was a coup. Like Stowell, Elliott was a pipe-smoker, an ex-Marine, and a graduate of St. Paul's and Harvard. Even though he loved BBDO, he was taken with the energy and thrust in his new agency, remarking that people answered memos the day they received them.

Elliott flaunted his Scottish heritage even more than Ogilvy, naming his weekend home "Highland Fling" and telling everybody he was born on Robbie Burns's birthday. He bought a crofter's cottage in northern Scotland, chaired the Scottish National Trust in the United States, and started traditions of walking the halls at

Christmastime behind a bagpiper and celebrating major agency events with pipes. A masterful public speaker, Elliott was a father figure at staff meetings and an admired company spokesman.

With General Foods and Shell on board, Ogilvy continued his hunt. Jean Clark, the wife of American Express CEO Howard Clark, got her new husband interested in Ogilvy in 1962. She had been working for Ogilvy as a volunteer during his stint as head of a campaign to involve the public in Lincoln Center, and they were neighbors in Greenwich. At his wife's urging, Clark called Ogilvy, who said he didn't think he was interested—in those days the account was too small. The Clarks persevered, however, and Ogilvy went to their house for an informal talk.

"In the first place, he's got a lot of charm," Jean Clark recalls. "We're sitting in the library. He puts all this stuff on the floor and lies down, and starts to describe the things he would do. You couldn't not get excited about what his ideas were"—ideas prepared for a client he said he wasn't interested in serving.

Stowell was against taking a tiny travel business with little potential. Ogilvy waited until Stowell went on vacation and then accepted the $1.8 million Travelers Cheque business, which had been at Benton & Bowles. He initially saw it as a travel account, to go with KLM Royal Dutch Airlines, P. & O. Orient cruise lines, the U.S. Travel Service, Puerto Rico, and the British Travel Association. The agency came through with two of the most famous campaigns in advertising history: "Don't leave home without it"* and people with recognizable names but nonrecognizable faces asking "Do you know me?" Actor Karl Malden was so authoritative in the Travelers Cheque commercials that some viewers wondered if he was the president of American Express. Before long Clark was attributing sales increases almost wholly to advertising. By the 1980s, American Express had replaced General Foods as the agency's largest client, and had become a creative showcase that attracted other new clients.

American Express built its business in part with an effective O&M direct mail letter that started: "Quite frankly, the American Express Card is not for everyone." Direct mail, Ogilvy's "first love,"

---

*"Don't leave home without it" (for the charge card) flexibly accommodated travel ("without us") and travelers cheques ("without them").

was a legacy from his days of door-to-door selling and his studies of John Caples. He set up a Direct Mail Department in the agency early in the 1960s, and clients quickly discovered how to integrate direct mail into their advertising plans. After a time, the agency acquired public relations and promotion companies to provide these services to clients and broaden its base beyond advertising.

As Ogilvy had candidly admitted, marketing wasn't his strong suit. Once these new clients were landed, he involved himself only occasionally in the creative work, certainly not the TV commercials. He was terrified to go to General Foods, says Bill Phillips, a fiercely competitive P&G-trained marketing pro who ran the General Foods account and became one of Ogilvy's successors as chairman. "David was always scared. All of a sudden he was working for these big companies. It was like going to work for God." He referred to the Maxwell House people as the "Brahmins" of General Foods, and was visibly relieved when he went to the office one Sunday and found people writing a presentation for a new Maxwell House product. "Thank goodness somebody's here working."

Sears Roebuck had tried national advertising, with disappointing results. Its chairman wasn't sure there was a way to tell the Sears story right. *Life* magazine felt there was an opportunity beyond the local price-oriented advertising the company was doing and, with the help of the chairman of Time, Inc., arranged an introduction for Ogilvy. Ogilvy suggested they hire the agency for 90 days, enough time to do its homework. After copy chief David McCall discovered that Sears sold more diamonds than any other retailer, and more mink too, he turned out 30 advertisements along those lines: "How to buy mink at SEARS . . . and why not this stole for Christmas?" Sears's first-ever national program started in 1961 and, when research showed it was upgrading Sears's image with consumers, eventually grew to $70 million. Many of Ogilvy's early creative successes had depended on the upscale audience delivered by *The New Yorker*. Not this time. Now the magazine wouldn't run the campaign—Sears wasn't a Fifth Avenue retailer. Ten years later, in leaner times, it was begging for Sears advertising.

These huge companies invited Ogilvy to speak at their meetings and welcomed his personal visits. "Every agency president I ever talked to promised he'd stay in the picture after we gave him the business," Bill Williams, the CEO of Campbell Soup, observed, "and the only one who kept his word was David Ogilvy." But his creative contributions were not as sure-footed as they had been for Hathaway and Schweppes. "I understand you're looking for a new promise for Prime," he told me, referring to a new General Foods dog food. "I will work on it this weekend." The most famous copywriter in the business would be working on my client's product! Monday morning, he came into my office and placed a sheet of paper on my desk. "I have been working on your problem all weekend. I've come up with dozens of ideas. None of them are any good, save one," as he turned the sheet over. There it was—"The prime minister of dog food." All I could do was wince and say we'd consider it seriously.

For Shell, Ogilvy suggested "What's so super-duper about Super Shell?" Jock Elliott told him he didn't think it was such a super-duper idea. For Mountain Dew, Pepsi-Cola's soft drink with a hillbilly image, he proposed an outhouse with one wall opening to show people passing out bottles of the yellowish beverage. The copywriter conceded it was a clever idea but reminded him Mountain Dew looks like something a nurse takes from you in a bottle. He so hated a commercial showing a plumber sobbing because Liquid Drano in effect put him out of work that he stalked out of the screening room and kicked a nearby wall. When the record high test score came in, he sent the writer a note: "You were right. I was wrong. Congratulations. David."

Ogilvy's aim was better with image businesses. He typically wrote the initial ad in a campaign, and must have savored writing "Send me a man who reads" for an International Paper corporate series. Learning from research that the Dutch had a reputation for being reliable, he proposed KLM as "The reliable airline of the careful, punctual Dutch," a theme still in use 40 years later. Although the account spent only a few million dollars, he turned down the much larger American Airlines business, explaining "What I lose in commission, I gain in vanity."

Much of the agency's early creative reputation was derived from its travel advertising, especially the "Come to Britain" campaign. Although Ogilvy didn't write its most remembered headline, "Tread softly past the long, long sleep of kings," about Westminster Abbey, the look and tone of the advertising unmistakably bore his imprint.

He continued to hammer away at new business, reminding his people, "sooner or later, all accounts will go." One account that came and went was Cunard Line, number one on Ogilvy's original target list. After many years, it moved from Ogilvy's agency to Ted Bates. Rosser Reeves sent proofs of the new Bates ads to his brother-in-law. The campaign introduced a new message—fly to the U.K. one way, return by Cunard—but otherwise was a dead ringer for Ogilvy's ads in type and style. Ogilvy called Reeves's office and spoke with his secretary. "I am so grateful to you for sending the new Cunard campaign. Please tell Rosser it arrived just in time. I'm editing my new book, and adding a chapter on plagiarism."

～

As recently as the late 1950s, there was little international advertising and few agencies that knew or cared much about it. There was plenty to do in the expanding market at home, and the global market was small and not well understood. In the United States, international advertising was small and known as "export" advertising. By the 1960s, that started changing. British and American agencies began to look overseas for agency partners to serve their multinational clients. Mather & Crowther in London naturally looked at Ogilvy, Benson & Mather in New York, and OBM naturally considered Mather & Crowther. The U.S. offspring had now grown bigger in terms of billing than its parent, but relative to its competition, Mathers was a much bigger agency in England than OBM was in the United States. More important, Francis and David maintained a fraternal correspondence that forged an understanding even while the U.S. company's increasing independence was pulling the two agencies apart.

OBM had taken its first step outside the States in 1960, opening an office in Toronto to serve Shell. Ogilvy, eager to make his mark in Canada, planned to spend quite a bit of time in Toronto, even to the point of being seen to have a residence there. To make this scheme affordable, he asked his creative emissary Joel Raphaelson to live in an apartment big enough to accommodate him on visits, and invited the Raphaelsons to his home in New York to get some idea of his tastes: rooms with right angles (no rounded corners or other oddities), no dark colors, no wall-to-wall carpeting. And, most important, the hallways must not smell of cooking.

To head his new Canadian outpost, Ogilvy recruited a former client, Andrew Kershaw, who had hired OBM when he was with the British Travel Association in London. Short and dynamic, Hungarian by birth, a British commando during World War II, a dedicated opera lover, and another pipe-smoker, Kershaw had taken on British mannerisms before emigrating to Canada and becoming a naturalized citizen. Decisive and unconventional in his thinking, he was brilliantly insightful on marketing and creative issues and is credited with spotting the potential of the "Don't leave home without us" line for American Express. More than anyone other than Ogilvy, he supported the emerging direct marketing discipline. Although Kershaw started as a loyal disciple, he and Ogilvy would eventually part ways in their approaches to growing the business.

Talks of a far more significant move—a full merger between the New York and London companies—had been on and off for several years. In 1963, they were on again. On a fall day, the entire staff of Mather & Crowther, about 550 people, gathered in London's Festival Hall to hear David make the case for a closer association. Francis had given the potential merger the code name "Colossus," explaining grandiosely that "it would bestride the dividing seas." As the parties drew closer, David cabled Hotspur's words from *Henry IV, Part 1:* "Out of this nettle, danger, we pluck this flower, safety." Colossus became HOTSPUR.

The Brits didn't want to merge with anyone but were worried that some American agency would try to buy them and figured it would be better to join forces with Francis's brother. Some felt a merger would change the character of their agency. Would the headquarters be in London or New York? Who would be its leader? David had said he would be content to see his brother as the first chief executive, but that did not dissolve unease among the London staff as to where the true leadership would reside.

It was high drama when David walked onto the Festival Hall stage, conspicuously took off his blazer, and put up his first slide: "What we have learned about advertising that sells." His prospective partners were about to be bombarded with state-of-the-art thinking in their business and the results it can produce. "It was the first time I had ever seen a presentation like it," says a Mather & Crowther man who was there.

I thought it was absolutely amazing—I was bowled over. David had drawn all these conclusions about what worked and what didn't work in advertising, with stories and lots of examples of good advertising. At the end, he posed a question: "Does it work?" And then he went through a whole series of charts of client sales rocketing. I thought it was absolutely riveting theater.

Apparently others thought so too. A tour de force, it melted opposition to the merger; discussions continued in back rooms of the Savoy Hotel.

In the midst of negotiations, Francis, then 60, died. Although he had been a heavy smoker (two packs a day for 30 years) and died of lung cancer, his colleagues believe he drank himself into the grave. Just as David was growing more successful, Francis was becoming jaded and bored. David made a trip to London to see his brother just before the end. One month later, on a *CBS Reports* program on smoking and advertising, Ogilvy said: "I watch these commercials. I see the handsome athletic young man drawing in a mouthful of cigarette smoke and then inhaling it down into his lungs, and I'm appalled to think that I belong to the profession which can perpetrate that kind of villainy." He acknowledged that his U.S. agency had handled a cigarette account (Spud mentholated cigarettes) until "inescapable" conclusions of the 1962 Royal College of Physicians Report prompted the decision not to accept any cigarette advertising, although London kept its profitable cigarette business for several years.*

Francis's death deprived Mather & Crowther of its leader and the potential merger of a special tie. The U.K. directors had expected that Francis, the elder brother, would be the guiding light of the combined agency, and that London, as the bigger and older company, would be dominant. David had a great deal of style and charm and some selling experience, but not the heavyweight credentials needed to run a big international operation. If he hadn't been Francis's brother, many believe, he might not have been considered for the position. But, in fact, it was the other way around. Even before Francis died, some of the younger English directors found the ambition for growth in New York, personified by David, refreshing.

---

* Years later, the U.S. company suspended the policy and took on a cigarette account, arguing the dangers of smoking were well understood and the policy had been compromised by cigarette clients in other countries.

The Brits revered Francis but thought less highly of his eccentric brother, despite his great success in America, and never fully accepted him. The man who won them over was Jock Elliott, who came over later and met with the senior staff in a conference room in the office. Elliott made what seemed an impromptu speech, as all his talks appeared to be. His meticulously thought-through talk, spoken with dignity and humor, impressed everyone. At the end, people were thinking, if this is the American who's boss in New York, we won't mind working for him.

Francis's name appears only briefly in his brother's autobiography. When he died, David at last acknowledged his debt: "A quirk in the character of all Ogilvys makes it difficult for us to say anything pleasant about each other; we play an elaborate game of sarcastic denigration, to conceal our mutual devotion. But in death, I will allow myself to admit that Francis was the great hero of my life and, for the last 30 years, my best friend." He acknowledged that his brother had been greatly admired and liked by the staff, and was "a much bigger person than I had ever realized, may God forgive me."

Francis adored his younger brother. When David came to London, he would find his room stuffed with expensive flowers. Always confident that David would succeed, at one point Francis wrote that he wished their father were alive, to tell him of the American success and hear him gloating about the American "O."

Negotiations between the agencies continued, and the agreement was finally signed in October 1964. Ogilvy & Mather International Inc. was incorporated in New York with David Ogilvy as chairman and chief executive and Donald Atkins of Mather & Crowther as vice-chairman. In 1938, Francis had predicted that someday an English agency would invade the American field. His brother had led the invasion; the merger secured its future. The London staff bulletin noted: "David Ogilvy is not an American; he is not an Englishman; he is happily, for variation's sake, a Scot."

"If God is on the side of big battalions, and that seems to be the case," Ogilvy trumpeted, "the path of wisdom lies in becoming one of the big battalions." The combination created the ninth-largest advertising concern in the world, the biggest in Europe, employing 1,600 people. The 50–50 merger was sold to the London office as a brilliant achievement, a "true alliance of equals."

~

Nothing would change the agency more than going public. Not
that there was much choice or that many of the principals objected.
British exchange control made a public stock offering a condition of
allowing the sale of a British company to a new *American* parent.
Papert, Koenig, Lois, a small but fast-growing start-up, had become
the first advertising agency to sell itself to public markets in 1962.
PKL couldn't afford the escalating salaries of creative people and
thought it might be able to use its stock as an incentive. Four agencies followed, with no apparent ill effects. Hostile takeovers had not
been invented, even for companies with hard assets. For service
businesses, whose assets go down the elevator every night, they were
inconceivable.

Ogilvy wanted to go public. He started writing memos about it
in 1964, urging the agency not to be so late in the procession as to
miss the market. He pointed out that he invested all his capital
($6,000) in the agency, bought stock in succeeding years, and
wanted to sell some to diversify his estate and become more liquid.
"All my eggs are in one basket." He figured his holdings at $1.8 mil-
lion in "public" value ($12 million in today's dollars). The only
downside he saw was the requirement to disclose profits and remuneration of top people. Nevertheless, he emphasized: "LET US
NOT MISS THE OMNIBUS."

The public offering of Ogilvy & Mather International, Inc. took
place in 1966, with the stock listed on exchanges in London and
New York, the first for an advertising agency. Client billings were
$150 million, double the amount of four years earlier (and four
times larger than PKL) with after-tax profits of $1.4 million on $24
million in income. The bankers were First Boston in New York and
N. M. Rothschild and Kleinwort Benson in London. Ogilvy was
chairman and chief executive as well as the principal stockholder; he
had stepped down as chairman of the U.S. company the prior year,
to serve only as its creative head.

By 1970, the agency could run a full-page advertisement in *The
Wall Street Journal,* reporting on its most profitable year. Ogilvy told
security analysts that half the clients were charged fees, not commissions, and fees made it easier to run the business. "I like being able to

go to a client and advise him to increase his advertising expenditure without him suspecting my motive. I also like to be able to go to a client and suggest that he reduce his advertising expenditure, without having to apologize to our stockholders."

The instant financial reward of taking a company public was not to everyone's taste. Stowell believed a professional services firm could not ethically serve the interests of both shareholder and client and resigned in protest. At Ogilvy's insistence, he stayed on the board and accepted his shares, but he remained an uncomfortable presence with no responsibilities, smoking his pipe and making solemn pronouncements. His conservatism began to offend Ogilvy, who ultimately sent others to ask for Stowell's full resignation.

Public ownership made little difference in how the agency was run, but it did attract Warren Buffett as an early investor. "I like royalty-based businesses," he explained, (referring to commissions as royalties), despite Ogilvy touting the virtues of fees. Buffett came to New York once a year to meet with the management team and asked a lot of questions. Although he liked what he saw, he debated the wisdom of acquiring other agencies. "Why don't you buy the *best* agency? Buy your own shares." After Ogilvy had sold much of his own stock, he would introduce Buffett as "the fellow who has made more money out of Ogilvy & Mather than I have."

With Stowell gone, the remaining directors became boldly expansionist. The next move was the purchase of the other English parent, S.H. Benson in 1971, which was losing money but owned a valuable building in London. Since the leasehold was worth more than the agency and could be sold, the agency itself would cost almost nothing. Bensons also owned several neglected agencies in Southeast Asia countries that appeared so inconsequential the Ogilvy people called them the "Mickey Mouse countries."

Ogilvy was bitterly opposed to the buyout. He felt Bensons was poorly managed, and he especially didn't like the real estate part. It was the first time his board had opposed him, and he was furious. He walked out of the meeting and didn't return for the birthday party planned for him that evening, but went to see his sister in Devon. The acquisition went through, but, oddly, without the valuable London building—the board agreed that would be too adventurous. (Rothschild's bought it and made a fortune.) For a while, the idea was to unload the Benson agencies in Southeast Asia. Instead, Michael Ball, a charismatic Aussie who had launched successful Ogilvy & Mather outposts in Australia and New Zealand, transformed them into first-class profitable agencies, building what would become the largest agency network in the Asia-Pacific region. Throughout the 1970s, other regional "Barons" were building the network across Europe and Latin America.

The fact that the company was created by a merger of equals created an international mentality that would serve it well with multinational clients. Ogilvy people sensed they couldn't order one another around—they had to work together. International management supervisors watched over the interests of a growing roster of multinational clients; no other agency served so many global marketers. Despite a late start, Ogilvy & Mather was to become one of the top three international agencies.

~

Having set a vast expansion in motion, Ogilvy was not entirely happy with the consequences. The principles traveled well, but the founder did not. He was terrified of flying and would go to staggering lengths to avoid getting on an airplane. Rather than fly a few hours to the office in Houston, he would take a two-day train trip through Chicago and Dallas and stay for five or six days, instead of making more frequent short trips. In India, where train stations were filled with masses of people sleeping on the platform, he journeyed by train from the office in Delhi to the one in Chennai (Madras)—at 72 hours, the longest train trip possible in that country. Almost all the directors of the Indian agency escorted him, the king with his retinue.

Ogilvy accepted his fear of flying as irrational but was unable to conquer it and flew only when absolutely required. Generally abstemious, drinking only a glass or two of wine on occasion, he might need to pour himself several martinis on a plane. When bad weather prevented him from taking a boat to Scandinavia, he sent a Telex: "Tempest in the North Sea. Taking flight to Stockholm. Please pray for me."

Beyond his traumatizing fear of flying, he was at heart a colonialist, most comfortable where the British Empire had ruled, especially

Canada, India, and South Africa. He visited the agency's offices in South America less willingly, and derided its entry into Japan as a "cesspool." He ridiculed an entry into Russia: "What are we going to sell? Fur hats!"

In New York, Ogilvy turned the U.S. agency over in 1965 to a team with Jock Elliott as chairman, Alan Sidnam (a senior executive from Benton & Bowles) as vice-chairman, and Jim Heekin as president. Heekin, a very able, bold account manager, had been promoted when his client Lever Brothers became for a time the largest in the agency. A talented account man with strong strategic and creative instincts, Heekin made several unwise moves, including a power play to become sole boss of the office. Ogilvy fired him and brought Andrew Kershaw down from Toronto to be president.

After establishing himself in New York, Kershaw teamed with Jimmy Benson (no relation to S. H. Benson), who was building the network in Europe. Together, they began driving for growth, arguing that the only way to make more money year after year was to buy other agencies. Page considered it a Ponzi scheme, a way to create the illusion of dynamic growth. Kershaw then put forth the idea of several competing agencies under the same company umbrella, like Marion Harper's Interpublic Group. This strategy led to the purchase of Scali, McCabe, Sloves, a hot creative agency that was promised total separation except for financial matters. When the Ogilvy directors gathered at the Hotel Dorset to toast the "marriage," Ed McCabe, the iconoclastic creative director of SMS, raised his glass and responded: "OK. But remember"—wagging his finger—"separate bedrooms!"

Ogilvy disliked both the concept and the execution. From the outset, he insisted that his company should be "One Agency Indivisible." ("Under God?" a client mused.) It is hardly surprising that he would reject the apostasy of other agencies with different philosophies being invited into his sacred domain. He ridiculed Scali, McCabe, Sloves as "children playing in the sandbox," was furious about how much its principals had received for selling their agency,* and fought the acquisition at board meetings and by memos: "There can be only one true church."

---

* Each of the founders received $3 million (nearly $11 million in 2008 dollars).

Ogilvy's position was that his principles had been shown to work. They had provided a solid foundation for growth. Why must we welcome diversions in the name of growth, itself a debatable philosophy, in a company dedicated to placing client interests first? he wondered.

He lost not only the battle but the war—Kershaw and his allies continued to buy agencies with different names and philosophies, and Ogilvy's breach with his former disciples widened. Now, in the 1970s, Ogilvy & Mather itself was a long way from the boutique he worried might go under. It had become one of the largest worldwide advertising agencies, with red-carpeted offices all over the globe. In the United States, the acquisition of a Los Angeles agency brought the Mattel account (with the Barbie doll). Hal Riney opened an O&M office in San Francisco, soon to change the image of Gallo with his contrarian advertising for Bartles and James and other Gallo brands. Ogilvy admired Riney's campaigns, which were perhaps reminiscent of his own early image successes. Ogilvy Direct, his "secret weapon," grew to become the largest—and most highly awarded—direct response network in the world.

But it was all very big. Ogilvy passed the chairmanship of Ogilvy & Mather International, the parent company, to Jock Elliott and took the new role of international creative head, with a mission to raise creative standards in the agency's dozens of offices around the world. Ogilvy's was a powerful voice, but the role wasn't enough to satisfy him. And he saw his company as increasingly divisible.

∼

Starting in the late 1950s and into the 1960s, Ogilvy had started pulling back from management responsibilities and becoming more visible than ever outside—with speeches, interviews, and public service projects. He chaired the United Negro College Fund in 1965, and chaired a Citizens Committee to Keep New York City Clean, sharing credit with the Sanitation Department for improving the city's cleanliness rating. (Ogilvy changed just one word in Elliott's talk about the "Don't Litter" advertising program—from "people who litter our streets" to "barbarians who litter our streets." The headline in *The New York Times:* "Barbarians litter our streets."

Ogilvy's Lincoln Center committee was able to report that public awareness of the new arts complex had been boosted to 67 percent, with a typical Ogilvy touch: "the same percentage as have heard of the Pyramids." He persuaded the New York Philharmonic to advertise its full season program—a first. His letter to fellow agency heads appealing for support of the orchestra from their clients promised: "Bernstein is Box Office. Bernstein is Hot." Using a special research study, he told the National Automobile Dealers Association that car dealers were seen as less honest or trustworthy than undertakers, service station managers, or plumbers, and advised them to deliver better service ("Emulate the great surgeons who know that it pays to give their patients post-operative care") and upgrade their advertising ("Stop the schlock, sleazy, bargain basement, fast-buck advertising and start respectable advertising.")

He told the Magazine Publishers Association that TV commercials had made Madison Avenue "the arch-symbol of tasteless materialism" and suggested stricter government regulation. The Harvard Business School Club heard from him about opportunities for rapid advancement in advertising. "The average age of our Vice Presidents at Ogilvy, Benson & Mather is only 41. Almost all of them became Vice Presidents when they were still in their thirties. Our youngest Vice President is 31."

Elected to the Copywriters Hall of Fame in 1965, Ogilvy accepted with the words: "I detest awards except when I win one." Soon after Ellerton Jette of Hathaway got him elected a trustee of Colby College, he confronted Colby's president with 12 ideas on how to run the college better.

The head of the CIA, Allen Dulles, volunteered to get Ogilvy U.S. citizenship because of his help to the OSS during the war. He declined, explaining later that he didn't plan to run for public office so he had no need to be a citizen, but also complained about being ignored by the British government.

His Majesty's Government wants exports, which require marketing. But HMG scorns the king of all British marketers. Provoking me to defect? Here in America, I am employed as a senior advisor by Sears Roebuck, IBM, General Dynamics, J.P. Morgan, Campbell Soup, General Foods. No other Englishman has ever occupied a position of such influence in American business.

In 1967, Ogilvy was finally honored at Buckingham Palace with a CBE, Commander of the British Empire, recognizing his work in promoting British exports. When he received his CBE, the Queen asked about his work; he said her expression in response to his reply he was in advertising was "a mixture of incredulity, horror and amusement."

Asked to consider playing the lead in a Broadway comedy called *Roar like a Dove,* set in the Scottish Highlands, Ogilvy explained, in a characteristic non sequitur: "I turned it down. The play failed."* He was invited to the White House twice. On one occasion, he danced for three hours, then left and joined a postparty gathering with Ted Sorensen, Arthur Schlesinger, and other bereaved members of the assassinated President Kennedy's staff. "The grandest evening of my life." The secretary of commerce asked him to prepare a presentation on the Kennedy Round of GATT (General Agreement of Tariffs and Trade) negotiations in Geneva, named for the president. The round was considered a success.

The *Reader's Digest* paid Ogilvy $10,000 for a full-page love letter, "Confessions of a magazine reader." It was, he said, the magazine he most admired.

> They know how to present complicated subjects in a way that engages the reader.
>
> They are on the side of the angels. They crusade against cigarettes, which kill people. They crusade against billboards, which make the world hideous. They crusade against boxing, which turns men into vegetables. They crusade against pornography.
>
> They crusade for integration, for the inter-faith movement, for the Public Defender system, for human freedom in all its forms.

Ogilvy said that he admired the editors' courage in opening readers' minds on delicate subjects, liked their sense of humor, and found the magazine easy to read, from the table of contents on the cover to the clear language inside. "The best advertisement ever written for the *Digest,*" said the editors.

---

* It opened May 21, 1964, and closed June 6.

Ogilvy vacationed in Barbados with the international social and political couple Ronald and Marietta Tree ("rubbing shoulders with visiting aristocracy from England, and black men of high degree") and in Montana (bird watching, camping at 8,500 feet, walking six to seven hours a day—"very fit.")

But he couldn't forget Lancaster County, and wrote an advertisement praising the area: "Escape to the Nineteenth Century in Pennsylvania." In 1963, he bought a second farm among the "fecund Amish" with his second wife. Anne loved the farm and furnished the two houses on the property with old furniture with claw feet and hung pots and pans on the walls. There most weekends with Anne's young children, they led a simple life with no socializing: gardening, walking, riding, and sleeping. It was more housework for her, but she had a splendid horse to ride.

Ogilvy's first farm had been farmed for him by a son of his friend Ira Stoltfus, an Amish bishop and one of his "life heroes." This new one, on 101 acres, was farmed for him by Ira's grandson, also named Ira, who grew so attached to the New York advertising man that he and his wife, Fannie, considered naming their second child David Ogilvy Stoltfus. In the end, they couldn't bring themselves to appropriate both names; their son's middle name is David.

Ogilvy bought six workhorses and a pony he named Pompey, explaining to Ira that it was the name of a Roman general. Pompey pulled Anne's two little girls around in a small black cart. There was a Guernsey cow Ira milked by hand, sitting on a stool. "Oh, how wonderful to have milk fresh from the cow every morning," Ogilvy marveled. Ira often saw the Ogilvys stretched out on their backs looking at the sky and enjoying the country air.

A would-be novice farmer the first time around, Ogilvy's new status as a weekend farmer became clear at a party with locals. One of them asked:

"Mr. Ogilvy, I understand you have some sheep. How many sheep do you have?"
    "Not very many. I'm not a big farmer like you."
    "How many sheep do you have, Mr. Ogilvy?"
    "Just a few. I'm really an advertising man in New York."
    "How many sheep do you have, Mr. Ogilvy?"

"About 22, I think."
"Oh! What are their names?"

When he sold the farm in 1968, the New York advertising man put the brand name in the headline: "David Ogilvy's farm at Intercourse."

∾

Although Ogilvy had disarmingly painted himself as a bad manager and brought in Stowell to help run the agency, he was a remarkably instinctive leader. "I have been managing Ogilvy & Mather for twenty years," he wrote in 1968. "I have learned from my own mistakes, from the counsel of my partners, from the literature, from George Gallup, Raymond Rubicam, and Marvin Bower."

What followed in the red-covered booklet (red had become the signature color for almost everything) conveyed a "unity of purpose" to O&M offices around the world. "Principles of Management" talks about advertising agencies, but the principles apply equally to almost any professional services business.

> On minimizing office politics: "Sack incurable politicians.
>   Crusade against paper warfare."
> On morale: "When people aren't having any fun, they
>   seldom produce good advertising. Get rid of sad dogs
>   who spread gloom."
> On professional standards: "Top men must not tolerate
>   sloppy plans or mediocre creative work."
> On partnership: "Top Management in each country should
>   function like a round table, presided over by a
>   Chairman who is big enough to be effective in the role
>   of *primus inter pares.*"

And so on, outlining roles for leaders, creative people, management supervisors, treasurers, and researchers.

Ogilvy didn't use the phrase "corporate culture" until years later, but that's what he was nurturing. One employee who had worked at several agencies noticed the difference. "People I knew who worked at other agencies had a job. We had a mission, and it was different. No place else I've ever worked had anything remotely like it." Another agreed: "This isn't an advertising agency, it is a *club,*" referring not to exclusion (there were many women) but to an attitude about the founder and his principles.

As well as a reputation for sparkling creative work, the agency was developing a personality. Ogilvy's foreword for a recruiting brochure spelled out the high standards and humane attitude toward those who worked there that he expected of his people.

> We are looking for gentlemen with ideas in their heads and fire in their bellies. If you join Ogilvy & Mather, we shall teach you everything we know about advertising. We shall pay you well, and do our damnedest to make you succeed. If you show promise, we shall load responsibility on you—fast. Life in our agency can be very exciting. You will never be bored. It's tough, but it's fun.

"Magic Lanterns," Ogilvy's name for the slide-and-film presentations designed to build a "corpus of knowledge," were a large part of the personality. Lantern slides stated a principle, quoted research, showed a sales result, and illustrated the point with a print ad or commercial. His first Magic Lantern, "How to create advertising that sells," the one that impressed the staff at Festival Hall, was mandatory viewing by all new employees; there would be several dozen more such presentations on topics useful to clients—and prospects. While the ostensible purpose of Lanterns was knowledge and training, they proved to be seductive new business tools.

The manner in which Ogilvy stated his principles reminded some Catholics in the agency of the catechism. It is an anomaly that Ogilvy, a professed atheist, was fascinated by the structure of the Catholic Church and often borrowed its language. Reeves was in the "apostolic succession" from Claude Hopkins. A royal blue vest Ogilvy donned on state occasions resembled ecclesiastical vestments. He reveled in a magazine's labeling of him as "The Pope of modern advertising"

Soon after I joined the agency in 1963 as a junior account manager, I was called to the phone one evening while dining with friends. "I'm at the engraver's looking at the proofs of the coupon ad," said the copy supervisor. "You know where the two color pages come together? They're too far apart—there is too much white space in the gutter. We can shave each plate one-eighth of an inch and bring them closer. It will cost $300." I agreed that the fix made sense but pointed out this was not the main campaign, only a coupon ad, and this was just a test market. The change could be made later. "And the client has already approved it," I added.

The reproving response was swift. "David says (pause) it's never too late to *improve* an ad—even after the client has approved it." "Spend the 300 bucks," I agreed. Like the church, the agency had standards.

Part of the personality of the agency was lodged in a Belgian barber extricated from the Park Lane Hotel in New York by Ogilvy, who accused the shop owner of being a profiteer. Emil Vaessen was given the use of an office with barber chair, mirrors, and sink, and was on his own. "Our Classy Clipper" announced the staff newsletter *Flagbearer*. Nobody in any communications business communicates like a barber; Ogilvy got all his haircuts from Emil and always asked for the "latest dirt." Emil is still there 42 years later, his services available to staff, clients, friends, and the lawyers upstairs.

For some O&M people, Rattazzi's, a dimly lit restaurant across the street from the agency's entrance on East Forty-eighth Street, known for its oversized martinis, was part of the scene. Unlike Leo Burnett, who enjoyed the cocktail hour with colleagues, Ogilvy took a dim view of camaraderie lubricated by alcohol. When he decided the agency should have its own cafeteria, suggestions for a name were solicited. Among the favorites: "Charlemagne East" (his claimed heritage), "The Hungry Eyepatch," and "Toady Hall," relating to his lofty principle: "We despise toadies who suck up to their bosses." Ogilvy announced he planned to eat there regularly and urged others to follow his example. One Rattazzi's regular solved the dilemma posed by the new liquor-free cafeteria by going across the street, downing his martini, and then returning to the agency for a tuna fish sandwich. Ogilvy, a frequent patron of the cafeteria, would take his tray, scan the room, and invariably sit next to the prettiest girl. He seldom entered Rattazzi's except to seek one of his executives on a business issue.

When the agency later added an executive dining room, Ogilvy visited the cafeteria less often. At lunch one day in the more exclusive setting, he observed a fellow executive sitting alone at a table reading his mail. "Sandy, you and I belong to two clubs, this and the Brook," he called across the room. "We don't bring our papers to the table there, and I don't think you should do it here either."

~

His second marriage was coming apart. Anne had been married to a Boston Cabot, was full of herself and stubborn, and wanted to do things her way. Now she was married to someone who wanted to do things *his* way. She was trying to do it all; he was self-centered and inconsiderate. Early in their marriage, she was taking courses at Barnard College to complete requirements for her Radcliffe degree. Ogilvy would announce he had invited someone for dinner, and she'd say, "You can't have him for dinner that night. I have a quiz the next morning and I have to be up at Barnard and I have to do my homework, and I can only do it at night because I have three little children here." Once they arrived at the opera house in the rain; he sprang out of the Rolls-Royce and bounded up the stairs, leaving her behind. Ogilvy had created a vision of a marriage with lots of time off and travel, then brought home two briefcases at night.

Everyone knew he was a difficult guy to be married to. Anne summed it up: "When he's nice, he's very very nice. When he's bad, he's horrid. Things with him are always heightened. Nothing is what you would expect." The couple enjoyed bicycle trips in France; one was the beginning of the end. Ogilvy found a château in 1966 and bought it, with proceeds from the public offering, without telling her. "That's when I knew the marriage was on the rocks," says his friend Louis Auchincloss, who represented David in the divorce.

Anne was against the château from the beginning. She was put off by the feeling that it was something of a monument to him, which wasn't far off the mark. She preferred their farm in the Amish country, where she rode her horse, or the summer house they rented on the Massachusetts North Shore. Nor did she aspire to the baronial life he wanted. They broke up in 1973, after having been married 16 years. Ogilvy, now 62, retreated to his château, from which he bombarded directors with memos. He called himself "The Holy Spook."

TEN

THE KING IN
HIS CASTLE

When guests are in residence, days at Château de Touffou might start with three jaunty tunes played on a *cor de chasse,* the circular hunting horn favored in Poitou, the "belly" of France, 100 miles southwest of Paris near Poitiers. The horn player, partly hidden in the morning mist, stands on the bridge over the dry moat, facing away from the house so the bell end points back toward the guests. His repertoire includes a drinking song from Bach's "Peasant Cantata" that he learned from Ogilvy.

After dinner, sometimes there is a concert in the courtyard under the night sky. Several horn players from nearby châteaux stand in a circle facing each other, horn ends facing behind them. On the ground by their feet, lighted candelabra. From dawn to eve, show business.

That was what it was like after Ogilvy retired to his château in 1973. If Ogilvy & Mather was his child, Château de Touffou* was his love. *"Il n'ya que deux châteaux en France,"* he proclaimed. There are only two châteaux in France, Versailles and Touffou. Parts of it date back to the twelfth century. He called it a *"folie de grandeur"*

---

* *Tous fou* (pronounced Too-Foo) means "everybody's crazy," which has nothing to do with the name of the château but is a corruption of its earlier names.

and professed to disdain the châteaux of the Loire as Johnny-come-latelies, only 300 years old.

Why France? For one thing, Ogilvy didn't really get along with some of his English partners, who revered his brother and regarded him as an upstart, never inviting him to address the staff. But he also loved France: the landscape, the food, the wine, the architecture. He knew the climate to be good for gardening, and would for the first time perhaps get his hands dirty. He understood French from his days as a chef in Paris (but spoke it reluctantly and infrequently). And France had no capital gains tax. He was less enthusiastic about the country's politics. When Mitterand and the left wing won the 1981 election, Ogilvy almost expected Russian tanks to appear in Paris, and sent a succinct Telex to the agency's treasurer in New York: "Mitterand is going to soak the rich. I am rich."

Although not of the scale of the great French châteaux, neither is Touffou, with 30 rooms, simply a great country house. Looming high on the hill overlooking the river Vienne, a tributary of the Loire, Touffou presents a sweeping vista of the rolling French countryside. With no electric lines or modern houses in view, one can imagine being back in an earlier century. The François I bedroom commemorates a supposed visit of the French king. Approaching from the small town of Bonnes a mile or so down the hill, the visitor first sees the blue-gray slate-roofed turrets, then the worn apricot-ochre stone battlements. Some of the walls, designed to repel attacks during the Middle Ages, are ten feet thick. It is surrounded by a wide dry moat in which prior owners kept wild boar.

Ogilvy said he borrowed $500,000 to buy it, furnished, with 150 acres; he spent a great deal more restoring and fixing it up. It was never a ruin; German soldiers billeted there in World War II, and it survived an RAF bombing raid. But the foundation and roof both needed major repairs. The French government paid half the costs, on the understanding that, as a *"monument historique,"* parts would be open to the public. Ogilvy would stand at the tall Renaissance window counting the tourists wandering into the courtyard below. "One franc fifty, three francs, four francs fifty. Today is a good day," he'd comment, as if these visitors were a significant source of his income.

High among the reasons for selling his company to the public was getting some money to buy Touffou. Few of Ogilvy's associates believe he took such a consequential step solely to buy himself a colossal home, but he certainly wanted to live more largely than his means had permitted. A great château made possible what he deemed an appropriate lifestyle. He had a big superego, explains one of his partners. "He was a person of big capacity. He wasn't athletic. He wasn't wrapped up in art or music. This gave him a kind of field to play on."

The seller was Enguerrand de Vergie, the head of the company that makes Suze, a bitter yellow liqueur believed by the French to have great medicinal powers in settling the stomach. When an embezzling employee almost bankrupted the company, most of de Vergie's personal fortune was sucked away and he was forced to sell his château. As part of the sale agreement, Ogilvy permitted him to live there.

Ogilvy loved telling visitors, "This place was 300 years old when Columbus was born. Would you like to see the dungeon?" Asked facetiously if someone was in the dungeon, he admitted it was empty at the moment, but like KoKo, The Lord High Executioner in *The Mikado,* he had "a little list of those who never would be missed"— such as art directors who set type in reverse. "Put *them* down in the dungeon for a few years." There is an anachronistic swimming pool. One of his irreverent colleagues couldn't resist: "Is this where you practice walking on water, David?" A short beat. "I don't practice."

Monsieur de Vergie, a prodigious hunter, had furnished the château with the horns of countless deer he had killed. Anne moved in only briefly, took down the horns and began to make changes in the dark interior, until she decided it was too damp and cold, moved out, and went home. Ogilvy went on to brighten the high-ceilinged rooms, add English and French antiques, hang a large collection of copper pans on the wall in the kitchen, and install a coal-fired Aga Cooker. It is surprisingly homelike and livable.

The vineyard that came with the château produced a classic story as well as grapes. Standing on the terrace, Ogilvy said to a guest: "You know that wine we had at lunch? It comes from grapes grown in that vineyard just across the river." Guest: "It doesn't travel very well, does it?" The vines were removed shortly thereafter.

With the help of a garden designer, Ogilvy created an informal English-style garden that somehow works in its French historical setting. A series of garden "rooms," enclosed by fast-growing thuya hedges, are filled with fragrant old roses, golden peonies, lupines, delphiniums, and, in memory of his mother, "Mrs. Sinkins" pinks (dianthus). Two "rooms" are dedicated to changing into and out of bathing suits for the pool. The pool is made invisible from the château by an optical illusion; the land slopes up, so swimmers appear as severed heads rolling across the lawn.

The garden, cited as one of the 25 best in France, is featured in gardening books. At the end of a lime tree allée, the Grecian goddess Diana the Huntress stands in sculpture with her bow and arrows. Ogilvy proudly showed off his garden, giving visitors a full tour, complete with the Latin names of dozens of flowers and shrubs. While being a life member in the Royal Horticultural Society does not necessarily attest to gardening expertise, Ogilvy did know horticulture. On a visit to the gardens at Wisley, he regarded the two long facing rows of herbaceous perennials: "The finest double border I've ever seen." He was told by his mother: "You have inherited my love of gardening, but your taste is entirely vulgar. You have no interest in plants themselves, all you want is to make a show."

~

Châteaux need chatelaines to run them. Ogilvy separated from Anne in 1971, moving out of their New York East Side brownstone into a furnished apartment, before going to live full-time in France two years later. He first met Herta Lans de la Touche, a slim, elegant brunette living nearby, when he bought Touffou in 1967. They were introduced by M. de Vergie, the prior owner. Now alone and lonely in a vast château, Ogilvy was susceptible and she was recently divorced. He said he could tell by looking at her that she wasn't totally happy. This time his romantic pursuit culminated with what she calls a business letter: "You should marry me because . . . ," listing fact after fact to make his case. He made the sale, and they married in 1973.

Herta moved in with her three teen-aged children, son Guy and two daughters, Isabelle and Laurence (known as Minouche). Ogilvy was a doting stepfather, especially to Minouche, the youngest; he would rib her, and she'd give it right back. It was a wonderful relationship. Herta was 25 years Ogilvy's junior but his match in most respects.

Including intelligence, said he. They both took an IQ test he found in the back of a book. He got a 96 ("par for ditch diggers"), and she got 136. It changed their relationship. "Suddenly she's pretty and clever and I'm ugly and dumb." Of German Dutch and Swiss English parentage, Herta was born in Mexico and considers herself Mexican. She describes Ogilvy as the most American Englishman she had ever met.

Everyone agrees he was lucky to find her. She knew how to deal with Ogilvy, a skill that had eluded his other wives. "She didn't put up with any crap from David," said a friend. When he started to get up in the middle of a meal because he was bored, Herta told him he could not leave the room while they were having dinner and could not allow her children to understand that is good behavior. When he started to misbehave, she would jolly him along. "Come on, David. You can't do that. This is what you've got to do."

Herta said that living with him was like living from one storm to the next. She didn't get upset, but made her views clear, handling his moods and demands with a knowing smile and without complaint, even when he'd ask for Grape-Nuts after she had been in the kitchen most of the day preparing a fine meal. She solved the problem of his behavior in restaurants, where he was impatient beyond the point of rudeness, by ordering the meal in advance so he wouldn't have to wait. She handled him perfectly, and he got to where he liked it. Before Herta came along, he was stomping out of meetings; she was a calming influence.

Touffou ran on her plan, with the help of a too-small staff, and she managed the steady stream of visitors with good humor—in four languages. She was determined to turn their medieval monument into a comfortable family home, softening its massive presence and giving it charm and style. Herta is expert at embroidery, creative in turning worn bedspreads into window curtains, inventive in converting unused rooms to useful purposes, and the epitome of the gracious hostess.

Ogilvy too could be a thoughtful host. Citing the Duke of Wellington's attention to detail as one reason for his success, he placed books in guests' rooms according to their individual interests. He met guests at the train station, dressed in old boots and roomy corduroy trousers. If someone else had brought them from the station, Ogilvy would appear on the château's second-floor balcony, raise both arms, and call out a dramatic "Welcome."

And there were guests—in the first year alone, 348 stayed at least two nights. His nieces from Scotland came for two weeks and stayed a year, to learn French. His Amish friends came to visit. Faced with the choice of jugs of water and wine on the table, the Amish men went for the wine, doing "as the custom says." Ogilvy extended an open invitation, rash but typical, to all the hundreds of Ogilvy & Mather people to come and see him when in France. Dozens took him up on it. People would invite themselves for tea and be coaxed to stay the night. One young couple asked if they could come for a night and stayed for six. He put some houseguests to work improving his dry moat—a dirty job—confiding that guests seldom outstayed their welcome if put to work. The house was always full; Ogilvy loved having people around.

Under Herta's guidance, visitors were treated with Old World courtesy. Bedspreads were turned down; often breakfasts of homemade croissants with homemade jam and honey were delivered on trays to bedroom doors. On nice summer days, idyllic lunches were served at long wooden tables on a terrace overlooking the river. Dinners were taken in a room lined with lighted shelves filled with Ogilvy's huge collection of East India Company blue and white porcelain, followed by coffee in the great living room with its comfortable upholstered sofas and chairs covered in a sturdy white fabric. There were flowers in each guest's room.

A visitor's day at the château might include exploring the gardens, rowing on the river in a small boat, bicycling though the countryside, croquet (long mallets, white trousers), walking the hills and woods, shopping at Poitiers or another nearby market, but most of all talking. Conversation was the sport at Touffou. An art director from the London office, invited to stay for a week, met Ogilvy in his office each morning. They talked until lunch, then got into his black Mercedes and went sightseeing, came back and talked some more—about advertising, companies, and, especially, people—until dinner, then into early hours of the morning. Ogilvy was full of energy, and the younger man had a hard time keeping up with him.

Ogilvy became a presence in the area, something of a local lord. Driving through town, he would look out the car window and wave in regal fashion at some passerby. With great satisfaction, he turned to one visitor and said, "That's the mayor. He hates me." The postmaster loved him. With the help of a secretary based in the Paris office, he conducted such an active correspondence from Touffou that the volume at the local post office increased enormously, and the postmaster got a promotion and a raise. In early years, Ogilvy would go up to Paris, to his apartment on rue de Varenne on the Left Bank, adjacent to the Rodin Museum (literally backing up to Rodin's *Gates of Hell*). He avoided the main agency office because he didn't get along with the managing director. Instead, he worked from his "spiritual home," the direct response unit, at a different address.

In the winter, Ogilvy accompanied his wife and friends on skiing vacations in Rougement in the Swiss Alps, "to escape the French tax collectors, who have gone mad."* How did this nonathlete feel about being at a ski resort? He read books. He wrote. He walked. He knew everybody around. "He could have been on the moon," says Herta, a lovely skier (in the best-looking outfit on the slopes). "He had a friend he adored, the best friend of his old age, Leonard Woods, of the [J.P.] Morgan family. He walked with Lenny. They talked. It was a completely intellectual life. They both dressed in L.L. Bean and read the same books. They were enchanted."

But Ogilvy increasingly preferred life at Touffou, where he spent much of the day in his study, a bright spacious room with a few chairs and a large antique writing table, decorated only with a big bunch of flowers. No formal desk set, just a real working surface. A fax machine in an adjacent room replaced the chattering Telex of earlier years. Ogilvy worked every day, battling the world in memos and letters—often 30 to 50 a day—and an occasional speech. After breakfast in bed, brought in on a tray by his gardener, he'd go for a walk. Then to his high-ceilinged office, with a constant breeze stirring white drapes through open windows, to see what faxes had arrived. He would sit down, light his pipe, take a sharpened pencil from the silver Tiffany bowl on his desk, and write. "I couldn't work without smoking a pipe." Midmorning, he'd come out for a cup of coffee. Then back to see if there was an answer to a fax. Lunch, listen to music, snooze, read, and work—until ten in

---

* Escape meant spending six months, plus one day, outside France.

the evening. He occasionally retired to bed wearing a white night-cap of the type Englishmen wore in Dickens's time.

Evenings when he wasn't working, Ogilvy and Herta would look at television together. Many commercials aroused his ire. "What are they advertising—tea, coffee, a lovely hotel room at the Ritz, or the idea of a half-naked girl?" he'd ask rhetorically. "Most of the people who are writing advertising today have never had to sell anything to anybody," he said in an interview with *Newsweek*. "They are think-ing, 'Is it witty? Is it charming? Is it civilized?'"

David was always writing, writing, writing, says Herta. He read everything that went on in the company and bombarded everyone with notes. He answered every fan letter that sounded intelligent. People wrote to say they were in advertising because they had written to him and he had answered, or they went to a speech and sent him a note and he had answered. "For his last 25 years, he gardened, he wrote, and he read," says Herta. "And people came, and that was it. He was a very hard worker. With him, everything was written down. Everything, everything, everything. Except the numbers. He was a word man, not a money man."

Except that he continually *worried* about money, and com-plained when the dollar declined against the franc (when he was paid in dollars). "I'm supposed to be terribly rich. I'm not, because I screwed up my financial affairs all my life." Louis Auchincloss, visiting at Touffou, told Ogilvy to stop complaining about money. "You're in excellent health, you have this glorious château, you have a devoted wife and everyone's admiration. Stop grousing." He did . . . for 15 minutes.

∾

With more free time, he could travel. Ogilvy had always wanted to visit his father's birthplace in Argentina and finally agreed to embark on the *Augustus,* an Italian liner traveling from Cannes. A few days later, he sent a Telex: "The Augustus is disgustus. I have disem-barked." Persuaded to try again by plane, he was met at the airport in Rio de Janeiro with a red carpet rolled out. He bent down on his hands and knees and kissed the ground. At the sheep farm in the Pampas where his father was born, he *cried.*

On his only tour of Southeast Asia, he took the *Queen Elizabeth 2* to New York, traveled across the United States by train, visited his wife's birthplace in Mexico, and sailed on to Sydney on the *QE2*. "Most of our fellow passengers were rich octogenarians with stentorian voices," he reported. "One woman had brought 69 evening dresses." He met with the prime minister of New Zealand, addressed the biggest audience the American Chamber of Commerce ever attracted in Australia, met with 27 clients, spent "long and happy hours" reviewing the creative output of each office, and endured three-hour cocktail parties. "My idea of life in hell has always been a perpetual cocktail party." He visited 16 cities, gave 46 speeches, and was covered on TV and the front pages of newspapers.

Ogilvy had little choice but to fly back. On the day of his return, the agency's Bangkok manager checked him in for a Singapore Airlines flight and went home. The next morning, Ogilvy called. A storm had come up, and he went to the cockpit and asked the pilot if he was going to take off. The captain assured him there was nothing to worry about, they'd be taking off any minute. "Not with me," said Ogilvy, who got off the plane and went back to his hotel.

He had started thinking about stepping down as chairman in 1972, telling the board he was not in a hurry to retire but listing 17 criteria to help identify his successor, from being a good judge of men to being able to travel: "The poor devil should not be afraid of airplanes." He concluded, "I have measured our present Chairman [himself] against this list of criteria. He seems to score reasonably high marks on about twelve of the seventeen. None of us scores high on all seventeen."

Three years later, at 63, he stepped down, acknowledging "I have been a non-playing captain for the last two years." To nobody's surprise, he nominated Jock Elliott—"a gentleman with brains"—as chairman. "He is much more *stable* than I am. He's got more wisdom than I have. His inter-personal relationships are better than mine ever were. I'm rather a cross-patch, and he's not; he's a pacifier. He's got a deep keel. I have always carried too much sail."

Well, not exactly nonplaying, even when no longer captain. Although he lost some presence in New York as he spent more time in France, without formal responsibilities other than board or executive committee meetings, Ogilvy's energy over the next 15 years almost seemed to grow as he tried to steer the agency he launched, gave interviews, wrote an occasional ad (including for the French Government Tourist Office), and accepted more honors and awards.

In a speech accepting the Parlin Award from the American Marketing Association, Ogilvy delved into the topic of leadership. He told the National Distillers convention: "You aren't selling whiskey—you are selling imagery." To the Proprietary Association convention, he said: "You can spot a good medicine writer by throwing him a bottle of your tablets. If he automatically reads the formula on the label, he is a professional. If he doesn't, avoid him." For his talks, as always, he took his jacket off to display his red braces, "so people won't think I'm an old fart."

The New York Times billed his talk to the 4As agency meeting as "Ogilvy's Farewell." He called that a slight exaggeration, but noted the news value in farewell appearances ("as Frank Sinatra discovered") and said he was thinking of saying FAREWELL in every speech he made. A "bread-and-butter letter" for Madison Avenue's kindness, it saluted his stimulating colleagues in the business— "most of them may be nutty as fruitcakes, but never dull."

Ogilvy made clear that he had not retired, only given up the role of chairman. "Now I'm working entirely in the creative area, which is what I'm best at." He appointed himself the agency's worldwide creative head, and assembled a handful of the agency's top creative directors in a Creative Council to meet with him twice a year to review worldwide output. He wrote dozens of red-bordered Creative Council encyclicals on hiring better people, typography, visual clichés, awards, "addy" versus editorial layouts, boring photos, training in direct marketing, avoidance of stereotypes, and a remarkable variety of other issues.

He continued to campaign against the acquisition of other agencies outside "The True Church" and attacked growth for the sake of growth, rather than the service of clients, but failed to derail this train. "I seem to be a perpetual pourer of cold water nowadays. In old age I find myself inclined to preserve and refine the institution we have built; I resist innovation which, in my view, would muck it up." He made his case to Jock Elliott:

If we are to prevent the eventual disintegration of our world-wide church into a Tower of Babel, we must continue our evangelism, make sure that every office is headed by a member of the True Church, and *not by a stranger* (ditto Creative Heads) and, never again entrust the supervision of offices to outsiders or lay brothers [not ordained by training in The True Church]. This error leads to schism, balkanization, apostasy, bankruptcy and ultimate disintegration.

Ogilvy took issue with the agency's long-range business plan, concluding that the company was being managed to impress security analysts and citing St. Paul in his First Epistle to Timothy: "The love of money is the root of all evil." (This from the seeker of "lucre.") He opposed diversification, deriding as "small beer" the purchase of a one-woman speech consultancy: "Read all about this Amazing and Irrelevant Diversification in our next Annual Report. The analysts will guffaw."

He continued to resist starting a second network of non-O&M agencies like Scali, McCabe, Sloves, arguing that it did no good for clients—indeed, it irritated them. Instead, Ogilvy urged the company to sell those agencies and use the proceeds to buy back the agency's stock. "My ambition for O&M is that it should be the best agency, not necessarily the biggest." He mused in a memo (not sent) as to why he remained on the board: "Because I identify with the Company. Because I need the money. And because I am useful. How does the Company use me? As a symbol of Creativity, and a celebrity for ceremonial purposes. But my judgment is rejected by the Executive Committee with monotonous regularity."

After failing to make much headway on strategy, Ogilvy turned his focus to people. At a 1984 international "jamboree" in San Francisco, he told the agency's 100 or so top people: "If you ask me what is our primary purpose, I would say that it is not to make the maximum profit for our shareholders, but to run our agency in such a way that our employees are happy." He was clear about what made an organization attractive to its employees: Absence of politics at the top. Pride in being part of the best agency. A feeling that the prime purpose is to do great work for clients. Success in new business. Firing "passengers," because their continued presence on the payroll offends people who actually work. Firing politicians, because they are "cankers." Fairness at the top. Integrity at the top. Fun. "Kill grimness with laughter."

Ogilvy loved to discover new talent, and wrote an uncommon recruitment ad:

Wanted by Ogilvy & Mather International: TRUMPETER SWANS

Trumpeter Swans are those rare specimens "who combine personal genius with inspiring leadership," said the ad, which went on to encourage "one of those rare birds" to write Ogilvy personally. The advertisement attracted attention if not job-seekers; it seems that few trumpeter swans answer help-wanted ads. Ogilvy lobbied directors to recruit more "high flyers," noting he had sent the same memo a year earlier but nothing had happened. "I never give up."

Campbell Soup invited him to consult on all their brands. He told the company they were underspending on advertising, their products needed improving, and the famous red and white soup label (made an icon by Andy Warhol) lacked appetite appeal—"it looks like an oil can." The company changed labels on several products after testing proved Ogilvy was right. It also created its own David Ogilvy Award for marketing, confident that as judge, he would be so objective that the award might go to other Campbell agencies. (It did.)

The leading talk show host of the era, David Susskind, interviewed Ogilvy for four hours on a program shown on two Sunday nights. Ogilvy talked about the advantage of being a Scot (it differentiated him), his Gallup experience, how he got ideas, his bad financial deals, and his persistent fear of failure. "I never thought what I was doing would be as good as my previous work."

Guy Mountfort, one of the British directors of the parent company, took Ogilvy's advice to pursue his real interest outside advertising. "We ad men are a dime a dozen. You ornithologists are rare birds," he wrote. Mountfort went on to become one of the founders of the World Wildlife Fund and recruited Ogilvy to its prestigious board and executive committee. Ogilvy seldom missed a WWF meeting, and there were many. He organized a two-day brainstorming session at the château, volunteered the agency's services, and solicited financial backing in one of the most persuasive of his long-copy ads ("Back from the dead"). "I have written hundreds of ads for dozens of clients," he said. "This is my favorite. The more exposure it gets, the more animals and birds will be saved from extinction." Then, quoting from the ad: "Remember, extinction is forever."

Ogilvy loved the cause and the heady company and meetings at Buckingham Palace, chaired by Prince Philip, the Duke of Edinburgh, who publicly acknowledged Ogilvy's good ideas: "Although he wasn't himself a conservationist, he could see the point and contributed enormously."

Privately, the two men never seemed to get along. Told that Philip had said nice things about him, Ogilvy said that he was under the impression Philip considered him "a blithering idiot." Ogilvy had strong opinions on what WWF should be doing, views that Philip did not always agree with. The Duke of Edinburgh was inevitably the center of attention when he was in the room, a position Ogilvy preferred for himself. He felt Philip was a bit of a bully and started bad-mouthing him, which didn't go down well with other WWF board members or the staff. For whatever reason, he was off the board—a shame, since he was doing a fine job for the WWF, and had become deeply committed to its purpose. Disgruntling the duke probably didn't help Ogilvy's candidacy for knighthood.

~

It is not unusual for retired advertising grandees to write about their experiences in the business, as Ogilvy did soon after stepping down as chairman. Unlike *Confessions of an Advertising Man,* his autobiography, *Blood, Brains and Beer* was, he conceded, "a flop"—both in its first publication and when republished 17 years later with a new title, *David Ogilvy: An Autobiography,* and puffed up with lists of favorite friends, flowers, and, of all things, recipes.

His partners urged him to consider updating *Confessions.* Ogilvy concluded that the agency didn't need another best seller but an entirely new book that could be used for business purposes. *Ogilvy on Advertising,* published by Crown in 1983, was lavishly illustrated with advertisements (seven with nude women to make a point about European advertising) and, unlike *Confessions,* included campaigns from other agencies. It is even more of a how-to book than its predecessor: how to produce advertising that sells . . . get a job in advertising . . . run an advertising firm . . . get clients . . . pick an agency . . . compete with P&G . . . and do better advertising, direct marketing, research, and promotion.

A chapter on six giants who invented modern advertising describes Albert Lasker, Raymond Rubicam, Bill Bernbach, Leo Burnett, Claude Hopkins, and Stanley Resor. "All six of them were Americans. All six had jobs before they went into advertising. At least five were gluttons for work, and uncompromising perfectionists. Four made their reputations as copywriters. Only three had university degrees." In other words, except for their birthplaces, they were all just like him. The book inveighs against billboards ("Who is *in favor* of them? Only the people who make money out of them"), political advertising ("Can you imagine Abraham Lincoln hiring an agency to produce 30-second spots about slavery?"), and testing commercials by the recall method (citing a creative director who claimed he could get high recall by showing a gorilla in a jockstrap).

"The book of David," as *Madison Avenue* called it, was judged "as fine a primer on advertising as has ever been written." John Caples said it was "the most exciting and instructive volume about advertising I have ever seen" and "a must for every ambitious advertising man." In a peculiar comparison, *The London Standard* named Ogilvy "the Einstein of Advertising." He admitted the obvious: "All my books are thinly disguised advertisements for Ogilvy & Mather."

~

"When I got to IBM, I thought culture was just one of those things like finance and marketing that you managed in an institution," says Lou Gerstner, who became friendly with Ogilvy when Gerstner was building the major businesses at American Express—with much-admired O&M advertising, and later engineered a historic turn-around at IBM as its CEO. "At the end of my time there," he continues, "I realized that culture wasn't part of the game—it *is* the game in building and maintaining a successful enterprise." In Gerstner's view, Ogilvy built an institution by creating a powerful culture and creating a set of principles that are adaptable to the current environment. "They're quite eternal."

Ogilvy himself took on culture formally in 1985, in a dinner address to the agency's directors and top executives at Fishmongers Hall in London, saying he had read a book on corporate culture and wondered if the agency had one. "Apparently we do. We seem to have an exceptionally *strong* culture. *Indeed, it may be this, more than anything else, which differentiates us from our competitors.*" It starts with the working atmosphere: "Some of our people spend their entire working lives in our company. We do our damnedest to make it a *happy* experience for them."

> We treat our people like human beings. We help them when they are in trouble—with their jobs, with illnesses, with alcoholism, and so on.
>
> We help our people make the best of their talents. We invest an awful lot of time and money in training—perhaps more than any of our competitors.
>
> Our system of management is singularly democratic. We don't like hierarchical bureaucracy or rigid pecking orders.
>
> We abhor ruthlessness.
>
> We like people with gentle manners. Our New York office goes so far as to give an annual award for what they call "professionalism combined with civility."
>
> We like people who are honest. Honest in argument, honest with clients, honest with suppliers, and honest with the company.
>
> We admire people who work hard. Objectivity and thoroughness are admired.
>
> Superficiality is not admired.
>
> We despise and detest office politicians, toadies, bullies and pompous asses.
>
> The way up the ladder is open to everybody. We are free from prejudice of any kind—religious prejudice, racial prejudice or sexual prejudice.
>
> We detest nepotism and every other form of favouritism.
>
> In promoting people to top jobs, we are influenced as much by their character as by anything else.

The final section, "EX CATHEDRA," listed some of Ogilvy's "*obiter dicta*"—notably, and hardly for the first time: "We hire gentlemen with brains" and "Never run an advertisement you would not want your own family to see." His view was that advertising was an invited guest into the home and should have good manners.

Fun is part of the culture. Ogilvy enjoyed jokes, peppered his notes and memos with them, and saw the humor in most situations.

He felt creative organizations worked best if there was a spirit of fun, as in great research laboratories where scientists play practical jokes on each other.

Bill Phillips, one of his successors as chairman, captured the spirit in his mantra: "Work hard. Play hard. Sleep fast." His General Foods account group worked hard and late, so he replaced a conference table with a Ping-Pong table, covered for client meetings. Several offices produced Christmas revues; author Salman Rushdie was a writer for London's "Red Braces 1977." The New York Red Braces running team wore white T-shirts imprinted with red braces. When the jogging team in South Africa asked Ogilvy to write something for their T-shirts, he wrote back saying he hated T-shirts. The team ordered shirts reprinting his letter.

Ogilvy was convinced that keeping the best people is more a function of leadership than money.

∾

"It did not escape our notice that everyone in the upper levels of Ogilvy knew how to write—and write very well," said the head of an agency acquired by O&M. Asked what was different from BBDO, where he had worked for 20 years, Jock Elliott said "We write down what we know and believe."

Ogilvy was, above all, a writer, and his agency had a writing culture. He wrote like an angel, rhapsodized David McCall. "Even his memoranda were worth saving. He was capable of organizing his thoughts into brilliant prose even when he was dictating. His advertising copy came hard." Ogilvy always considered himself an advertising writer, never more. "If I were a really creative writer, like my cousin and great friend Rebecca West, I would probably prefer to seek fame as an author—instead of devoting my pen to the services of Rinso." But he wasn't and he didn't.

Ogilvy never wrote an advertisement in the office: "Too many interruptions." He started by looking at every advertisement for competing products for the past 20 years: "Study the precedents." Then he'd go to work on a headline. Finally, when he could no longer postpone the actual copy, he would start writing, usually throwing away the first 20 attempts. "If all else fails, I drink a half a bottle of rum and play a Handel oratorio on the gramophone. This generally produces a gush of copy." The next morning, he would get up early and edit the gush. "I am a lousy copywriter," he would say, "but a good editor."

Being edited by Ogilvy was like being operated on by a great surgeon who could put his hand on the only tender organ in your body. You could *feel* him put his finger on the wrong word, the soft phrase, the incomplete thought. But there was no pride of authorship, and he could be quite self-critical. Someone found a personally notated copy of one of *his* books in which he had written cross comments about his own writing: "Rubbish," "Rot!" "Nonsense." He would send his major documents around for comment, with a note: "Please improve."

Like his brother, David drafted in *pencil.* No typewriter, not even a ballpoint pen. Freshly sharpened pencils. Always in pencil, says a former secretary, because he thought that nobody was so good they should write in pen and not change things. After a secretary transcribed his hard-to-decipher handwriting to a typewriter, he was meticulous in making it attractive and easy to read. Double-spaced, short paragraphs, key phrases underlined, sections indented for further emphasis, sections separated by a row of spaced asterisks. With an occasional flourish, after a letter had been typed, he would sign his name in red. For urgent matters, he attached a small red card saying IMMEDIATE, a practice he picked up in Washington.

Everything was scribbled and rewritten and scribbled again. Ogilvy would go through a document and take out adjectives and adverbs, leaving nouns and verbs, to make it clear—and readable. Short sentences, short paragraphs, no circumlocutions. All those pure little pieces of writing that people saved were hard work. "When you read them, you think this must have been like Mozart's music, it came straight out of his brain," says a writer who worked with him. "But no. I couldn't believe how much trouble he had to get the sentence he wanted." Or the perfect word, *le mot juste.* The widow of a friend said his was the best condolence note when her husband died: "He was golden."

Just as he expected the agency's advertising to be clear and honest, Ogilvy expected the same in memos, status reports, and plans. "The better you write, the higher you go in Ogilvy & Mather. People who think well, write well. Woolly-minded people write woolly memos, woolly letters and woolly speeches."

The advertising business has historically provided incomes to writers until they published their books or because they elected to use their facility with words to sell, and Ogilvy's agency provided sustenance for a fair share of authors destined for literary fame. Ogilvy himself figures prominently in several memories.

Before Salman Rushdie was a lionized member of the literary establishment and threatened with a *fatwa* for his book *The Satanic Verses,* he was a copywriter with Ogilvy & Mather in London. His "Naughty but nice" line for the Milk Marketing Board's promotion of cream cakes was drawn from an old English quip. For Aero chocolate bars, the literary lion created "Irresti-bubble" and "delecti-bubble."

Another Indian-born writer, Indra Sinha, worked in the London office as well. Known for his translation of *The Love Teachings of Kama Sutra* and his novels *The Death of Mr. Love* and *Cybergypsies,* Sinha wrote three-page advertisements for the packaging company Metal Box, correcting misconceptions and reducing the guilt many people felt when using canned foods, with the line "Every time you open a can you save a little of your life."

Don DeLillo had what he calls a "short, uninteresting" career as a copywriter at OBM in New York in the late 1950s. Scenes in his first novel, *Americana,* drew on his advertising background. He wrote anti-littering ads for New York City, image ads for Sears, ceiling tile and insulation ads for Armstrong Cork, and an International Paper series featuring well-known writers, under the headline: "Send me a man who reads."

Before Peter Mayle went to France and wrote *A Year in Provence,* he worked in the agency's London office. After six months of correspondence with Ogilvy, he went to New York and worked "in the salt mines of trade ads and product leaflets" before being promoted to junior copywriter on Hathaway shirts, "Come to Britain," and Steuben Glass. None of the accounts was large, but each was one of Ogilvy's pets. Mayle describes presenting his first Hathaway ads, which he had rewritten a dozen times.

His secretary told me to go through to the office. It was empty. Puzzled, I was wondering what to do when a voice from the corner of the office said, "I am at stool. Pass your copy under the door." David was taking his ease in his private lavatory. I slid the copy under the door and waited. Eventually, the copy slid back, heavily marked with red pencil. "Off you go," said the voice, and off I went to study the penciled comments on my carefully typed text.

David had underlined a phrase I was particularly pleased with, and had written: Quack-quack. Belles lettres. Omit. There were other, equally pungent directions scattered throughout the short piece.

Edmund Morris, winner of the Pulitzer Prize and National Book Award for *The Rise of Theodore Roosevelt,* was hired as a copywriter on the "least glamorous" account in the agency, IBM recruitment, advertising jobs in IBM facilities around the world. He appealed to Ogilvy to get a chance to do some work in TV and eventually worked on Good Seasons salad dressing but was always thought of as the "long copy" man.

Writer and illustrator-cartoonist Bruce McCall appears regularly in *The New Yorker* with humor pieces, topical covers, and freestanding art. Some consider his campaign that introduced Mercedes-Benz in the United States—demonstrating the car's superior engineering on test tracks and the open road—the single most influential car advertising of its time. McCall acknowledges that he copied Ogilvy's lead in writing ads that "got the argument up off its ass and in there swinging from word one." One ad, for the most expensive Mercedes, the Grand 600, was returned with a note from Ogilvy: "Illiterate!!!" McCall was told to avoid unctuousness in addressing millionaires: "I'm a millionaire—how would you speak to me?" That unlocked his paralyzed central nervous system, says McCall.

Ian Keown, a copywriter on British Travel Authority, Puerto Rico, and KLM Royal Dutch Airlines and author of four KLM travel guides, now writes travel books. For a double-page spread of "trooping the color" in London for British Travel, with guardsmen coming down the Mall, Keown took a headline from Gilbert & Sullivan: "Tan-tan-tara, zing boom, zing boom." Ogilvy said, "Not tan-tan-tara, *tin*-tan-tara." He was right.

The idea of publishing Ogilvy's more remarkable memos in a book had been discussed on several occasions. Some doubted it could be done, arguing the good stuff wasn't publishable, and the publishable wasn't that good. It was decided to try anyway, for his seventy-fifth birthday, in 1986. What emerged was a stylish production, edited by Joel Raphaelson, that went beyond memos to include speeches, parts of the Aga Cooker manual, and papers on management and corporate culture. Raphaelson came up with the title—*The Unpublished David Ogilvy,* meaning not published in the public press.

The memos ranged from two words to several pages—on leadership, his own shortcomings, things to do on his visits to offices, how to write, what to look for in a creative head, useful books on advertising, and 37 questions to his creative directors, ending with "Have you stopped beating your wife?" The book was privately printed and presented to Ogilvy in London at a gala black-tie birthday party on a Thames riverboat. After two weeks of nervous waiting for reaction to a book published under his name (without his permission), the verdict was delivered: "My best birthday present ever." The book was eventually published commercially, by Crown.

The London office, with which he had a difficult relationship, celebrated this birthday with an advertisement. The headline read: "Stubborn, irreverent, uncompromising, unpredictable, brilliant, impudent, contrary, provocative, infuriating." Three long columns of quotes and praise surrounded the second line of the headline: "Fortunately, his employees take after him."

Now in his late sixties, Ogilvy still felt guilty because he was not working in some formal capacity, "exacerbated by the knowledge that at least one of my partners thinks I am gaga." Then the head of the agency in Germany suddenly resigned, and a young account director was appointed to succeed him. The board asked Ogilvy if he would help the transition. "I felt like an old archbishop who suddenly has a chance to get a parish." For most of a year, he commuted between Touffou and Frankfurt. Every Monday, he would take the train to Paris, travel across Paris on the Métro (with suitcase) from the Gare de Luxembourg to the Gare du Nord, and board the train to Germany, reversing the journey on Friday. He spent his days in Frankfurt counseling the new managing director, meeting clients, talking with creative people, and reviewing their work. He was happy, and his memos showed it.

A similar appealing opportunity opened up a few years later when a region director left the company. Ogilvy quickly accepted invitations to succeed him as chairman for India and South Africa. It was more spiritual leadership than oversight, but he threw himself into it. He spent time in both countries, working long days and dining almost every evening with young agency staff. The director in South Africa said the agency grew better with every visit. During his two extended trips to India, Ogilvy was treated like a god or, more precisely, a guru. Not just as any guru, said an Indian colleague—a "Maja Guru," the great guru, who "distills knowledge and above all shares it with everybody." To get to India, Ogilvy flew from France, since there was no practical alternative, and traveled within the country mainly by train. Car rides in India scared him.

Honors continued to pour his way, with election to the Advertising Hall of Fame, the Direct Response Hall of Fame, and Junior Achievement's U.S. Business Hall of Fame. He became a trustee of the American College in Paris and was inducted into France's Order of Arts and Letters. Ogilvy acknowledged he was the first living honoree in *Fortune*'s National Business Hall of Fame not to be inducted in person. "I am also the first who lives in Europe and suffers from an acute fear of flying. This living recipient of the award might not be living after four flights. He might have died of fright."

But he felt his views within the agency increasingly ignored, especially on issues involving growth. He feuded with former disciples frustrated by his conservatism and was thwarted by a new wave of creative people who dismissed his principles of advertising. But Ogilvy found it emotionally difficult to walk away from his baby. "For 30 years I have secretly felt, '*L'etat c'est moi, et je suis l'etat.*'" Now, in his 70s, it was important for him to feel needed and useful, but it was difficult to involve him except as a ceremonial figure. "Please find something for David to do," pleaded Herta. He still traveled to London and New York, meeting with and impressing clients, but less often.

There had been two attempts to capture his likeness in a formal portrait, plus a sculptured bust. None quite satisfied. Then, in the 1980s, the agency had a great success with an American Express campaign featuring photos of recognizable celebrities in sports, politics, and entertainment, shot in inventive poses by the editorial photographer Annie Liebovitz. How about getting Liebovitz to shoot a portrait of Ogilvy at the château? Ogilvy felt close to the client. A photo might be less subjective than a painting.

He agreed, and Liebovitz arrived at Touffou, bringing several Ralph Lauren shirts for him to wear. "I'm not going to wear someone's brand," he grumbled. Then she asked him where he'd like to be photographed. "In a carriage with four horses." In the absence of a suitable carriage, she posed him in the doorway of the tool shed, dressed him in clothes she had brought, and insisted he leave the top button of his trousers open. The artificiality of her idea irritated him, and the trouble began. They fought for two days. He refused to be photographed in a kilt. She refused to take no for an answer and left in tears. "Karsh took a great photograph of Winston Churchill," he wrote after she'd gone. "I bet the session did not take two days, and that Karsh did not show up with a 'stylist' to dress the old man." When the proofs were sent to France, he reported that his family thought they made him look old. Everyone in New York commented on how young, vital, and handsome he looked. He was 75.

∾

The 38-minute film opens with a man striding across a field, then stopping to address the camera. He is wearing a cardigan sweater over a shirt and tie. He talks of his passion for gentle landscapes, as in the South of England where he grew up and later in Lancaster County in the Amish country, and now here in France. "I am David Ogilvy, and this is Touffou." The film was produced five years earlier, when he was 70.

After that opening segment, Ogilvy goes inside and settles onto a couch in his living room. He tells the viewer he'll start with the story of his life ("70 years in seven minutes"). The next part takes place in his study, where he restates his beliefs about advertising, illustrated by favorite TV and print examples. He then moves outside to his garden, where he sits down and delivers the most moving and enduring segment of the film.

The Gothic main building at Fettes, Ogilvy's school in Edinburgh, said to be the model for Harry Potter's Hogwarts School of Witchcraft and Wizardry.

London's Fleet Street around the time of the founding of Mather & Crowther, in 1852.

(Right) *Elder brother Francis, with his actress wife Aileen, son Ian (later an actor) and daughter Kerry Jane, at a 1950s wedding.*

(Below) *27-year-old David Ogilvy comes to America, in steerage, in 1938.*

(Above) *Ebullient and kilted at a 1948 party with first wife Melinda (far left), in Lancaster, Pennsylvania.*

Characteristic early 1950s portrait—tweed suit, pipe, and display of already-famous advertisements, like the arrival in the United States of "The Man from Schweppes."

The man in the Hathaway shirt

CANADIAN MEN are beginning to realize that it is ridiculous to buy good suits and then spoil the effect by wearing an ordinary, mass-produced shirt. Hence the growing popularity of HATHAWAY shirts, which are in a class by themselves.

HATHAWAY shirts wear infinitely longer—a matter of years. They make you look younger and more distinguished, because of the subtle way HATHAWAY cut their collars.

The whole shirt is tailored more generously, and is therefore *more comfortable*. The tails are longer, and stay in your trousers. Even the single-needle stitching has an auto bellum elegance about it.

Above all, HATHAWAY make their shirts of remarkable *fabrics*, collected from the four corners of the earth.

Broadcloth and Lawns from England, voile and woolen taffeta from Scotland, Sea Island cotton from the West Indies, hand-woven madras from India, oxfords and hand-blocked silks from England,

exclusive cottons from the best weavers in North America.

You will get a great deal of quiet satisfaction out of wearing shirts which are in such impeccable taste.

HATHAWAY shirts are made by a small company of dedicated craftsmen in the little town of Prescott, Ontario.

At better stores everywhere, or write WELLINGTON-HATHAWAY, Ltd., Prescott, for the name of your nearest store. Prices from $6.95 to $25.00.

Can you find the president of the agency in this 1956 staff photo? (Top right)

The most memorable headline in the car business, for Rolls-Royce. 1960.

1976 inductees into the Advertising Hall of Fame—agency heads Ogilvy and Bill Bernbach, and Quaker Oats marketing chief Victor Elting.

Château de Touffou, Ogilvy's home in France, to which he retired in 1973. Parts were built in the twelfth century.

Herta and David Ogilvy were married the last 26 years of his life.

Speaking at an agency training program, trademark red braces and makeshift tie clip (a Bulldog paper clip) on display. 1980.

Fiftieth anniversary of Ogilvy & Mather (1998). Ogilvy's son David Fairfield Ogilvy and wife Herta are third and fifth from left. From right: former chairmen Bill Phillips, Ken Roman, Jock Elliott (rear), and current chairman Shelly Lazarus.

In later years, in his garden at Touffou.

Grooms from neighboring châteaux occasionally played concerts on the cor de chasse, *the French hunting horn.*

Well, there we are. I hope you don't make as many mistakes as I've made. I made some frightful mistakes, like turning down an obscure little office machinery account company that I'd never heard of before. That was called Xerox.

I was always a terrible coward about firing non-performers. I frittered away far too much time on things which were not really important. I failed to recognize some big ideas when they came along—may God forgive me.

I made a mistake when I gave up creative work and concentrated on management. I regret that.

I was always petrified of losing accounts . . . Now wait a second. . . . In my heyday I resigned five times as many times as I was fired.

Here at Touffou I've succeeded in forgetting all the disagreeable aspects of the agency business, like losing accounts and losing good people, which is worse.

I've forgotten the hellish pressures. Sixteen hours a day, six days a week, and three briefcases.

I've gotten a lot of happiness out of advertising, like seeing poverty-stricken Puerto Rico become a little less poverty-stricken as a result of our advertising.

I've never been bored by my job. Above all, I've made some wonderful friends, friends with my partners and with our clients and with some of our competitors.

I'd like to be remembered—as what?—as a copywriter who had some big ideas. That's what the advertising business is all about. Big ideas.

Ogilvy described *The View from Touffou* as his last will and testament. It was not the last of anything, but the testament never changed over the remaining 18 years of his life.

Asked in an interview when he was 75 to what he owed his success, Ogilvy responded:

First of all, I'm the most objective man who ever lived, including objective about myself. Second, I'm a very, very hard worker. I really work very hard when I'm doing a job. Next, I'm a good salesman. I used to be good at getting new business.

I had a reasonably original mind, but not too much so. Which helped, not being too original. I thought as clients think. I also thought as women think. I had a terrific advantage when I started in New York. I'd got a gimmick—my English accent. I've always had an eye for the main chance. When I'd go into a meeting, a dinner party, or a reception, or a cocktail party, I could always smell the billing if there was any at the party.

I came into advertising from research and that gave me great advantage. And I had a short period in my life, maybe ten years at the outside, when I was pretty close to being a genius. Then it ran out.

As with his garden, Ogilvy's life can be seen as divided in rooms. Growing up in England. Experiencing life as a chef, salesman, researcher, farmer, and intelligence officer. Building an advertising agency and becoming recognized. In the last room of his life, Touffou provided him with a lifestyle he considered "close to paradise."

ELEVEN

MEGAMERGERS AND MEGALOMANIACS

*E*very February, around the start of the Chinese New Year, it had been a custom for the agency's Hong Kong office to design a small scroll depicting an animal on the Chinese calendar, with an interpretation of the kind of year it would be. 1989 was the Chinese Year of the Snake. In New York, it was the year the agency planned to move its headquarters into Worldwide Plaza, a new skyscraper on the West Side in an area formerly known as Hell's Kitchen. The Chinese artist put the two events together in a drawing of a menacing black and gold snake wrapped around a red Worldwide Plaza. It was almost too prescient.

The phenomenon of agencies merging started in the United States in the 1960s. Ogilvy & Mather was among the early ones. But what happened in London in the 1970s was on a far greater scale. There, the brothers Charles and Maurice Saatchi started aggressively buying U.S. agencies, aided by lofty valuations in the U.K. stock market, a strong British pound, and inventive financial instruments. Saatchi & Saatchi was already established as London's creative hot shop, with campaigns for British Airways and Margaret Thatcher's Tory party ("Labour isn't working"). Now on an acquisition binge, it was hauling in large U.S. agencies, including Compton, Dancer Fitzgerald Sample, and Backer & Spielvogel. Some of these agencies' owners wanted to cash out, and the Saatchis had the cash, wrote Randall Rothenberg in *The New York Times.* The agency's nickname was "Snatchit and Snatchit." In on it all was Martin Sorrell, the agency's chief financial officer, often referred to as the "third Saatchi."

One merger was motivated simply by a desire not to be acquired by strangers. Worried about becoming targets, three U.S.-based agencies—BBDO, Doyle Dane Bernbach, and Needham Harper Worldwide—banded together in 1986 to form The Omnicom Group. Known as the "Big Bang," the merger created the world's largest advertising company . . . for two weeks. Then Maurice Saatchi persuaded Bob Jacoby, CEO and principal shareholder of Ted Bates, to sell his agency for $507 million, vaulting Saatchi & Saatchi back to the top. Jacoby put $110 million into his own pocket—a personal windfall that led clients to suspect they were paying their agencies too much and, in many cases, to act on that suspicion by reducing agency compensation. A joke went around in the business that all the agencies would eventually merge until at last there was only one. Then all clients would merge until at last there was only a single client, which fired its single agency and took its advertising "in-house."

These events inspired a caustic comment from Ogilvy: "Megamergers are for megalomaniacs. These big mergers do nothing for the people in the agency. It's quite the opposite. They do nothing for their clients. And it remains to be seen if they do anything for the shareholders. So I'm against them."

Sorrell then struck out on his own. He had invested in a tiny British manufacturer of supermarket shopping baskets called Wire & Plastic Products. But Sorrell, a short, intense workaholic with a photographic memory, inexhaustible energy, and a Harvard MBA, had little interest in shopping baskets. WPP Group, as it was renamed, was to provide the financial mechanism to acquire companies providing unglamorous but profitable marketing services such as sales promotion. Under this umbrella, it quickly made 15 small acquisitions.

That was just the start. In 1987, WPP startled the advertising business on both sides of the Atlantic by bidding $566 million for the JWT Group, which included J. Walter Thompson, a huge worldwide agency with deep roots in London, New York, and

Chicago. A minnow was going after a whale. But JWT was under-managed, losing clients, and financially vulnerable, and it tumbled. It was the first hostile takeover in advertising. "Advertising agencies as an investment . . . had, at long last, arrived," wrote Richard Morgan in his book *J. Walter Takeover.*

The JWT Group also comprised a small creative agency, Lord, Geller, Federico, Einstein, which had launched the IBM personal computer (and was the group's most profitable unit). At his first meeting with Sorrell, Dick Lord asked to buy back his agency. "I'm a buyer, not a seller," Sorrell replied. He told Lord to cut the agency's profit-sharing contribution to employees from 15 percent to 4 percent—and give him a list of people who got bonuses. With more confrontations and feeling like an indentured servant, Lord quit and formed a new agency—with 43 people who followed him out the door, but without IBM. Sorrell claimed they had plotted to ruin his business; after highly publicized litigation, the court case was settled. But it provided a sense of WPP's management style.

~

Rumors of a possible takeover of Ogilvy & Mather had caused its stock to surge in 1987. A group of former Ted Bates executives, including Jacoby, who had been forced out following the controversial sale to Saatchi, tried to raise money in London to go after O&M. A team of legal and financial advisors was assembled under the code name Yorktown ("The British are coming") to run defense scenarios. An amateur plan that never materialized, the Bates caper was a fire drill for the real thing.

Then, in late 1988, unsettling rumors started again, but now pointing to WPP, which had acquired ten companies following the Thompson coup. Sorrell was telling analysts he aimed to make WPP the largest marketing services company in the world, the JWT turnaround was ahead of schedule, and he was getting ready for another acquisition, listing criteria that fit The Ogilvy Group all too well.

The financial community was not convinced about the company's vulnerability or Sorrell's ability to mount a successful attack. "Ogilvy is no ailing sitting duck," observed Alan Gottesman of Paine Webber. "There's no parallel with JWT in terms of how screwed up they were. There are no extra layers at Ogilvy." *The Wall Street Journal* noted the financial community's infatuation with Sorrell: "so strong, that at times it seems almost blind." On the London Stock Exchange, WPP had traded above 60 times 1986 earnings. Said Gottesman: "If God went public at 60 times earnings, I'd have a problem with it."

However, after years of doing well, the Ogilvy Group's share price was lagging. Profit margins had been temporarily depressed by recent acquisitions in sales promotion and marketing research. And, like other agencies, it was facing a profit crunch because of a widespread slowdown in client spending. Still, the annual report showed revenues of $838 million and record earnings. The company was growing with its 3,500 clients around the world, bolstered by its commanding position in direct marketing and a growing presence in other profitable services.

The "Yorktown" team reassembled. In January 1989, the board adopted a shareholder rights plan, more ominously known as a poison pill.* Throughout the winter, speculation continued as the stock price bounced around. This was no fire drill; somebody was buying. I had recently succeeded Bill Phillips as chairman of the parent company, now known as The Ogilvy Group, and would be leading the defense.

In March, at the urging of advisors, I accepted Sorrell's invitation to lunch at the Sky Club in New York. After admitting he had accumulated some of the company's stock, Sorrell brought up merger—four different ways—and talked about the "inexorable logic" of a combination. There may be logic, I replied, but it was not inexorable.

April 29, 1989, was a gray Friday. I had just returned from London, where I met with financial analysts to correct two spreading assumptions: that Ogilvy was a poorly performing company and that it might be responsive to an approach by WPP. My presentation seemed

---

* Throughout history, spies were issued poison pills to eliminate the possibility of being interrogated if captured. On Wall Street, they are designed to make unfriendly approaches more expensive to the acquirer by providing shareholders with rights to buy more stock in the event of an acquisition.

to go well. Titled "Apples and Oranges," it made the case that our advertising margins were equal to those of the best-performing agencies (apples to apples), but a big research company we recently acquired from Unilever (an orange, not an apple) was still learning to operate on its own. I made it plain that the agency saw no benefits, for shareholders or clients, in merging.

When Sorrell learned that I was in London, he suggested we meet again, but I put him off and called New York to solicit advice from the merger and acquisition partner at Debevoise & Plimpton, our longtime corporate law firm. "You have to call him back and make it clear where you stand. Tell him the company plans to remain independent, it is a board decision, and it is your job to carry it out. Your policy is not to be sold, and you don't want any miscommunication. Tell him that you don't want to be rude, there's just no point in getting together." I called Sorrell at his home and delivered my script. "That is said in a vacuum," he replied. "You're a public company; you owe it to the shareholders and yourself. We have a fair and full offer."

Then he dropped a bombshell. "I've had indirect communication from people inside the company, at high levels, that they would welcome an approach." One of Sorrell's tactics is to try to destabilize his target, to make it more vulnerable. He had picked up on some friction in our New York management group; also, several executives had been wondering what would be so bad about a takeover. Sorrell asked to sit with me on the Concorde on my return to New York to discuss his offer. I told him firmly that that wasn't going to happen, but we wouldn't treat the matter lightly.

Not to be put off, Sorrell continued. "My plan has the simplest criteria, it's not highly leveraged. Our companies have similar strategic directions." Then he dropped another bomb. "We're prepared to offer $45 a share." Ogilvy stock had been selling in the low $20s and had risen to $27 in recent months on the rumors. For the first time, a price was on the table. "Message received and understood," I replied, and hung up.

The next morning, Sorrell was on the phone again, ostensibly answering an imaginary call from me. "I appreciate your calling to seek clarification," he said. "I want to make it clear that any proposal would keep the structure as it is now, unless Ogilvy feels different.

People would stay in place, unless Ogilvy feels different. I'm happy to talk with the board, with you. We're flexible about the $45, the nature of the offer, about incentive plans." I put him off again but carefully, given my fiduciary responsibilities to shareholders, telling him it required thoughtful consideration by our board.

~

Returning to New York after the London analyst meetings, I drove to Troutbeck, a corporate meeting center a few hours from the city, to meet with my management team for a long-scheduled review of the agency's key people. The meeting had been postponed several times because of the pressure of business, and was almost canceled again because of the storm clouds. But we had a business to run, and the meeting went ahead.

The "bear hug" arrived by fax the first afternoon of our meeting. A Wall Street term, a bear hug is no love letter, as Andrew Ross Sorkin explained in the *Times:* "One part Emily Post and two parts Machiavelli, these oh-so-cordial notes are sent by unwanted suitors in an attempt to broker a peaceful deal. But they always carry an implicit threat: Rebuff this advance, and you're in for a fight."

The letter came on my private fax machine in New York. Five minutes later, there was a call from London asking if it had been received. Sorrell was stepping up the pressure. I instructed my secretary to send copies to Skadden, Arps, Slate, Meagher & Flom, a top merger and acquisition law firm that had joined our legal team, and our two investment bankers: Shearson Lehman, recently acquired by client American Express, and Smith Barney, another client ("They make money the old-fashioned way. They *earn* it."). We believed in using our clients' products, and aberrational circumstances like this were no exception. S.G. Warburg, in London, completed the banking team.

The fight for independence had begun. Sorrell's letter repeated the $45-per-share offer and observed that WPP and Ogilvy & Mather were "natural partners." It went on to propose roles for the agency executives—and the founder.

> On consummation of the merger we would very much like to invite David Ogilvy to assume the position of Chairman of The WPP

Group, and would be honored if he would accept so that the clients, employees and shareholders of both The Ogilvy Group and WPP would benefit from his unparalleled experience and vision. This would also ensure a prominent means of maintaining The Ogilvy Group's creative heritage and closer contact with one of the industry's greatest personalities.

If there was one point on which everyone might agree, it was that there was *no* chance that David Ogilvy would accept that invitation. It was a clever ploy by a predator, hardly to be taken seriously. WPP stood for everything Ogilvy had publicly opposed: financial holding companies, agencies with different philosophies under the same umbrella, and the drive for growth and size. His negative views on mergers and money managers were thundered in speeches and interviews. He told *Advertising Age* that losing the agency would be like seeing one of his children being sold into slavery, then added that clients wouldn't approve:

> Clients never like mergers. They hate them. They don't like their accounts being sold. I don't blame them. If my doctor said he had sold his patients to another doctor, whom I had never met and must consult for all future health care, I wouldn't jump up and down with joy.

Ogilvy had almost met Sorrell the prior year, at a World Federation of Advertisers meeting in London. When he saw his picture next to Sorrell's in a trade publication as the only representatives of the agency sector, he withdrew. "I won't appear on the same platform as this gnome." This was the first of a number of Ogilvy's less than admirable public allusions to Sorrell's height.

Ogilvy admitted he had planted the seeds that made his agency vulnerable. "The worst thing I did when I was Chairman," he wrote directors as rumors smoldered, "was to go public. My only excuse is that unfriendly takeovers had not been invented in those days. EXCULPATE MY SIN!" His protestations were disingenuous. Beyond being the principal exponent of going public, he was well aware that a public offering was a *condition* of the original merger with Mather & Crowther. Later, in 1976, when the board considered going private, he had explicitly stated that he was *not* an advocate. Now it was too late—and too expensive—to undo what had been done.

Now that the fight was on, it was time to unleash Ogilvy to fire a broadside. We chose the *Financial Times,* to reach investors on both sides of the Atlantic. When the reporter called, Ogilvy was ready. His position had been previewed in his "megamergers are for megalomaniacs" diatribe, which appeared in *The Times* in London as well as in our 1986 annual report. Now he repeated these sentiments and directed his attack to Sorrell.

> I got my clients—he buys his. This odious little shit is money driven. He has no interest in doing good advertising, which is my obsession. I spent 40 years building Ogilvy. The idea of this little chap taking it over gives me the creeps. Remember when Jesus turned the money-changers out of the temple.

Strong stuff picked up in the press everywhere, softened only by changing "odious little shit" to "odious little jerk." Ogilvy later corrected the misquote, insisting on the more graphic noun.

Returning Sorrell's attack, we took the unusual step of releasing the WPP proposal to the press, accompanied by a statement characterizing it as "a sales pitch which suffers from serious flaws in business logic." I released a letter to Sorrell saying his statements were "inaccurate and disingenuous" and left a totally false impression regarding our communications. Ads were prepared, with headlines like "Hostile to our clients, hostile to our employees, hostile to all we stand for." Ogilvy suggested side-by-side photos of Sorrell and himself. Under Sorrell's, a quote: " . . . the most despised man on Madison Avenue." Under his: "The most sought-after wizard in American advertising." Advertising wasn't going to be the answer to hard financial facts. None of the proposed ads ran.

Over the next 18 days, the story was widely reported, as the tension built and we explored defenses: stock buybacks, "white knights" and "white squires,"* recapitalizations, leveraged buyouts. No stone was left unturned; near the end, I called Mike Milken, the junk bond king and financial guru. After studying our financial state-

---

* A white knight is a company or person ready to help another firm with an investment. A white squire is similar, except that it acquires only a minority stake and has no interest in taking over a company (Warren Buffett, e.g.).

ments, he asked, "Do you have any preferred stock?," referring to a possible defense. None, I said. "Too bad." WPP had offered so much money, in cash, that our choice came down to accepting its offer or being sued by angry shareholders. "A firestorm of litigation," predicted one lawyer. Sorrell's offer had risen to $54 per share; $862 million to get $32 million in earnings. WPP would pay a premium price for a premium brand.

The next step was a negotiated agreement. To prepare for my meeting with Sorrell, I raised 65 possible issues in a discussion piece, "What would life be like under WPP?" Known for adversarial relationships with people who work for him, Sorrell was on his best behavior when we got together, expansive and reassuring. Nothing would change except for ownership, he promised. WPP would bring its financial skills; otherwise the company would be run much as before. He would not interfere or call on clients unless asked to do so by the officers of the company. I reported those assurances to the executive committee and scheduled a board meeting for May 15 to consider and act on the bid, just prior to our annual shareholders' meeting.

~

Directors came to the board meeting drained by the pressure and emotions of the 18-day battle. Now there was a last-minute competing offer. Phil Geier, chairman of the Interpublic Group (McCann-Erickson and other agencies), had called to discuss how he might help foil WPP. I told him it was late in the game but agreed to look at what he had to offer. Interpublic wasn't our ideal choice for a merger partner, but at least Geier understood the business and would be better than WPP. The board would consider his proposal at our meeting the next day.

The meeting was in the agency's tenth-floor conference room at 2 East Forty-eighth Street, a nondescript Emory Roth–designed 1950s structure we had occupied for 35 years. We had run out of space, with operations spread in ten other buildings around New York, and were in the process of moving everyone to our new offices at Worldwide Plaza. In the meantime, the Forty-eighth Street offices were rundown, and the air conditioning was erratic.

There were 40 people in the room: five teams of investment bankers and lawyers plus directors of The Ogilvy Group and also of Ogilvy & Mather Worldwide, which represented the bulk of the group's revenue and profits. Region heads flew in on short notice from London, Frankfurt, Paris, Toronto, and Hong Kong. The agency's director for Latin America was recovering from a skiing accident and would follow the proceedings by speakerphone from his home in São Paulo.

I opened the meeting at 2 P.M. with a review of the situation, including the last-minute Interpublic offer, and reported that the clients we had heard from said they were deeply concerned—the whole affair was taking people's eyes off the ball and they didn't see the benefits—but none was prepared to take any action other than to say they were "assessing their position."

I then turned the meeting over to Shearson's J. Tomilson Hill. The Ogilvy people had never met anyone like Tom Hill, who, with his slicked-down hair and patterned braces, resembled Gordon Gecko in the movie *Wall Street*. A street-smart financial pro, Hill talked about the Interpublic offer, higher than WPP's but based on stock with no consideration of the possibility of losing business because of conflicts between clients of the two firms. He held up Geier's letter distastefully with two fingers, as if it were something dirty, and dismissed the offer as "this airball!"

Interpublic's stock offer, with no assumptions of client losses, wasn't as strong as WPP's clean all-cash proposal but couldn't be rejected as long as it appeared to be larger. Geier had to be persuaded to withdraw to permit a reluctant peace with WPP, so the agency could get back to business. The meeting was adjourned several times to talk with Geier on the phone. Time dragged on, pizzas were ordered, and everyone waited for Interpublic to take what seemed the obvious action.

At one point, someone turned to Ogilvy and asked how he felt about the offer to become chairman of WPP. Few who were present have forgotten the scene.

Should I accept? Ogilvy asked, turning to the directors. He had been suggesting he might be open to the idea.

Hans Lange, who ran the German company, started. "You have always been against megamergers. If you accept, what would I tell my young tigers? This is a blatant use of your name. You talk about giants—this belittles you."

Peter Warren, a veteran of the agency in London going back to Mather & Crowther and recently named chairman of O&M Europe, agreed wholeheartedly. It was against all the principles Ogilvy had professed over the years, he said.

Jules Fine, one of the earliest people to join the agency in New York, known for his integrity, followed with characteristic directness: "How can you sell your birthright?"

Ogilvy, looking worn and tired, addressed the group from his chair. He started slowly.

> He [Sorrell] knows finance. I can help the image of WPP, and be helpful in preserving our ethos and culture.

After this warm-up, he asked for understanding.

> I'm underemployed, and still have ambition. I don't want to retire, and I need a job.

Parenthetically, about another part of WPP:

> I've always liked JWT. I'm hard up. I've mismanaged my money. I have a castle and a young wife, and I need the money. Greed [pause]. There's also some vanity involved.

Then the stunning finish:

> You people have no right to tell me at this point in my life what's right and wrong for me. As for Sorrell, maybe I can reform him.

We felt guilty, remembers Fine. "It was pathetic, but we had to support him. It was his company, and he built it."

A little after 10 P.M., Geier withdrew the Interpublic offer. The board reconvened in the conference room, now filled with empty pizza boxes and uncomfortably warm. I reported the Interpublic news, restated the WPP offer, and the board voted unanimously to accept it. Around 11:30, nearly ten hours after the meeting had started, I called Sorrell, who had been waiting nearby. Within 20 minutes, he made his triumphant entrance with Bruce Wasserstein, his aggressive First Boston investment banker, in tow.

~

The next day, May 16, I went before the last shareholders' meeting of The Ogilvy Group and reported that the company had lost but they as shareholders had done very well indeed. The final price was $54 a share, double what it had been before the start of all this. A pot of gold for Ogilvy shareholders, including many employees. For WPP shareholders, the high price would make the deal an expensive Pyrrhic victory for several years. Unlike the underperforming J. Walter Thompson, which owned an undervalued property in downtown Tokyo (which was sold for a large profit), Ogilvy & Mather was tightly managed and had no undervalued assets. This time Sorrell had no quick fixes to pay back his huge borrowings.

The following day I called a meeting of 125 of the agency's officers in the auditorium of the nearby McGraw-Hill building, to explain what had happened and introduce their company's new owner. Ogilvy came into the meeting looking and feeling terrible. People went up to him to try to get a comment, and he waved them away. It was like approaching the family at the scene of an accident, said one observer. I opened the meeting by explaining that the lawyers hadn't permitted me to say much publicly while the battle was on. I outlined the financial facts of life, described WPP's assurances about "autonomy," and introduced Sorrell, who affirmed those assurances. Then the floor was opened to questions.

A questioner asked Sorrell what he planned to acquire next. He had completed his goals, he responded, and planned no further acquisitions. From the middle of the audience came a stage-whispered comment from the founder: *Just like bloody Hitler after Czechoslovakia.*

Three days later Ogilvy accepted the invitation to be chairman of WPP.

It was the biggest takeover in advertising history. More than the end of The Ogilvy Group's independence, it portended an era of holding companies frantically acquiring ad agencies and related companies. Within a few years, scores of independent agencies would be gobbled up or combined among themselves, to join WPP, Omnicom, Interpublic, or other big holding companies. It was a world Ogilvy would never recognize or understand, except for Sorrell's answer when asked why he had paid $800 million: "To anyone who has the first understanding of the value of brands, it should seem a nonsensical question."

Ironically, in the 1970s, Jock Elliott had discussed merging with J. Walter Thompson, under the code name TOTO ("in toto.") The agencies shared several clients, and a plan for management had been worked out: Elliott would be chairman for five years, followed by the younger Don Johnston of JWT. The Thompson board voted yes to a man. The Ogilvy board was a unanimous no. "We were very arrogant," Elliott explains. "We thought we were the best agency." Largely unaware of the excellent Thompson agency in London, the New Yorkers referred to JWT as J. Walter Tombstone. If that merger had gone through, it would have created the biggest agency—too big and expensive for WPP to have even considered.

❧

Predictably, the period after the acquisition was painful. Something intangible but powerful had been lost: the agency's pride and identity. It left many people feeling diminished; some were seen crying at the shareholders' meeting. Even the press took sides; *Advertising Age* headlined its story "A giant bows to jackasses." Inevitably, there was fallout among top executives. Some, like Jody Powell, President Jimmy Carter's former press secretary, who had built our Washington public relations office, departed immediately. Others, like European regional director Peter Warren, our worldwide PR chief Jonathan Rinehart, and Brendan Ryan, who ran the big American Express and General Foods accounts, left over the next months.

What Ogilvy saw as a happy place that people loved and sacrificed for, Sorrell saw as an indulgent country club. He doesn't have advertising in his veins, Geier said of Sorrell. "But he wears a green eyeshade well." That description didn't bother Sorrell: "I like to count beans." Within days, pressured by heavy debt and a recession, he started backing off commitments, violating the "autonomy" clause by going directly to clients or agency executives and refusing to rein in his heavy-handed financial people. Ogilvy executives around the world began leaving. Feeling that my ability to lead the company had been undermined, I accepted an offer to join our client American Express in a senior communications role. Sorrell accepted my recommendation for a successor and appointed Graham Phillips, a tough, seasoned Brit who had run our agencies in the Netherlands, Canada, and the United States.

~

Despite his new role as "nonexecutive" chairman of WPP (Sorrell was still CEO), the effect of the takeover on Ogilvy was traumatic. His baby had been kidnapped; the center of his life was gone. With customary hyperbole, he said he cried himself to sleep every night for several weeks. Then, one day, it was over. He went for a long walk, and when he came back he was fine. Ever the pragmatist, he accepted the reality of what had happened and went to work for WPP.

A few weeks after the takeover, Ogilvy was due to be recognized with a new award created by Seagram memorializing Bill Bernbach, for Excellence in Advertising. Edgar Bronfman Jr., president of Seagram, a client of both Ogilvy & Mather and Doyle Dane Bernbach, had invited Ogilvy to be the first honoree. At the presentation dinner, former copy chief David McCall, now the head of his own agency, introduced his former boss. "He has spent his life raising standards. Professional standards. Personal standards. Even standards for having fun. The old Scottish proverb 'Be happy while you're living, for you're a long time dead,' was very much a part of our lives at Ogilvy." McCall concluded: "David Ogilvy has character. His agency has character. And, he has improved the character of an entire business."

It was apparent in Ogilvy's acceptance speech that Sorrell, who can turn on the charm if needed, had somehow charmed him. Ogilvy rained praise on his new boss, proclaiming Sorrell the smartest man he had ever worked with in advertising, further bruising his already black-and-blue former partners in the audience. Later he told an interviewer that advertising was filled with dumb, boring nonentities, the only exceptions being Sorrell, Hal Riney (the con-

trarian creative leader of Ogilvy's San Francisco office), and himself—by implication denigrating all his other longtime partners.

Money erased his admiration for Esty Stowell, as Ogilvy had expressed years earlier: "With a sigh of relief I turned over to him the
management of every department in the agency except creative.
From that point on, our agency began to grow in bigger chunks. A
very able man." Now the paragon "who contributed most to our
early success," who made the agency acceptable to big clients and
personally brought in General Foods, was described as someone who
had done *nothing* and won *no* new clients.

What was Stowell's offense? As a matter of principle, he had
stepped down as president over the issue of going public but held all
his shares. Ogilvy, who had sold most of his shares over the years,
was incensed. "Do you know how much money he made!" he
moaned to almost anyone who would listen. "He held his shares and
made millions!" (It was $28 million.) Why did Ogilvy not hold his?
"I was always terrified the thing would go bust."

In the middle of the takeover battle, I had called the château to
talk with Ogilvy. Herta answered the phone and said how upset he
was about what was happening to his company. I said I certainly understood, but at least he had made money this time on the rising
share price. "He sold it all two weeks ago," she replied.

The takeover destroyed a part of Ogilvy. He had already begun
to feel lonely in France and separated from the business. But this
was something else. His secretary in France, Lorna Wilson, says she
can mark the beginning of his decline to that period. "The agency
was the most important thing in his life. It was the nearest thing he
could have to childbearing. He felt he'd brought Ogilvy & Mather
into being and nurtured it, and it had been brutally taken away
from him."

Despite his fulsome praise at the award dinner, Ogilvy's attitude
toward Sorrell was ambivalent. He admired the man's intellect and
financial success but hated what he stood for. Sorrell took away the
one thing that kept Ogilvy going: his agency. He felt the ethos
would change. Ogilvy & Mather had been a company people were
proud to work for, proud of what it stood for, and now his baby had
been bought at a bazaar by someone who was essentially an accountant. Sorrell responded with forbearance in dealing with the

grand old man, winning him over with many kindnesses, including a nice salary.

Jeremy Bullmore, the head of J. Walter Thompson in London, adored being on the WPP board with Ogilvy, and they became great friends. Ogilvy liked that they had both been copywriters. But Bullmore understood that his new pal had lost something from his prime, as he helped him with a speech that had become a "repetitive regurgitation" of others Ogilvy had been making for some time. An agency veteran who saw Ogilvy, in his role as chairman, try to explain away WPP's poor results at a meeting in London thought how sad it was that Sorrell was using him in that way. Why did he accept being chairman of a company whose purposes he abhorred? *I don't know why Martin Sorrell wants me,* he complained. Respectability, he was told. *What am I doing it for?* "$200,000." *How did you know that?* "Everybody knows."

Ogilvy believed he had no other choice. He hadn't managed his money well, as he often admitted, and there were expenses. He wanted Herta to be able to stay on at Touffou, during his life and after, which wasn't inexpensive. He swallowed what he felt he must, to keep the wolf away from the palace gates. Others were blunt in saying that Ogilvy sold his soul and questioned whether he genuinely believed it was in the best interests of the company, its staff, its shareholders, its clients—or in *his* best interests. He hurt for his company and his partners but was beguiled for the moment by a clever man who knew how to charm and flatter . . . and make money.

It soon became apparent that Ogilvy was over his head on financial matters, and the financial community started to demand a stronger chairman. When he came off the WPP board several years later, he was relieved. "Martin never asked my advice, and told me nothing. I wasn't allowed to go near JWT. That left me OMW [Ogilvy & Mather Worldwide], and the little subsidiaries—I never even met them. My relationship with OMW was ambiguous. I have my own culture and it is not the same as Martin's."

❧

Ogilvy had been invited to address the firm's long-scheduled worldwide management meeting in New York in November 1989, just six months after the takeover. The atmosphere as he rose to speak was hardly upbeat, with the wound not yet healed among many in the audience. His started with The Joke, almost the *only* joke he ever told and one he trotted out for all occasions, appropriate or not.

> I don't know if you've ever been in Tonga. I have.

The audience, 125 senior managers of the agency, laughed in recognition as he pushed on.

> It's an island in the Pacific. My wife and I have walked about on Tonga. They have a royal family there. They are huge. They're giants, both the queens and the kings, and the present king, who is a huge man, paid a state visit to London.
>
> It's one of London's great shows. Great pageantry. The tradition is that the Queen drives to Victoria Station. The Queen arrives in a royal coach. Red carpet on the platform. Introduces him to the prime minister and governor. He's put in the back of the beautiful state landau pulled by horses. The Queen sits beside him. They drive out of the station, and they drive to Buckingham Palace and have lunch.

At 78, the large-boned frame had diminished a bit and the waistline had expanded. Ogilvy wore reading glasses with heavy horn-rimmed frames and his hearing wasn't quite what it used to be, but the feeling was one of power rather than the look of an old man. This was a blazer and no-tie day. The rumpled jacket came off, as it invariably does in speeches, and was dropped with a calculated toss on a nearby chair.

> It's a great thing to watch. The sovereign's escort, with the breast plates and plumed helmets. Flags. The Tonga flag is flying. Crowds are waving . . . singing, cheering. The monarch, the sovereign, is in the back of this lovely carriage, with the King of Tonga beside her. Six horses, open carriage. Six horses pulling them, Windsor Greys I suppose. Ridden by postilions.
>
> As they went along the Mall, before they got to Buckingham Palace, one of the horses farted as no horse has ever farted before. [Great laughter.]
>
> The Queen and the King of Tonga were absolutely asphyxiated. [More laughter.]
>
> Finally, when the wind mercifully blew it away, the Queen said to the King of Tonga, "I'm so sorry about that." [Pause.]

"No need to apologize," replied the King. "I thought it was one of the horses."

An explosion of laughter followed, though almost all present had heard it all many times before. The man who brought civilized good taste to advertising got away with it again.

> I probably won't be at the next one of these, so it's not appropriate for me to just stand here and tell jokes. I'm not going to give you an oration. I'm going to give you some hard-working advice on some specific subjects. You can do with it what you like. And I'll do it in about ten minutes. It's all about people.

Ogilvy fingered the set of nesting Russian dolls that had been placed on the lectern, using them as a jumping-off point.

> Who do you think are traditionally the most important people in our pecking order? I hate pecking orders, but all institutions have them.

This was a new theme, and everyone listened closely.

> I think that the general unspoken tradition has been that the big shots, the top-notch people, were the heads of offices. And that's wrong. I mean, there are heads of office and heads of office. A lot of heads of offices I've known in my days were mere administrators. If you have a pecking order, I suggest this: I'd put at the top new business producers, if you're lucky enough to have one of those rare birds.

Next in Ogilvy's pecking order were those who watch over big international clients. After that, "creative genius." Then heads of offices.

> Of course, occasionally we get a head of office who is also a new business producer.

Slyly:

> I was one of those.
> Occasionally, we get a head of office who is also a creative genius.

With a smile:

I was that too.

The familiar, self-aware show of ego was greeted with laughter.

Ogilvy moved through other people issues, urging his audience to hire fewer MBAs and more people with unusual backgrounds

> like tobacco farmers in Pennsylvania. Get some people from other countries. And particularly get some from India. And from South Africa. I name them because I have a vested interest—I'm chairman of both those companies, and they're full of very remarkable people. If you started showing up at your clients' offices with some Indians in one hand and some South Africans in the other, they will be interested. It's not like showing up with a bunch of goddamn MBAs.
>
> Look inside the agency. Nobody's too young for that and, I hasten to add, nobody's too old for it either. Why do we have this odious habit of putting all our old people out to pasture when they're still young, and replacing them with baby zeros?
>
> Take care of any new terrific person who has been recruited. Make him read my books. For crying out loud! [Roars of laughter.]
>
> [Holding them up one at a time] *Confessions of an Advertising Man—by David Ogilvy! Ogilvy on Advertising—by David Ogilvy! The Unpublished David Ogilvy!*
>
> I keep writing these books, and they're widely read all over the world—except by the employees of Ogilvy & Mather! They're absolutely stuffed with priceless information. And if you read them, you won't be so callow and ignorant.

Then culture: "differentiates us more than anything else." Treating people humanely. A confession about the benefits of a happy agency.

> If you have a gentle, kind, human agency, you won't have to pay so much. And it attracts the best employees, and it attracts the most attractive clients. It will also give you a happier time through life.

Next, a "new preachment" in favor of cutting salaries rather than firing people.

> I think the most cruel thing you can do to people, especially I am sad to say, to men, is to fire them, to put them in a situation where they don't work. Always do your damndest to avoid condemning people to the hell of unemployment. [Pause.]
>
> I've finished. I can't think of anything else to say.

His company's 125 most senior people, assembled from dozens of countries, rose to their feet, applauding. A magnificent performance, one agency veteran remembers thinking at the time. Everyone was down, and he picked them up.

It was not his last speech. Nor the last time for the Tonga story.

~

It soon became clear that WPP had overreached. Its stock plummeted over the next four years, and it had to renegotiate its banking covenants. But it managed to pull through and get back in the acquisition business, buying two more major agencies, Young & Rubicam and Grey Advertising, and dozens of marketing services and "new media" firms. So much for the plan that was "complete" with the takeover of Ogilvy & Mather.

In the fall of 1991, Ogilvy attended a party celebrating the Chicago agency's fifteenth anniversary. That office had a tradition of handing out annual awards recognizing memorable "goofs." The awards were called "Hankies," named for Hank Bernhard, the office's founding head. For this occasion, Ogilvy was awarded the first Grand Hanky. His grand goof? Going public. His two-word acceptance speech: "Nobody's perfect."

TWELVE

A DISEASE CALLED ENTERTAINMENT

*T*he "creative revolution," as it was known, first swept over the business in the 1960s. Copywriters and art directors became known as *creatives*. In many cases, *creative* became synonymous with *entertaining*. Ogilvy was not impressed. He was put off by the revolution's flashy show-biz techniques with no evident payoff in sales. "There is a disease called entertainment infecting our business" was his increasingly frequent lament in interviews and speeches.

The disease was spread, in Ogilvy's view, by various annual awards that advertising people conferred on each other. That humor and dazzling TV production techniques were most often rewarded was bad enough. Ogilvy mistrusted the long-haired, trendy "creatives" from the start. Self-congratulatory award dinners only confirmed his suspicion that the lunatics were taking over the asylum.

His first move, to ban Ogilvy & Mather people from entering these contests, caused a minor mutiny. Winning an award bestowed prestige and added to the winner's value in the job market; like Academy Award nominations, mere entry of your work counted for something. In 1970, Ogilvy countered by establishing his own award—for *results*. The David Ogilvy Award recognized the Ogilvy & Mather campaign that did the most to improve a client's sales or reputation. The winner received a small red plaque and $10,000 cash.* "If you, my fellow copywriters or art directors, want to win the award," he admonished the troops, "devote your genius to making the cash register ring." *Make the cash register ring* joined the agency's lexicon.

The first award recognized a campaign for Tijuana Smalls, a new small cigar from General Cigar. It was a success at the start, and hard evidence gave credit to the advertising. But the product didn't live up to the advertising. Smokers tried it and didn't come back; a year later, it was quietly withdrawn. If the cigar didn't make it, though, the award did. The prize focused the agency's efforts, gave tangible recognition to its most effective campaigns, and impressed clients. Some complained when "their" campaign didn't win or, worse, wasn't even put up for consideration. It didn't entirely mollify the creative people, who still wanted to win the esteem of their peers that came with the highly publicized industry-wide award dinners. So Ogilvy relented, saying they could enter awards contests "if you win"—while advising them to pack the juries.

The agency—and Ogilvy's reputation—had been built on sparkling creative work. Starting in the 1970s, he became increasingly concerned that the pendulum was swinging in the wrong direction and the agency's advertising was becoming dull, even if effective. "We are not producing enough remarkable campaigns to win the new business we need, or to satisfy some of our present clients," he wrote directors in 1974. He called it the most important problem confronting the agency, launching a series of "ESCAPE FROM DULLSVILLE" memos, and urging the organization to emulate creative organizations like *The New Yorker* and Bell Labs.

Concluding that the agency was producing too many campaigns that were strategically sound but not brilliant, he created an agency award for "show-case advertising." The first award went to the Bangkok office for its campaign for a local beer; the commercial proudly promoted Singha beer as being as native as Thai foods and Thai customs. Nobody was quite sure what "show-case" meant, and the award never gained the traction of his award for sales, but the

---

* $50,000 in 2008 dollars.

creative work did take on new sparkle with the arrival of new people stimulated by his new charge.

∼

Events offered support for Ogilvy's skepticism about creative awards. A 1969 parody of a 1930s Busby Berkeley musical featuring lines of high-stepping chorus girls, for Contac cold capsules, swept the awards. A creative consultant rated the "Cold Diggers of 1969" campaign as not just the best of the year but one of the best of all time. Despite such acclaim, sales slid and the agency was fired. A knowledgeable drug advertising writer had predicted the result: "The customer is sick and in pain. You don't laugh or sing. You promise *relief.*"

Several years later, the authors of the book *Advertising in America* showed how Alka-Seltzer fell into the same trap with its memorable and highly awarded "I can't believe I ate the whole thing" commercial. "The more those ads ran, the more Pepto-Bismol was sold. We all laughed at the miserable victim, but when we became miserable ourselves we thought 'Alka-Seltzer thinks it's all a big joke and doesn't take my symptoms seriously. I want something serious to fix me up.'"

Ogilvy rubbed it in with his analysis of prestigious awards known as Clios, named for the Greek muse of history. "Agencies that won four Clios had lost the accounts," Ogilvy reported gleefully. "Another Clio winner was out of business. Another Clio winner had given half its account to another agency. Another refused to put his winning entry on the air. Of 81 television classics picked by the Clio festival in previous years, 36 of the agencies involved had either lost the account or gone out of business."

Notwithstanding such results (or Ogilvy's fusillades), the Clios continued to thrive. In 2007, 19,000 entries from 62 countries competed for the votes of 110 judges. Entertainment became an increasingly important ingredient of advertising, especially with big-production, high-priced commercials for beer and soft drinks show-cased on the National Football League's Super Bowl. Columnists and viewers weigh in on the "best" commercials on what some call "The High Holy Day of Advertising."

In 1990, Dullsville apparently escaped from, Ogilvy produced a 19-page paper warning about "wallowing in an epidemic of 'creativity.'" He told everyone to go back to research, pay attention to his Magic Lanterns, and stop pursuing awards. He also quoted his brother Francis: "Those who close their ears will continue to skid about on the slippery surface of irrelevant brilliance." An Indian copywriter in the New Delhi office wrote to say "CLARITY is more important than CREATIVITY." Ogilvy purred: "I kissed her on both cheeks."

❧

By 1991, when Dewitt Helm, president of the Association of National Advertisers, asked Ogilvy to address the ANA convention in Phoenix, there were few who did not know what he stood for. Helm faxed the invitation. "One of my better efforts," he recalls. "I told him the concept was to have Charles Kuralt or Barbara Walters interview him and Mary Wells Lawrence [president of Wells Rich Greene]. A statesman and a stateswoman."

"I have four conditions," Ogilvy responded. "I'm sure you can't meet them."

"Try me," said Helm.

> I don't want to be interviewed by somebody who knows nothing about advertising.
>
> Why should I share the spotlight with that Lawrence woman—I want to go on solo.
>
> My title is "We Sell. Or Else." And don't tell me that "Or Else" isn't a sentence.

"Absolutely," agreed Helm. "What is the fourth condition?"

"Hell, I've forgotten." Ogilvy then asked Helm, "Have the clients gone crazy? Who is approving this junk called advertising?"

Ogilvy arrived by train from New York and Chicago, complaining he was getting too old to travel with a heavy suitcase. A bronchial cough contributed to his fatigue. As a former chairman of the agency, I had been invited to the meeting. In his hotel room, Ogilvy lay down on the bed and rambled.

"I've been a lousy investor. J.P. Morgan lost 23 percent on my account in one year. I just made out my will. I don't know how much money my son has. How much to leave him, I don't know. I need enough for Herta to go on living at the château. She didn't like it at first—now she loves it."

He picked himself up to meet with two other former chairmen, Jock Elliott and Bill Phillips, consumed a prodigious lunch, and by evening had perked up. The cough abated, and he was first to arrive at the cocktail reception. Still in good humor the next morning, he went off for a private interview with Joanne Lipman, the bright young advertising columnist for *The Wall Street Journal.* Their talk outside in the Arizona sun was a preview of his talk that afternoon. Now 80, he had become if anything even more outspoken and more indifferent to the sensitivities of his targets. He said to Lipman:

> There's more bad advertising than there has ever been. It's high-brow, obscure and doesn't sell. Clients share the blame, because some young idiots at client companies have cut agency pay so sharply that agencies can't afford to hire good executives. It's very stupid of them.

Lipman was enchanted by the man she described as "the legendary adman and father of modern advertising." The interview left the usually skeptical reporter starry-eyed: "A reporter's dream. My life is complete."

Time for Ogilvy's address. After an introduction by Ross Love of Procter & Gamble, the ANA chairman, he stood up, removed his blazer, dropped it on a nearby chair, and sat behind the low coffee table that had been set up for him. Before launching into his "crusade" for advertising that sells, he made a typically extravagant gesture: "If you heard Jim Jordan's speech yesterday, you don't need to hear mine today. Because Jim said exactly what I am going to say, except he said it better."

Jordan's agency, Jordan, Case, McGrath, was known for its hard-selling copy, framed in an unadorned and, in some views, dated style. Jordan had sold its philosophy hard in his talk. "Advertising agencies in 1991 have about as screwed up a sense of priorities as any enterprise I'm aware of. Agency principals perceive that their agencies will get more business if their work is perceived as chic, on the cutting edge, funny or entertaining than it will if the ads merely *sell* a lot of stuff." He urged them to return to fundamentals and *build brands*—singing from Ogilvy's songbook.

"I have come to the conclusion that Jim's speech was the most valuable I have ever heard anywhere in my life in advertising," Ogilvy pronounced, making a lifetime friend of Jordan and impressing everyone else. Now his crusade was ready to get underway. He told the audience it had a war cry—"We Sell. Or Else."—and he was not going to jump on any fashionable bandwagons going elsewhere.

> Down with advertising that forgets to promise the consumer any benefit. Down with creative show-offs. Too clever by half.
>
> If you spend your advertising budget entertaining the consumer, you are a bloody fool. Housewives don't buy a new detergent because the manufacturer told a joke on television last night. They buy it because it promised a benefit. If I could persuade the lunatics to give up their pursuit of awards, I would die happy.

Copywriters and art directors were not his only targets. He warned advertising managers what would come from demanding "fashionable" advertising.

> Unless this epidemic is checked, it may kill advertising because the reports from BehaviourScan* will convince heads of manufacturing companies that advertising has no effect on sales.

The speech over, once again Ogilvy prompted a standing ovation with a slight upward gesture of his outstretched hands.

∾

Some creative people agreed with Ogilvy, especially those who, as awards judges, had sat through hours of the stuff he was castigating. Others were outraged. "What unmitigated gall," exclaimed one. "We're supposed to take criticism from a guy who lives in a castle called Tofu [*sic*]?" The major complaint was that the 80-year-old ad-

---

* A testing service that measures shopper behavior in stores.

vertising luminary had been out of the mainstream too long to make such harsh judgments, and that the business had changed since he left it. Most respected the man more than they agreed with the message.

It was time to stop scolding, Ogilvy was told by an agency friend. "No one in his right mind can deny the correctness of what you say about current advertising, but the thrust of your recent messages is relentlessly *negative*. If you continue on this track you risk being dismissed as a cranky, irrelevant curmudgeon." What the business needed was "an evangelist/prophet to revive the commandments of selling. Not a stone-flinging David, but a tablet-toting Moses." Ogilvy accepted that he had been a scold and promised to be less negative. But he couldn't do it. "I fear I am now too old to stop speaking so negatively. It has become a function of frustration."

Before the annual Cannes Festival, the advertising community's grandest gathering and distributor of its most prestigious awards, Ogilvy was quoted in the French magazine *Figaro* about how prizes distorted the business. When the agency's Paris office won the 1991 Grand Prix with a commercial depicting a woman and a lion fighting for a bottle of Perrier, his reaction surprised everybody: He was more excited than anyone. Conceding that the prizewinner went against all but one of his guidelines, he nonetheless judged it as "one of the best we ever made—a simple, strong idea." The ultimate principle.

Ogilvy maintained that his critics were wrong on one point—that his obsession with selling could *only* lead to very dull advertising. "Every ad I ever created for every client was a selling ad—and none of them were dull. Indeed, they were so non-dull that I became a creative super-star. (Loud laughter from my sisters in England.)"

Later in 1991, at the Bill Bernbach Award for Excellence in Advertising dinner, Ogilvy asserted that Bernbach was a misunderstood man. "Bill was the guru of phony creatives. The pretenders adored him, but he didn't adore them."

The following June, Ogilvy summoned more than a dozen of the agency's top creative directors and client service executives from around the world to the château. There he told them to get off the awards kick and get back to basics. He preached about his advertising philosophy for five solid hours. It was a good conference, said one creative director, even if less actually a conference than an obeisance to "the only remaining man of creative stature" in advertising. Ogilvy summed up the failure of his counterrevolution in one sentence: "The Creative Head of New York left the Touffou Jamboree after lunch—to attend the Cannes Festival."

∿

In fact, Ogilvy was more than a scold. As advertising leaned in directions he deplored, he began to build anew on two rocks of certainty: research and direct marketing. He didn't get his hands dirty preparing research questionnaires, as in his Gallup days, or writing a direct mail letter. He was an evangelist/prophet.

He had set up a direct mail department in the early 1960s and supported this discipline decades before most others recognized its potential. O&M Direct grew to become the world's largest direct marketing agency—and the most highly-awarded for its results for clients. As its godfather, Ogilvy gave it credibility. When he started appearing at its meetings, suddenly other senior staff started showing up too. He was vocal in criticism as well as encouragement: "Who wrote that presentation? I'm falling asleep." Ogilvy described his office in Paris at the direct marketing affiliate, rather than the main agency, as "my spiritual home."

One of his memos had observed in passing "In direct marketing, you sell or else. Meaning your work is accountable." O&M Direct knew a good thing and adopted it as their motto: "We Sell. Or Else." It soon became Ogilvy's final battle cry. He was unable to attend his induction into the Direct Marketing Hall of Fame in 1986 (he was in India) but sent a videotape ripping into the world of "general advertising" and telling the direct marketers they would inherit the earth.

> You direct response people know what kind of advertising works and what doesn't work. You know it to the dollar. The general advertising people don't know.
>
> You know that fringe time on television sells more than prime time.
>
> In print advertising, you know that long copy sells more than short copy.
>
> You know that headlines and copy about the product and its benefits sell more than cute headlines and poetic copy.

You know to a dollar.

The brand advertisers and their agencies know almost nothing for sure, because they cannot measure the results of their advertising. They worship at the altar of creativity, which really means original-ity—the most dangerous word in the lexicon of advertising.

They opine that 30-second commercials are more cost effective than two-minute commercials. You know they're wrong.

And so on, on the comparative merits of *knowing* versus *opining*.

Why don't you save them from their follies?

Ogilvy's formula for salvation was to integrate the separate direct re-sponse unit into the main agency and insist that *everyone* serve an ap-prenticeship in direct response before being allowed to create general advertising. (Several years later, the agency's advertising and direct marketing units in New York were merged under single leadership, but there was no rush of advertising copywriters signing up for ap-prenticeships.)

Ogilvy told the audience he had taken a correspondence course from Dartnell in direct mail, and it became his "first love." He cred-ited personalized mailings to new business prospects with helping his agency take off in its early days: "My secret weapon."

> For 40 years, I have been a voice crying in the wilderness, trying to get my fellow advertising practitioners to take direct response seri-ously. Today my first love is coming into its own. You face a golden future.

How could anyone working in what had been termed a "below-the-line" business* not be moved by that rosy forecast? Ogilvy had been prophetic. Over the decades, direct mail had broadened into direct marketing on TV and in newspapers, moved smoothly into digital marketing and on the Internet, becoming the fastest-growing adver-tising medium.

---

* Nonadvertising functions like sales promotion or public relations.

Ogilvy had long preached that all copywriters should study the bible of the direct marketing business, *Tested Advertising Methods* by John Caples, and wrote an introduction for the book's fourth edition, quoting his favorite Caples fact: "I have seen one advertisement sell 19½ times as much goods as another." He said an earlier edition of the book taught him most of what he knew about writing ads. He meant that *literally.* "Experience has convinced me that the factors that work in mail-order advertising work equally well in *all* advertising."

When Caples died in 1990, Ogilvy was asked to deliver the eulogy. In a taxi to the memorial service, he said that he hadn't given much thought as to what he would say. Decades of admiration came to the rescue. After extolling Caples as the nicest man he had ever known, Ogilvy declared he was very simply the best and for that reason had plagiarized his work unashamedly. "Why steal from anyone but the best?"

~

"How do you know?" That was Ogilvy's quintessential question. A discussion of an ad would get around to something like this.

> *Ogilvy:* Why don't you put the name of the product in the headline?
> *Copywriter:* Because if we leave it out, more people will go on to read the whole text.
> *Ogilvy:* How do you know?

The copywriter never knew. So Ogilvy turned to his other rock of certainty, research, to find out. The Gallup experience made a lasting impression on the man who started with an inquiring mind. He never forgot that before he was the most famous advertising man in the world, he was a researcher.

Ogilvy's attempt to make the practice of advertising more professional began with research and the knowledge it unearthed. His findings were set down with dogmatic flourish: "We pursue knowledge the way a pig pursues truffles." Research was embedded in his creative philosophy: "Look before you leap," a line that embodies two thoughts—look deeply into the research, then take an adventurous creative leap. Ogilvy credited research as another of the secrets that helped build his agency.

As with direct mail, the marketing research community was short on self-esteem. Researchers felt that their work, often vital, was seldom recognized. Everyone was taking the bows except them. In 1994, to rectify this and recognize his proselytizing role, the Advertising Research Foundation created the David Ogilvy Research Awards "for the effective use of research in developing successful advertising." Ogilvy added a proviso: "I don't want to give the award unless there is a good sales story."

Unwilling to fly to the first awards presentation but seeing a fresh opportunity to attack creative awards, Ogilvy sent a videotape.

> Nowadays, you know, the creative departments and agencies are dominated by specialists in television. Their ambition is to win awards at festivals. They don't give a damn whether their commercials sell, provided they entertain people and win awards. They won't have anything to do with research if they can help it. These creative entertainers have done the advertising business appalling damage.

He went on to talk about one of his pet projects, saying that while many clients spent a portion of their money on long-term research and development, no agency did anything of the sort. Ogilvy wasn't talking about testing individual campaigns; he was referring to basic research into the nature of things, like the work done at the fabled Bell Labs for AT&T.

> How are we going to revive the use of research in the creative process? I hope my award will help, but it won't be enough. Here's another idea. Six years ago, I persuaded my partners to set up The Ogilvy Center for Research and Development. This center did good basic work, not related to specific brands. It got off to a good start but the last recession forced us to give it up. Why don't you guys get together and start it up again? This time confine research to creative questions. To do that, you will need a staff of psychiatrists to deal with the creative lunatics and you will have to arm yourselves with bludgeons to make them do as you tell them.

Launched in 1984, The Ogilvy Center was essentially one man in San Francisco, Alex Biel, a respected researcher who had worked at several agencies, including O&M, before setting up on his own. Under Biel, the center commissioned several studies on what makes advertising work: physiological reactions to advertising (e.g., brain waves), the correlation between people liking an ad to its ability to persuade, determining if advertising made a measurable contribution to return on investment. The impact of these reports in the industry was such that, at one point, Young & Rubicam was citing Ogilvy Center studies. In the early 1990s, owned by a WPP parent in huge debt and bearing no discernible connection to income, the center was closed.

But the ARF Ogilvy Research Awards survived and prospered. Ten years later, Microsoft joined to help publish a book on the benefits of the awards launched in Ogilvy's name: *Learning from Winners: How the ARF David Ogilvy Award Winners Use Market Research to Create Advertising Success.*

In the 1950s and 1960s, academicians—notably Lloyd Warner, an anthropologist and sociologist, and Ernest Dichter, a Freudian psychologist and the father of "motivational research," had identified and studied another, softer side of advertising. In Biel's view, campaigns by Burnett, Bernbach, and Ogilvy really spoke to what Warner and Dichter were learning on the research side with depth interviews: "They were talking to the inner man, realizing that people didn't buy brands just for rational reasons."

Biel admired Ogilvy's personal commitment to research and his eponymous center but was puzzled by disparity between the research he favored, such as "promise" testing, and the advertising he created. "Promise testing" asks consumers to rank simple statements about a product's benefits. The advertising is presumably built on the winning promise. But the campaigns he created didn't do that. "The advertising that Ogilvy made was a monument to the *personality* of the brand," says Biel. "But to hear David talk, you would think that functionality was what drove advertising."

Asked why mothers would pay more to dress their children in Viyella, a luxurious British wool-cotton blend and an early client of the agency, when they could get clothes made of DuPont's Orlon, which cost less and was just as soft and warm, he replied: "Two reasons. First, lamb's wool. Women are very emotional about lamb's wool. And second, SNOBB'ry." So much for the rigid advocate of reason over emotion.

But research is where he started. He understood the importance of the unconscious in the creative process, believing that most business-men relied too much on rationality to find new ideas, and was convinced that "nothing is more dangerous than an ignorant unconscious." Facts were needed. When creating his own ads, he would immerse himself in the research, then take a long country walk or open a bottle of wine, to open "telephone connections" with his unconscious.

Most of all, he wanted to *know*. Ogilvy said he once asked Sir Hugh Rigby, Surgeon to King George V, what makes a great surgeon. Sir Hugh replied, "There isn't much to choose between surgeons in manual dexterity. What distinguishes the great surgeon is that he *knows* more than other surgeons." Ogilvy extrapolated from that a lesson for the advertising business, relating a discussion with a copywriter who said he had not read any books on advertising but preferred to rely on his own intuition. "Suppose," said Ogilvy, "your gall-bladder has to be removed this evening. Will you choose a surgeon who has read some books on anatomy and knows where to find your gall-bladder, or a surgeon who relies on his intuition?"

When the company acquired Unilever's Research International unit in 1986, Ogilvy went to its annual meeting and was spellbound. After listening to an expert talk about advertising research, he leaned over and said in a loud stage whisper to Biel: "Find out everything that man knows about advertising."

$\sim$

Following the takeover, Ogilvy turned to his new job as WPP's "non-executive" chairman. It was a largely ceremonial position—running the company was Sorrell's job as chief executive. Ogilvy would chair board meetings and represent WPP to the financial community. Poor casting. Those weren't his strengths. But it gave him a role.

Sorrell was the face of the company. Despite considerable financial skills, he had dug himself a deep hole. "Wagons Are Circled at WPP Group" headlined *The New York Times* in 1991, reporting the company was on the verge of a financial crisis and predicting that

Sorrell might be forced out. *The Economist* noted "a humbling year" for Sorrell and WPP. Shareholders were concerned by a steady exodus of senior executives, especially from O&M, and a share price at a five-year low. JWT needed the financial belt-tightening WPP could provide, wrote *Advertising Age,* "but Mr. Sorrell's reputation as a financial genius began slipping when he bought Ogilvy Group." Sorrell admitted in hindsight he had paid too much. Jock Elliott disagreed: "They simply borrowed too much—in effect, the entire amount. Such was the fiscal custom of the 80s."

As chairman, Ogilvy signed the 1991 WPP annual report, noting the decline in earnings and writing that it would have been a lot worse if staff had not performed so nobly. "We owe them our gratitude. *I admire their guts.*" Loyal to Sorrell in public, Ogilvy told *Adweek:* "At these times we look for someone to blame, and that person is Martin. I think it's rather good to have Martin's kind of financial discipline right now." He acknowledged Sorrell's mistakes but didn't join the talk of pushing him out:

> I don't want him out. I get on with him. It was awful at first. He thought he was getting an old fart who would cause no trouble. I told him an old fart may become a nuisance. I went to a hotel room with him and two other directors, and we went at it all day. He's a curious man. Appeared to pay no attention. Six months later, he had done everything we asked. We told him we had to have proper Board meetings; now we have too goddamn many—one every month. We made him start a Compensation Committee. I'm simply astounded at the salaries.

Taking control of salaries was one way WPP chose to recover from its debt binge in the 1980s. Another was staff cuts. Sorrell conceded the impact on clients: "a debt-laden agency is vulnerable to the criticism that its fee will go not to pay for great advertising, but rather to pay down bank loans." WPP was not alone in facing such a problem. As *Adweek* pointed out:

> In the early '80s, ad agencies were on a fairly even footing with each other. Their operations were basically the same, and they shared two important characteristics: virtually no debt and good cash flow. What happened was that some sharp financial talent (Martin Sorrell was perhaps the epitome of this) caught on to ways in which cash flow could be used to expand the business.

Ogilvy's role as WPP chairman had not turned out as he expected. It was, he said, little more than ornamental—"not to say farcical." He complained about the modest pay and his minimal influence, at WPP and at Ogilvy & Mather, and was uncomfortable finding himself chairman of a company in dire straits.

By 1992, WPP was again negotiating with banks to avoid liquidation, a second refinancing in a year. "WPP begging bowl out again," reported the British press, noting Sorrell's "cheekiness." Finally, in August, shareholders approved a rescue plan, giving the bankers nearly half of the heavily indebted company. Ogilvy had been to the meeting where the bankers insisted he be replaced as chairman. Nearly deaf in one ear, he cupped the other and feigned total deafness: "Chairman? Did I hear Chairman?" But he agreed to step down and become president emeritus and a consultant. After the meeting, he walked over and shook hands with all the bankers; the other directors just stood there. "Class," one participant observed.

Although Ogilvy was miffed at the slight from the money men, he admitted in private that the change was necessary. He had been telling the board that WPP was a financial holding company, and it must have a financial man as chairman. "I know absolutely zero about finance." He lobbied to stay on the board, despite friends telling him he was being vain and greedy. Either that or return to Ogilvy & Mather as creative head. "I'd die of misery if I was completely cut off from the business. I have so few other interests." He wondered if a man of 81 could still be good at anything in advertising, "or is it *ipso facto* that you're useless at 81? They're out there saying, for God's sake, get rid of that old codger. I've had to become very outspoken. There is still very much I would like to do and not many years to do it."

∾

His WPP role, wrong from the start, went away. As for advertising, his dislike of travel—and his age—took him increasingly out of the game, although he showed no less interest. He turned his attention back to Ogilvy & Mather. "It is lovely for me to be back to one loyalty—to OMW 100 percent." He jumped back in, complaining "some baboon in the New York office" added seven words to the award in my name: for a campaign that produced results and "*did so in an outstanding manner.*" He said he judged the entries for 1992 and found it impossible to assess the "outstanding manner" ingredient.

Thinking he could stay in touch with advertising in the United States while living most of the time in France was clearly unrealistic. He was never in touch with American popular culture; distance and age further removed him from the latest advertising developments.

He had started formalizing his creative philosophy in 1968 with a 19-page booklet. "Few of my Principles are mere expressions of opinion," the introduction stated dogmatically. "Almost all of them are rooted in fact." He said the facts were derived from picking other people's brains, experience, and exposure to research—and confirmed by Gallup & Robinson.

The section on TV is notable for explicating rational techniques, such as product demonstrations and problem-solution mini-dramas, while undervaluing emotion. The product of a print generation, Ogilvy took longer to appreciate television and the power of music in evoking emotion. He was convinced music didn't sell anything: "Can you imagine walking into a Sears store and being approached by a sales person who suddenly bursts into song?" When someone he respected made a case for music, Ogilvy simply got up and left the room.

Throughout the 1960s and 1970s, many of the "creative" agencies dismissed the advertising coming from Ogilvy & Mather as pedestrian and uninspired. They conceded Ogilvy's pronouncements might attract clients but noted his "rules" had tarnished a reputation for creativity. Mary Wells Lawrence, a founder of Wells Rich Greene, saw him as a giant and someone she could relate to but felt he never grasped the changes in the U.S. culture in the 1960s and 1970s.

The same kinds of changes were taking place in British advertising. After the mid-1950s, everything in London had transformed. Pop art and rock bands like the Rolling Stones exploded on the scene. Mary Quant and Vidal Sassoon helped make fashion affordable to young people. In this visually driven revolution, photographers and art directors took the lead. Ogilvy was brilliant with words, points out London creative director Don Artlett, but his "visual vocabulary" was limited. "It only extended to how you could make the words readable, or more readable." Although Ogilvy created several visual icons, he never understood the importance of art direction as communications.

The creative direction would begin to shift in the 1980s and 1990s as Ogilvy became less involved in the leadership of the agency. Some of its best work was coming from offices farthest from his reach—from the Asia-Pacific region, London, and Hal Riney's agency in San Francisco—paradoxically, work that he admired.

When Scali, McCabe, Sloves agreed to sell its agency to Ogilvy & Mather in 1978, they went to great lengths to make sure both parties understood that no one from O&M was ever to set foot on the premises. "It was David we wanted no part of," says Ed McCabe, a founding partner and creative director. "Had he ever been seen in or around our offices, we genuinely felt it would damage our creative reputation." When McCabe finally met Ogilvy, he expected him to be like Bill Bernbach, somewhat cool and aloof. Instead, he found him to be "charming, witty, entertaining, intelligent, down-to-earth."

McCabe, a fairly typical representative of the creative community, doesn't see Ogilvy as the world's greatest copywriter. "But in most other categories, he was an absolute genius."

Ogilvy was still much in demand as a speaker, although he was now recycling prior talks, such as his 1992 talk to INSEAD, the pre-eminent European business school, on how to succeed in advertising. He lifted the "Bees in My Bonnet" section from his talk to the ANA for a 1993 speech in London. *The Executive's Book of Quotations* (1993) gave him the lion's share of ad entries, including a jingle he attributed to an anonymous dairy farmer:

Carnation milk is the best in the land.
Here I sit with a can in my hand.
No tits to pull, no hay to pitch.
Just punch a hole in the son-of-a-bitch."

Meanwhile, the fortunes of two major agency holding companies were crossing trajectories. Saatchi & Saatchi, which had started the takeovers (with Martin Sorrell as chief financial officer) and had grown to become the biggest advertising conglomerate in the world, was imploding. After acquiring 37 companies, many for too much money, and overreaching yet further with an offer to buy the prestigious Midland Bank, Saatchi's stock had lost 98 percent of its value. In 1994, angry shareholders forced Maurice Saatchi out as chairman. With his brother Charles, who also resigned, he set up the New Saatchi Agency.

WPP, however, was continuing to recover. By 1996, its stock was the best performer among agency groups, albeit well below its record high. The London *Daily Telegraph* described Sorrell as "the architect both for the house that collapsed and its rebuilding." It was the purchase of Ogilvy that "made him rich and the shareholders poor." But the turnaround was solid, and industry analysts started to speculate when Sorrell would make another acquisition.

~

Despite his speeches and his role in India, the 1990s were almost all downhill for Ogilvy. As WPP started to recover, he began to decline. Although he was in good humor, he didn't look well. He appeared frail, despite having put on weight. At times, a tremor caused his head to shake uncontrollably, making it appear that he was saying "no." "I can't help it. It's like a siege." The fading of his terrific memory was manifested in an inability to remember names, and he took to asking about "the Hungarian" or "the tall gloomy man with the beard" or "the barber" (referring to a creative director who wore shirts with collars like a barber's). A colleague meeting him at the Stanhope Hotel in New York noticed he and Herta both had daiquiris in front of them. Ogilvy downed his, then finished off half of Herta's. Then he had another. It was very unlike him.

There was a sense of failing powers. "I don't know much about anything except senility," he wrote a colleague, "and I know a great deal about that." When the O&M board met at Touffou for its 1994 meeting, Ogilvy seemed in good form, telling them things they had often heard, but freshly. While the mind appeared fine, he knew he wasn't really sharp. "I am feeling my age, not only in my body but also in my head," he wrote a former colleague. "I have stopped driving cars and cannot remember the names of women sitting beside me when they come to dinner here."

He worked in the garden, even during the hot weather ("hot as the hinges of Hell") and ignored drought restrictions about not watering, waiting until after the gardener had gone home to water 200 newly planted roses. He still loved the company of his stepchildren, grandchildren, and children of friends, at times rolling on the floor with them at games and at others treating them as adults. Now he doted on his step-grandson, his first: "the joy of my life, even if he's not mine. He thinks my name is 'Hello.' He has me under complete control. I get my marching orders from him."

. He continued to fret about money. "My problem is poverty," Ogilvy wrote an O&M alumnus with undeclining hyperbole. "OMW pays me $300,000 a year. I must summon up courage to ask for more. It would not cost the agency much, because my expectation of life is slim, but I'm afraid Martin will veto it." He finally screwed up the courage to ask Sorrell to rectify his pension and keep in mind that he started the agency with nothing, built it to the third largest in the United States, and got 29 of its clients by himself ("probably the world's record for one man").

By 1995, he had come to grips with the reality. "I am now OUT, truly retired. That isn't easy for me, after 46 years." He kept asking visitors about people and what was going on in New York. "Digging, digging, digging," as someone described him. On his eighty-fourth birthday in June, surrounded at Touffou by family, children, grandchildren, and a handful of former colleagues, Ogilvy regarded the arrival of a birthday cake apprehensively. "If anyone sings that dreadful song, I'll leave the room."

For his next birthday, the agency produced a 20-minute videotape in which top people in many agencies, past and present—some he didn't even know—expressed what he meant to the business. *Advertising on Ogilvy* was also shown at a black-tie event at the Smithsonian, where he was to get an award in absentia from its Center of Advertising History. He sent a Telex saying the part of the film he liked best was when the narrator said he was the most famous advertising man. "If that is true, and I don't doubt it for a minute, I will tell you why I am the most famous. It is because I have outlived my elders and my betters."

∼

Ogilvy observed that the agency had been managed over the years by "a series of five friends," naming the first five chairmen. Then the chain was broken. After three years of increased meddling and brutal financial pressures, Graham Phillips resigned when told as CEO that he couldn't give a budgeted raise to a director. So much for the agency's promised "autonomy" within agreed-to budgets.

Phillips was succeeded—for the first time—by an *outsider.* In 1992, Sorrell recruited Charlotte Beers from Tatham-Laird, a medium-size agency in Chicago. Beers, an articulate, charismatic woman who had also headed the 4As agency association, had a reputation for winning new business. Ogilvy talked with her for seven hours, found nothing to disagree with, and was impressed right away. "She is the best chief we've had since I gave up the job," he wrote, airily dismissing his four successor-friends. But she had never run an international agency like Ogilvy & Mather. Of more significance, Sorrell had violated Ogilvy's principle: "to make sure that every office is headed by a member of the True Church, and not by a stranger."

The honeymoon didn't last long. Beers didn't answer Ogilvy's memos. Ignoring his specific request, she closed down *Viewpoint,* the agency's respected journal of opinion. She killed his "We Sell. Or Else" slogan without explanation. He asked her to stop people from talking about the "new" Ogilvy & Mather and referring to the "old" Ogilvy & Mather in a disparaging way. But, he wrote a former colleague, "If an agency hires a CEO from the outside it is inevitable there will be a major change in the corporate culture and almost everything else. These changes are hard to swallow. I still believe in Magic Lanterns, but the new management isn't interested in such things. Our old agency has changed faster than I expected." This lament turned into a direct attack on Beers: "Her version of Brand Stewardship has not brought in a single new account in two years . . . she has abolished everything which I think is valuable in Ogilvy & Mather." Beers left after four years.

Sorrell made a better decision in promoting Shelly Lazarus to chairman. A 25-year veteran of the agency (another "friend"), Lazarus had proven herself on the American Express account as well as heading the New York direct response unit, and was the main force in winning the $500 million IBM account in 1996, the largest single piece of new business ever won by any agency. She had grown up in Ogilvy's culture and understood Ogilvy's place in it.

Before Lazarus took over as chairman, she wisely traveled to France to spend three days with Ogilvy at the château. He didn't talk about the creative work. He didn't talk about the clients. His single-minded advice was to pay more attention to *people,* importuning that whatever time she spent worrying about them or giving them more opportunity or rewarding them was never enough.

Several years earlier, when the agency lost part of the prized American Express account just after Lazarus had taken over the New York office, Ogilvy called her at home to ask how she was. She went into a full financial analysis, noting how many people might be cut, how they might be moved. Ogilvy just listened. When she finished her monologue, he came back: "That's fine. I don't really care. I called to find out how you are. Clients come, they go, they come back, we'll get a new one. It really doesn't matter. The only thing that can actually affect who we are as a company is if you feel any less excited or committed. If the only impact of this is that American Express pulls its business, we'll survive." American Express did come back several years later.

In 1997, *Blood, Brains and Beer* was republished, with a new preface, as *David Ogilvy: An Autobiography.* It didn't sell much better than the original, but did include a message on selling: "I keep on beating the drums for advertising that *sells,* and flogging those who think that advertising is entertainment. I will go to my grave believing that advertisers want results, and the advertising business may go to its grave believing otherwise."

In early days, the entire agency held its annual staff meetings in the auditorium of New York's Museum of Modern Art. In 1998, it returned to MoMA to celebrate its fiftieth anniversary with a gala party in the sculpture garden for 1,500 staffers, alumni, and friends. Lazarus, in a bright red dress, introduced Herta Ogilvy—the founder himself was feeling his years, and not well enough to travel. There were celebrations in several hundred Ogilvy offices around the world. *Advertising Age* published a 28-page supplement of history, nostalgia, classic O&M ads, and testimonials.

Lazarus tried to involve Ogilvy, but he remained fixated on the past, not recognizing that the world had progressed. He was showing his age, forgetting names and repeating himself. He admitted that he got rattled, his memory was "hopeless," and he tired easily. He was depressed and in the early stages of Alzheimer's. The damp rooms at Touffou didn't help his chronic bronchitis, and he couldn't stop smoking. Herta closed the apartment in Paris; she couldn't leave him at Touffou for long periods.

~

Longevity fascinated Ogilvy, who railed about "the conspiracy against old men" and collected stories of people who were productive into their 80s and 90s. Such as Konrad Adenauer: "He was 87 when he gave up the job as boss of Germany. Put that in your pipe and smoke it." And John D. Rockefeller, who started Standard Oil, became one of the richest men in the world, and lived to be 96: "Had he retired at 60, nobody would have heard of him." And his client Helena Rubinstein, who worked until she was 90: "When she died she was still the prime mover in her company, all over the world."

Ogilvy saw long life solely as an opportunity to *work* longer. "If you work to age 85 or more, you have, in effect, two careers, one after the other. Your normal career, which lasts 40 years until you're 65, and then your second career, which is, say, 20 years. You outlive your competitors, and you achieve more. And when you finally give it up at 85, you're famous." He talked about how he had applied for a job in London in advertising at 17: "Thank God they turned me down. I would never have gotten the education that taught me two things . . . to have exorbitant standards, to try and do everything you did better than anybody's ever done it or will ever do it again; and secondly, to work myself to death. Well, not to death, to life!"

As his mind started to go, he watched two movies over and over. One was *Witness,* the story of a young Amish boy from Lancaster County who witnesses a murder, with mythic scenes of Amish barn raisings that allowed him to wallow in Lancaster memories. It's less clear what he saw in *The Sound of Music,* the wholesome Rodgers and Hammerstein musical with Julie Andrews as a nun, then governess, for the von Trapp family in Salzburg in the late 1930s. It was the same show from which his brother had bolted, grumbling about kids and nuns. Glorious music? The Austrian countryside? Certainly the anti-Nazi subplot. Maybe he just liked Julie Andrews. And he was always fascinated by the Catholic Church.

His son flew almost weekly from the United States to be with him. Their relationship over the years had grown from problematic, when Ogilvy divorced Fairfield's mother and left him at 16, to close as they reconciled in later years.

By 1997, Alzheimer's had taken over and the mind was gone. He recognized only a few people. His asthma, aggravated by lifelong smoking, had turned to emphysema, and he was on oxygen, spending much of his day in bed or on a chaise longue, like a magnificent beached creature—not sure who he was or where he was. He was content, and the family was often with him, but he had lost the center of his life. "We wives came into his life, but his life was the agency," says Herta, with understanding. He was 86 years old.

THIRTEEN

THE BURR OF SINGULARITY

*D*avid Ogilvy died on July 21, 1999. A blessing, said Herta. At the end, he could barely breathe. With his emphysema, he was no longer allowed to smoke, but he sneaked cigarettes as soon as she left the room. Alzheimer's had robbed his mind. He was 88.

It was headline news around the world. In America, where he first became famous, he was ADVERTISING TRENDSETTER and FATHER OF THE SOFT SELL. In his home country, where he was less well known, British papers nonetheless crowned him MR. ADVERTISING. To the Scots, he was ADVERTISING'S "GODFATHER." Even in Brazil, where he never visited, he was THE LAST OF THE PIONEERS. In India, where he was revered, he was predictably ADVERTISING GURU. Australia called him THE LAST OF THE GREATS. France, his adopted country, bid L'ADIEU to A FATHER OF MODERN ADVERTISING.

"He will be the last advertising man whose death will be marked on the front page of *The New York Times*," quipped agency head Jerry Della Femina. "That's it folks, everybody else gets the back page."

The Burnett agency placed a full-page ad in trade publications.

David Ogilvy 1911—
Great brands live forever.
Leo Burnett

The funeral scene at Touffou was poignant. The coffin, covered in Ogilvy's Mackenzie tartan, was carried to the garden on the shoulders of young, hefty family members, followed by two bagpipers playing a lament, "Dark Isle," and placed underneath the catalpa tree where Ogilvy liked to sit.

The weather was glorious. Fields of sunflowers in full bloom set off the beauty of Touffou. He had written instructions years earlier on how his death was to be managed: no mourning, no black, no sadness, no pomp nor circumstance—and no religious trappings of any kind. So when two of his friends on the way to the service came upon a prominently displayed three-foot-high rustic cross made of two tree branches, one mused, "How does that square with his instructions?" "Well, you can change your mind," responded the other. "When did he change his mind?" "This morning." Herta, having done everything his way for 26 years, apparently decided to do the funeral her way.

A curé from the village, assisted by a minister, conducted the ecumenical service, attended by an eclectic gathering of some 40 family, friends, and locals—the mayors of Bonnes and Sauvigny, the postmaster, workmen, and gardeners in dark, baggy suits. The person who wept most openly was Lami, Ogilvy's first gardener at the château. After the service, the coffin was shouldered again and carried out of the garden, as the pipers played happy airs. Ogilvy was cremated, at his request, his ashes buried at Touffou. He had told his secretary that the best thing to do would be to just put him in a cardboard box and bury him. She says he wanted it to be simple and environmentally friendly, so he could blend in with the earth.

~

How relevant is Ogilvy's creative philosophy today? Even he would have a hard time reconciling it with a younger audience or products he wouldn't understand—especially technology. He would applaud some of today's advertising for its inventiveness in delivering a message. But he would deplore much for being self-indulgent, obscure, wasting a client's money, and neglecting the purpose of advertising: to sell a product or a service or an idea.

Technology in particular would baffle him. Ogilvy didn't use a typewriter or, for that matter, even a ballpoint pen—only freshly sharpened pencils. In the early days of the agency, when television was still a novelty, a staff memo would go around announcing when a client's commercial was to be aired. The day the first Dove commercial was announced, Ogilvy came storming into the media department saying he couldn't get his set to work. A staffer came to his office, changed the dial from Channel 1 (no station) to Channel 2 (CBS), and a picture appeared. "It's so nice to have a television expert in the agency," said a grateful Ogilvy.

He was a print man and, unlike Bill Bernbach, he never really embraced television. Although he took credit for dreaming up the idea of the Pepperidge Farm wagon, he admitted that he never wrote a good TV commercial. At one point, he had a film editing machine installed in his office; it was strictly for show. He scarcely watched TV. "It has been brought to my attention that some of our creative people who make advertising for television do not own a television set," he wrote in one memo. "The excuse may be that they have no appropriate place in their homes for a TV. I have never found this a problem. I keep my TV set in my wine cellar." The trend toward visual, posterlike magazine and newspaper ads also escaped him. In his universe, art directors were not the equals of copywriters.

Many creative people are quick to dismiss Ogilvy as not relevant today—indeed, not relevant for decades—because of his fondness for what they call his "rules" (a word that he quickly stopped using). Oddly, they almost always cite just one: Don't run text in reverse (white letters on a black background or over a dark color). A creative director visiting the château said he had a bad dream in which a kilted figure appeared and pointed a bony finger at him. "YOU!" it spoke. "You reversed the body copy." Just as odd, avoiding text printed in reverse is probably the one rule that most often makes sense if you want people to read what you have written. The best creative people understood his principles as guides to what works best most often, not inflexible do's and don'ts never to be breached.

Although he, along with Bernbach, was a maverick and a pioneer, Ogilvy was not on the front lines of the creative revolution of the 1960s and 1970s. If anything, he was trying to hold back the flood of more visual, more emotional, more humorous advertising that gave higher priority to entertainment. Slow to accept new things, he didn't grasp changes in the U.S. culture or the ways in which communications had to adapt.

So what is Ogilvy's legacy?

He created a half dozen campaigns, revolutionary at the time, that added an element of quality and good taste into American advertising. *Always give your product a first-class ticket through life.* But it has long been evident that Bill Bernbach had a greater influence on today's standards for good advertising. Bernbach attracted more disciples, particularly among copywriters and art directors, than Ogilvy.

Ogilvy's legacy goes beyond print ads or TV commercials. "Like the great granite heads of Mount Rushmore," wrote Jeremy Bullmore, "it is the scale of Ogilvy that we wonder at—not the detail."

Perhaps his most enduring contribution was the concept of brand image, now mandatory in marketing discussions and reaching beyond advertising even into politics. He didn't invent the idea, but he championed it as early as 1955 in speeches and articles. *Every advertisement must contribute to the complex symbol that is the brand image.*

Ogilvy made the practice of advertising more professional. The Advertising Research Foundation's annual award in his name testifies to his importance in placing high value on the use of consumer research to guide the development of advertising. He mandated his agency to build "a corpus of knowledge." *We pursue knowledge the way a pig pursues truffles.* He led the industry toward payment by fees, like doctors or lawyers, for work performed instead of by commissions on client spending.

His embrace of direct marketing, with its ability to measure results, was ahead of its time. *We Sell. Or Else.* He brought the discipline into the mainstream of advertising and was elected—as a "general" advertising man—into the Direct Marketing Hall of Fame.

Throughout his professional life, Ogilvy campaigned to reinforce the purpose of advertising—to sell a client's product, service, or idea—rather than seek awards and recognition for creative inventiveness. *Make the cash register ring.*

The Associated Press suggested that his greatest legacy may have been his approach to advertising that assumed the intelligence of the consumer. *The consumer is not a moron, she is your wife. Never write an advertisement you would not want your own family to read. You would not tell lies to your wife. Don't tell them to mine.* Ogilvy's lobbying against billboards as despoiling the landscape was another such appeal to the conscience of his fellow practitioners. He was a consumerist before it had a name.

He showed a respect for good manners in advertising, in dealing with clients, and in treating employees, often referring to them as partners. *I admire people with gentle manners who treat other people as human beings.* Lofty statements like these influenced many men and women to choose advertising as a career.

He laid the foundation for a global brand. His original proposition for Dove—*one-quarter cleansing cream to keep skin looking younger*—has been strong enough to extend to other personal care categories beyond soap and make Dove the leading personal care brand in the world.

Ogilvy & Mather is his most visible legacy. Notwithstanding a reputation as a creative genius, his defining characteristic was as a leader. He articulated and inculcated principles of management that apply equally to other kinds of businesses, and devoted his career to building a major international agency, institutionalizing its values so deeply that, unlike many companies created by a charismatic founder, it prospered after his retirement, survived a hostile takeover, and remains highly respected today—with his name still on the door.

As the millennium approached, the trade press started making lists. *Advertising Age* picked the 100 "top" advertising campaigns of the twentieth century. Ogilvy & Mather had three: "Good to the Last Drop" for Maxwell House; "Do you know me?" for the American Express Card; and Ogilvy's "The Man in the Hathaway Shirt." Doyle Dane Bernbach had eight, including the magazine's #1 choice: Volkswagen. (Among the top 100 were several entertaining flops, notably Isuzu's lying salesman and Bert and Harry Piel for Piel's beer.) Bill Bernbach was selected as the single most influential creative force in advertising's history. Ogilvy was number four, behind (curiously) Marion Harper and Leo Burnett.

James Twitchell's *20 Ads that Shook the World* named "The Hathaway Man: David Ogilvy and the Branding of Branding" as one of those that changed the way we swallowed information from the world around us. *Adweek* asked professionals and students which individuals, alive or dead, made them consider a career in advertising. Ogilvy was first among both groups. The publisher of *Forbes* wrote that Ogilvy "gets my vote as the greatest advertising mind of the 20th century."

Confessions was reissued in the United Kingdom in 2004 and in the United States a year later, 42 years after its initial publication. Even the iconoclastic agency head Jerry Della Femina called it "the definitive 'how to' book on advertising." Almost as quotable as Ogilvy, Della Femina remembered hearing Ogilvy railing against young upstarts in the business and the inmates taking over the asylum. "He said it so brilliantly and so well that I got up and led the applause. Then I realized he was talking about me."

The economist Milton Friedman once reflected whether his own ideas in practice had been on the winning side or the losing side. Judged on this measure, Ogilvy loses in television advertising. Nor did he grasp new trends in print illustration. He wins on direct response, the spiritual parent of the Internet. He wins on enduring ideas: brand image, consumer research, respecting the consumer, agency compensation, global brands, building a corporate culture—and advertising that sells.

∾

Will advertising as Ogilvy knew it long survive in the new digital world? Mass audiences have been diluted by other entertainment and information options. Cable and satellite TV. Digital video recorders to watch whenever you want. Around-the-clock news from CNN. Plus blogs, iPods, instant messaging, and online video games.

It's not hard to imagine that advertising on the Internet will come to dominate the scene worldwide. Consider China, which in 2008 passed the United States in Internet users: 253 million. And that's only 19 percent of the country's population. Beyond the booming use of the Internet everywhere and the potential for growth in developing countries, advertising on the Web is booming as well. Online advertising in China is growing 60 to 70 percent a year.

But it would be unwise to vault to grandiose conclusions fueled by such numbers. Every time a new advertising medium appears, the end is predicted for whatever medium it appears to replace. When TV came in, it was going to be the end of radio. Radio didn't go away; it changed. There are now more stations with a wider variety of programming, and who would have thought that one day we might pay for radio via satellite? Classified advertising, a big revenue source for newspapers, has largely gone on the Internet, and big-city newspapers are merging or closing. But community and special-interest newspapers are growing.

A lot of money went out of the agency business when clients moved from commissions to fees, thanks in part to Ogilvy. One wonders how enthusiastic he would have been if he had foreseen the consequences of his bold action on this front. Cost-conscious clients now instruct their purchasing departments to analyze the prices paid to "vendors," and often advertising agencies are near the top of the list for cuts. At the same time, publicly held agencies or holding companies try to satisfy shareholders by holding down costs, which in agencies means salaries and rent.

Fewer people have to work harder and be more productive. Their e-mail in-boxes are jammed, and their BlackBerries are never far from their sides. But talk to any young lawyer or banker, even your doctor, and you'll find the same thing. It's not unique to advertising. The pace and speed of all business has accelerated, just as futurist Alvin Toffler predicted in 1970's *Future Shock*. Like all businesses, advertising is changing. This could be the most exciting time to be in advertising. Technology is creating new opportunities to reach consumers—and measure the benefits of spending.

What advertising delivers is *ideas*. And ideas grow best in agencies, where creative people can work with and be around other creative people, and where they can work on a diverse range of products rather than one single slice. Agencies are here to stay.

Ogilvy would not recognize much of the new landscape, but he would applaud the growth of disciplines that can be measured, such as direct marketing. He would chastise marketers for looking through the wrong end of the telescope, at how little they can pay their agencies rather than how much they can gain by investing in Big Ideas.

∾

By the mid-1990s, WPP started edging back from the brink of bankruptcy. A "near-death" experience, said Martin Sorrell, who not only survived calls for his head, *The Economist* reported, but "negotiated a fat compensation package for rescuing a company he had almost killed." And he was back in the acquisition game, bagging Young & Rubicam for $4.7 billion, the biggest takeover in advertising history. In buying big American agencies—J. Walter Thompson, Ogilvy & Mather, Young & Rubicam, and before long, Grey Global—Sorrell was gaining grudging respect for building one of the world's largest marketing services groups.

Musing on the need to balance creativity and discipline in creative enterprises, *The Financial Times* quoted Harold Ross, editor of *The New Yorker* in the 1930s: "What I need is a man who can sit at a central desk and make this place operate like a business office, keep track of things, find out where people are." What Ogilvy needed, the *FT* concluded, was "an odious little jerk." In the 2000 Millenium Year Honors list, Martin Sorrell, who bore that sobriquet, was knighted by Queen Elizabeth II, the ultimate honor that had eluded Ogilvy and one he had aspired to all his life. Not being knighted was one of his two major regrets. The other was his decision to sell his company to the public.

Why he was passed over for knighthood will never be known. Possibly it was due to his relationship with Prince Philip at the World Wildlife Fund. Perhaps it was the sensitivity of his work for British security, although his former boss at BSC became "Sir William" Stephenson. Perhaps he didn't meet criteria such as helping a British charity (he aided many in the United States). Evidently his promotion of British products in the States—Guinness, Schweppes, Rolls-Royce—did not count sufficiently. Nor did his "Come to Britain" campaign, which brought millions of American tourists across the Atlantic. He had to be content with the second highest honor, Commander of the British Empire. Not being a knight, he could never be called "Sir David." That disappointed him the rest of his life, although he was gratified to be able to pull rank with the British Embassy in Vienna, when told a replacement passport would take four days. "I am a Commander of the British Empire." He got it in two hours.

Jock Elliott, Ogilvy's friend and successor as chairman, "my deep keel," died in 2005. Respected by senior clients, Jock was admired for the unique quality of his public talks, his devotion to public service, and his collection of 3,000 books about Christmas, many of them first editions, including Dickens's *A Christmas Carol.* Ed Ney, former head of Y&R, called Elliott "the poet laureate of the advertising business." He followed Ogilvy into the Advertising Hall of Fame.

One of Ogilvy's favorites, Hal Riney, the gruff ad man who founded the agency's San Francisco office, died in 2008. Riney created brilliant campaigns for E. & J. Gallo and its Bartles & James wine coolers, helped reelect Ronald Reagan with his upbeat 1984 campaign "It's morning again in America," and launched the Saturn car. Riney was exempt from his dogma, Ogilvy said, explaining that if advertising had nothing but creative geniuses like Hal Riney, such dogma would be unnecessary. Asked why an independent cuss like him had joined a vast enterprise like Ogilvy & Mather, Riney responded: "I guess it was all that shiny paper," referring to the agency's thoughtful publications on every aspect of the business that bespoke a classy outfit, something he'd be proud to be part of.

In 2007, *Mad Men,* a U.S. TV series set on Madison Avenue in the 1960s—when Ogilvy was riding high—in a fictional agency called Sterling Cooper, was a big hit with its somewhat overblown portrayal of that era's smoking, drinking, and womanizing. It inspired designer fashions, window displays in department stores, and a mock issue of *Advertising Age,* and was exported to the United Kingdom, where BBC Four aired a special to give it historical perspective: "David Ogilvy: Original Mad Man." He would have hated the title and loved the attention.

The year he died, his agency decided to adopt the founder's signature

as its logo, keeping Ogilvy & Mather Worldwide as its name. *Ogilvy the brand.*

~

Great advertising, Ogilvy was fond of saying, has "a burr of singularity," something unusual enough to stick to the reader's or viewer's mind, the way a nonmetaphoric burr sticks to your trousers. A burr could be a visual device in a print advertisement, like the eye patch conveying the aristocratic aura and story appeal of the Hathaway man. Or a word like "diffident," characterizing buyers of the Bentley, a less showy car than the Rolls-Royce, its sister marque. Or an evocative image in a TV commercial, like the delivery man in a horse-drawn carriage delivering Pepperidge Farm breads.

Ogilvy was himself a burr of singularity, or perhaps many burrs—a self-proclaimed Scot who didn't much like Scotland and spent no time there; a Brit who felt least at home in his own agency's London office; an Englishman who conquered the U.S. advertising business on its own terms but never received the accolades or recognition in the United Kingdom that he felt he deserved; an expatriate who retired to France and said he loved the country but not the French people. In Herta's view, Ogilvy was "the most American Brit" and "the most British American."

David Ogilvy was a man of many paradoxes. An elitist name-dropper who instilled meritocracy in his agency. Open-minded about people but narrow about theories of advertising. An atheist who was fascinated by the structure of the Catholic Church, particularly admired Pope John Paul II, laced his memos with the language of the church and quotes from the Bible, and reveled in his appellation as "the Pope of Modern Advertising."

Conservative in tastes and attitudes, Ogilvy could be flamboyant in dress, eccentric in behavior, and radical in proposing new ideas. *Raise your sights. Blaze new trails. Compete with the immortals.* A model of civilized good taste, he often behaved like a spoiled child in restaurants and regularly told a joke about farting.

Ogilvy preached the importance of kindness and "gentle manners" but could be cruel in describing someone's personality or physical appearance: "the soul of Uriah Heep in the body of a baboon." A leader who inspired loyalty and valued it, he could fall in and out of love with his executives, in one flagrant case touting a recent arrival as his only worthy successor.

A champion of the rational sales message, he created the Hathaway eye patch from intuition and understood the power of emotion, encouraging a writer to appeal to "snobbery" in promoting Viyella fabric to mothers. Serious about the purpose of his business, he loved jokes and believed creative enterprises functioned best if the people who worked there were having fun.

A man obsessed with money, he paid himself modestly, forced agency shares on his partners, and instituted a profit-sharing trust for employee retirements when the agency was still small and its profits were not yet enriching him. He was a generous boss who would take a group to lunch at the best restaurant in Manhattan, then not allow them a drink before eating.

A lifelong smoker, he refused to accept a cigarette account when its health issues became known but continued to smoke himself, although his brother died of lung cancer.

~

Thirteen years before he died, Ogilvy wrote a memo headed "My Death." He stipulated that a memorial service would be permissible only under certain conditions.

> I don't want the ceremony to take place unless it is built around the following music, which would be expensive.
>   The Hallelujah Chorus, with professional chorus and big orchestra
>   "Rule Britannia"—all 3 verses
>   The audience to leave the auditorium to the happy strains of a high jig.

Two months after his death, at a high-spirited service at Lincoln Center's Avery Fisher Hall, the music was as ordered, played by a large orchestra with chorus and ending with the traditional "Bramble Bush" jig. The packed audience included family, clients, industry figures, current and former O&M people (many of whom hadn't worked for the agency in 20 or 30 years), and a large number of friends. Friendships can be more important than events, he wrote late in life. "So I have made an inventory of my friends"—and listed *several hundred*. He viewed his life as divided into a series of rooms: "20 different rooms, four countries, seven jobs." There were friends in each room, some remaining when he moved to other rooms.

Before the service, O&M directors from around the world gathered for lunch and traded "David" stories. One of the most characteristic came from Hans Lange, managing director of the agency in Germany, who had assumed that position as a young man. When Ogilvy was asked to spend some time in Frankfurt, he agreed and was given an office next to Lange. After a few days, Lange noticed cigars were disappearing from the box behind his desk and left a note in the box: "David, if you want a cigar, let me know and I'll get you some." The next day, when he opened the box, his note was gone, a new one in its place: "Hans, it wasn't me."

Some people felt Ogilvy might have done something more important than advertising. His sisters put him down because he was in commerce—they were in the arts, and in their presence he often felt like a door-to-door salesman. Asked why he chose advertising when he could have done well at anything, he responded: "You're quite wrong. Advertising is the only thing I could have done well."

When it became clear that he and his agency were great successes, he was asked to what he attributed this. Three things: "I worked very hard. I had some talent for the trade. And I was very lucky."

A reporter in Edinburgh once inquired of Ogilvy what he would like as his epitaph. He began by quoting Dryden's translation of lines by Horace:

> Happy the man, and happy he alone,
> He, who can call today his own:
> He who, secure within, can say,
> Tomorrow do your worst, for I have lived today.

Then he changed his mind, turning back to an old Scots saying: "Be happy while you're living for you're a long time dead."

Assessments of David Ogilvy's happiness may vary, but no one will disagree with the conclusion by an American friend from his Oxford days: "He has done rather well for an immigrant, don't you think?"

AFTERWORD

(MORE)
UNPUBLISHED
DAVID OGILVY

*O*n his seventy-fifth birthday, in 1986, Ogilvy was presented with a privately printed book—*The Unpublished David Ogilvy,* a selection of memos, letters, speeches, and articles from the files of his partners. He said it was his best birthday present ever.

Research for this biography unearthed further unpublished (with one exception) examples of his unique style, with its mixtures of little-known fact, historic analogy, apt if obscure allusions, surprising format, charm, and impertinence.

Memo to an agency TV producer

December 17, 1953
All my life I have been fascinated by monkeys.

Chimpanzees are my favorites.

I like to attend their daily tea-party at the London Zoo. It is a formal affair. The chimps behave with impressive decorum, except that every now and then the senior chimp turns a plate full of stew upside down on his head. This is what I like to see.

I wonder if you could use chimpanzees in T.V. commercials. They smoke cigarettes. They love bread and margarine.

∽

Commander Edward Whitehead was president of Schweppes U.S.A. and the model in Schweppes advertising—for which he was paid a talent fee, according to union rules. On June 18, 1954, Ogilvy sent two letters to Whitehead.

Dear Dr. Jekyll:
In a separate letter, I have written to Mr. Hyde, the President of Schweppes U.S.A., enclosing copies of the model release.

This letter is about your model fees.

If you are paid $25 an hour for print and $15 an hour for radio, your total take for the work you did during your recent visit to the United States would be $1,567.70.

The whole matter of your remuneration as a model is a delicate and prickly one for the agency to discuss.

Dr. Mr. Hyde:
In your official capacity as President of Schweppes U.S.A., I must call to your attention a matter which, unless promptly settled, might place your company in jeopardy.

Our Schweppes model, a two-headed fellow by the name of Whitehead (or Jekyll) has refused to sign a model release unless it specifies he see a proof of every ad in which he appears.

This is a most unusual situation, but I must admit he is a most unusual model. Never, in all my experience, have I seen an agency clear advertisements with a model—not even with Baron George Wrangel of Hathaway fame.

Would you please try to persuade the model to sign this release and to waive such specifications as would erect impossible obstacles in the process of getting good advertising approved and running for Schweppes here.

∽

Letter to an editor at The New Yorker

August 18, 1955
We want to be the first agency to use limericks in advertising. I am not sure which client (present or future) is likely to be the beneficiary of this idea, but let us suppose—for the sake of argument—that it would be Schweppes.

Now, as you and I know, most good limericks tend to be a little shocking. And what I want to find out is this: how straight-laced would The New Yorker be about this?

Your editors frequently print cartoons which are mildly pornographic, but nobody objects because they are so witty—and because your readers are ipso facto grown up.

Would you apply the same kind of standard to advertising?

I have no desire to be pornographic for the sake of pornography. I dislike the Spring Maid advertising, because it tends to be dirty without being witty.

I attach a collection of ten limericks. They are all classics. And they represent the depth of impropriety to which we would ever go with our campaign.

Three of the collection submitted for review

I sat next to the Duchess at tea;
It was just as I feared it would be,
    Her rumblings abdominal
    Were simply phenomenal,
And everyone thought it was me!

There was a young lady from Madras,
Who had a magnificent ass;
    Not rounded and pink,
    As you probably think—
It was grey, had long ears, and ate grass.

There once was a spinsterish lass
Who constructed her panties of brass.
    When I asked: "Do they chafe?"
    She said: "No, but I'm safe
Against pinches, and pins in the grass."

❧

Memo to Staff

December 15, 1958 (and re-sent almost every year thereafter)

CHRISTMAS CARDS

I am writing this note for the benefit of people who have joined Ogilvy, Benson & Mather since last Christmas.

I want you to know that we have abolished the convention of sending Christmas cards to each other.

The thing became absurd. There are about two hundred of us working here. If everyone sent a card to everyone else, it would add up to 40,000 cards—and cost us at least $10,000.

Very few of us can afford the time or the money to engage in such massive mailings. So, let us all say "Merry Christmas"—in person. Not by mail.

~

Letter to Randolph Churchill, in England

July 25, 1961
Thank you for your telegram. The cook delivered it to me on a salver in the middle of a game of croquet.

~

Letter to David Burpee, president of the W. Atlee Burpee Seed Company

July 1, 1971
My firm Ogilvy & Mather is a candidate for appointment as your advertising agency.

If this comes to pass, I shall be extremely happy, because I too am a gardener. I have been a Life Fellow of the Royal Horticultural Society for thirty-nine years.

My wife and I have just returned from visiting some gardens in England. The old roses at Sissinghurst and at Savill Gardens were glorious beyond description.

We spend our summers here in France, where we have 95 different kinds of rose—about 700 plants. The star today is Mermaid—six of them rampaging up a 15th Century stone wall, and covered with flowers.

I hope you will come and visit us here—whether or not you hire Ogilvy & Mather!

Burpee did award its account to O&M. Ogilvy visited David Burpee and wrote again on June 7, 1972, commenting on the company's penchant for cramming many products onto a single catalog page.

Helena Rubinstein was my client for sixteen years—between the ages of 77 and 93. She used to badger me about putting several products into every advertisement. I always told her it could not be done.

Then one day I said to her "Madam, I have thought of a way to do it."

I put twelve different face creams into one advertisement. It was very successful, and we used it for years. I will show it to you the next time we meet. You are right!

Here in my own garden the climbing roses are rampaging up the mediaeval stone walls, and the Russell lupins are in bloom. The gardener has just finished bedding out 5000 annuals from the cold frames.

I loved my day at Fordhook [Farms].

P.S. You have been head of your company for fifty-seven years. This must be a record. I cannot stop thinking about it.

~

From a memo to directors

December 21, 1971

HIS MASTER'S VOICE

I think you have on file a Xerox copy of my Magic Lantern. You can now buy a set of the slides, coupled to a stereo cassette tape with my voice reading the slides.

Just think how useful it would have been if Moses had recorded a cassette when he brought the tablets down from the mountain.

~

Memo to Directors

July 27, 1972

During the Kaiser's war, whenever one of Churchill's colleagues in the Cabinet got mad at him, he would write to them in this vein:

"We are on the stage of history. Let us keep our anger for the common foe."

With a little modification, we should sometimes say this to each other.

~

Memo to Directors

January 17, 1973

MOONLIGHTING

WE ENCOURAGE MOONLIGHTING, PARTICULARLY AMONG OUR COPYWRITERS.

It broadens their experience.

It gives them more sense of responsibility.

It increases their income—at no cost to us.

I learned this dodge from Dr. Gallup. He paid us miserably, but encouraged us to moonlight.

Rosser Reeves always did a lot of it. So did I. One year I made more—far more—moonlighting than I did at the agency. And it sharpened my wits.

Anyone who opposes moonlighting is a pettifogger.

Only two rules. Chaps must not moonlight on competing accounts or for other agencies, and they must not be caught doing the work in office hours.

~

From a memo to a chairman of O&M

March 30, 1975

Gerard B. Lambert of Listerine fame reorganized Gillette in 1932. He decided to change agencies. He went to see JWT, but he was so shocked by the opulence of their offices that he decided not to hire them.

Many years later he said to me, "If you ever start an agency, don't rent in one of those obvious plush buildings where all the other agencies are located. Take an old warehouse. Don't furnish it with antiques and thick pile carpet. Use old trestle tables. Make your agency look like the city room in a newspaper office. This will impress prospective clients. An atmosphere of hard work, with all the commissions going into service—instead of opulence.

Several times, over the years, I tried this on Shelby [Page, CFO], but never got anywhere. I am amused that you haven't either.

Another way to differentiate your agency would be to put the offices in a field, near a pleasant town like Princeton. The arguments against that are obvious, but they never persuaded me. One of the things I regret not having done.

In my next incarnation, I'm going to be a dictator.

~

From a memo to directors

August 20, 1975

GENERALISTS COST LESS

For thirty years, all agencies have been structured in more or less the same way. The steep rise in salaries and rent may force us to evolve a different structure—one which can be operated with fewer bodies.

When I worked at the Hotel Majestic, every cook was a specialist, and the kitchen was divided into departments—sauce, fish, vegetables, soup, pastry, and so on. Each department had three levels.

This classic set-up produced good cooking, but it was extravagant in manpower. It was only made possible by the fact that the cooks were paid low wages.

Today, French cooks are paid relatively high wages. As a result, no hotel or restaurant can afford the classic set-up. The specialized departments have disappeared.

The specialists have become generalists. The size of their brigades has thereby been drastically reduced.

When I worked at Ogilvy & Mather in New York, everyone was a specialist, and the agency was divided into departments—copy, account executive, media, research and so on. Every department had three levels, at least.

The classic set-up was extravagant in manpower. I wonder how much longer agencies will be able to afford the classic set-up. Will the specialists have to become generalists, so that numbers can be reduced? The same man would write copy, handle accounts, do media planning and research. This is how small agencies operate.

In the early days I used to write plans, handle accounts, supervise research and write copy.

On the little Hathaway account, a few years later, New York deployed three levels of account executives, and three levels of copywriters. We lost money. Then we put the account in the hands of one copy-contact man, and it became profitable.

~

Memo to Directors

October 6, 1975

When he was Chairman of Sears Roebuck, Charlie Kellstadt hired Ogilvy & Mather. I worked with him closely, and admired him greatly. Last week he died, aged 78.

He once said, "The first person to look out for is the customer. Next you take care of your employees. Third, you look out for your stockholders. But if you've done a good job on the first two counts, the stockholder has no worries."

One could apply this to OMI. It has always been Marvin Bower's* sermon to me.

Letter to managing partner of McKinsey

February 25, 1978
So you sent my Principles of Management to your partners. Well, that brings them full circle, because I wrote them after reading Marvin's WILL TO MANAGE, and he was kind enough to improve my draft.

Long live McKinsey.

∼

Memo to Directors

November 10, 1975

PROMOTIONS

When you face the problem of selecting people for promotion to high positions, it may comfort you to know that Louis XIV, the supreme autocrat, also found it difficult.

"Toutes les fois que je donne une place vacante, je fais cent mécontents et une ingrate."

Which may be translated, "Every time I make an appointment, I make a hundred people unhappy and one person ungrateful."

∼

Memo to Directors

May 5, 1978

PRESENTATIONS

On my recent tour, I was shown a great many case histories. I always wonder if they bore new business prospects as much as they bore me.

---

* Bower was the longtime head of McKinsey & Company, the eminent consulting firm.

Be that as it may, our presenters are still making the same old mistakes.

(1) They put up a slide full of words—and simultaneously say entirely different words. The result is total confusion.
(2) The slides are written in pretentious jargon. (I have written a note on this elsewhere.)
(3) The last slide in each case-history is headed RESULTS. It invariably claims that our campaign increased sales. After seeing several such slides, one's credibility is strained. And the new business prospect thinks, "If these jokers never give any credit to the efforts of their clients, I don't want them as my agency."

It was said in the Five Year Plan that we train our account executives better than we train our creative people. I wonder.

∽

Memo to directors when he was filling in as head of the German agency

March 31, 1979

"JUMPERS"

When you visit Daimler Benz factories, you see groups of two or three men standing with nothing to do; sometimes they go outside for a smoke.

These men are called JUMPERS. Their job is to jump in whenever a man on the line is taken ill or has to go to the bathroom. A jumper has to be able to do different jobs.

For the last seven months I have been a Jumper, taking Dieter's place on the line, on a stop-gap basis.

Not a bad way to use people like me—and you, Gentle Reader, when you are no longer in the "line."

∽

Memo to Creative Directors

July 1, 1979

ARE YOU THE GREATEST?

1. Are you creating the most remarkable advertising in your country?
2. Is this generally recognized, inside and outside your agency?

3. Can you show new-business prospects at least four campaigns which will electrify them?
4. Have you stopped over-loading commercials?
5. Have you stopped singing the sales-pitch?
6. Do all your commercials start with a visual grabber?
7. Have you stopped using cartoon characters when selling to adults?
8. Do you show at least six Magic Lanterns to everyone who joins your staff?
9. If they don't understand English, have you had all the Lanterns translated into their language?
10. Do you repeat the brand-name several times in every commercial?
11. Have you stopped using celebrity testimonials in television commercials?
12. Have you got a list of red-hot creative people in other agencies, ready for the day when you can afford to hire them?
13. Do all your campaigns execute an agreed positioning?
14. Do they promise a benefit—which has been tested?
15. Do you always super the promise at least twice in every commercial?
16. Have you had at least three Big Ideas in the last six months?
17. Do you always make the product the hero?
18. Are you going to win more creative awards than any other agency this year?
19. Do you use problem-solution, humor, relevant characters, slice-of-life?
20. Do you eschew life-style commercials?
21. Do your people gladly work nights and weekends?
22. Are you good at injecting news into your campaign?
23. Do you always show the product in use?
24. Does your house-reel include some commercials with irresistible charm?
25. Do you always show the package at the end?
26. Have you stopped using visual clichés—like sunsets and happy families at the dinner table? Do you use lots of visual surprises?
27. Do the illustrations in your print advertisements contain story-appeal?
28. Are you phasing out addy layouts and moving to editorial layouts?
29. Do you sometimes use visualized contrast?
30. Do all your headlines contain the brand name—and the promise?
31. Are all your illustrations photographs?

32. Have you stopped setting copy ragged left and right?
33. Have you stopped using more than 40 characters in a line of copy?
34. Have you stopped setting copy smaller than 10-point and bigger than 12-point?
35. Do you always paste advertisements into magazines or newspapers before you OK them?
36. Have you stopped setting body-copy in sans-serif?
37. Have you stopped beating your wife?

If you have answer YES to all these questions, you are the greatest Creative Director on the face of the earth.

&

Memo to the co-authors of Writing That Works

September 24, 1979

HOW TO WRITE

If you are looking for examples of bad writing by otherwise good men, here is one for your collection:

> Specifically, consumers' attitudes and usage habits are analyzed within the context of the major market entry's advertised product positionings.

Nine nouns in one sentence. He goes on:

> Product positionings are derived from the detailed assessment of the advertising currently utilized by advertised coffee brands.

Needless to say, he uses symbols instead of numbers—like MDM, TDM, SOV, MMDM. Which is OK if you know the code; I don't.

God knows what one can do in cases like this.

P.S. In spite of his writing, it is a valuable report and General Foods were grateful for it.

March 26, 1980

ENGLISH

In the draft of a new Lantern on sales promotion, I came across DELIVERY VEHICLE. . . .

Later in the same draft, the author kept talking about the REDEEMER.

Who do you suppose the Redeemer is? Jesus Christ, you suppose?

Not at all. The Redeemer is a person who redeems coupons at the supermarket.

Behold the Redeemer in his Delivery Vehicle.

∿

From a memo to the executive committee

February 28, 1980

ACQUISITIONS

As you can see by my [Creative Council] stationery, I don't know anything about finance.

But I have just read the biography of Lord (Roy) Thomson, the Canadian who went to Britain when he was about sixty and proceeded to make a huge fortune.

He did it by always borrowing every penny he could lay hands on, buying newspapers, and then managing them more profitably than their previous owners.

This is the classic way to get rich. Of course, a lot of people who play this game go broke. It is frightfully dangerous.

I doubt if we should take such risks with our stockholders' money, but if we did, we might get rich.

I am not an acquirer by nature. Not am I a gambler like Roy Thomson. That is why I am neither very rich or bankrupt.

However, those of you who are acquirers should, perhaps, price your offerings a little more in the light of future earnings, and a little less in the light of past earnings. Otherwise, you will always be out-bid.

P.S. I hope you will eschew acquisitions. Finance aside, I have always thought it a rickety way to grow. Good agencies are never for sale.

∿

Memo to a chairman of O&M

October 11, 1981

"The friends thou hast, and their adoption tried,
Grapple them to thy soul with hoope of steel."

Shakespeare

This should be the motto of everyone in our management.

The more hoops, the better. If a valuable man owes allegiance to only one person in management, and that person moves or leaves, he may not stay with us.

I do my best to grapple our best Creatives to our soul with hoops of steel.

Memo to directors, on the consequences of having issued a blanket invitation to O&M staff to drop in on him at his château in France

September 18, 1985

A GROWING NUISANCE

Visiting Touffou is now fashionable among the 9,000 employees of our 201 offices.

Too fashionable.

Two days ago I dared to say NO when a team of four New York creative people, in Paris for a shoot, invited themselves to stay at Touffou.

These visitors are often a damn nuisance. We have to entertain them, when we have other fish to fry. They have no conversation. When we give dinner parties for our French neighbors, it is difficult to integrate assistant account executives who cannot speak a word of French.

The burden on my wife-housekeeper is getting to be intolerable. Catering, laundry, planning.

I wish I knew how to damp it down without being beastly. Any help you can give me will be very welcome indeed.

Letter to a new entrant in a training program

September 22, 1977

I once asked King George's surgeon what makes a great surgeon. He replied, "A great surgeon knows more than other surgeons."

It is the same with advertising people; the good ones know more about advertising.

There seems to be no doubt that Ogilvy & Mather knows more than other agencies, and we go to great pains to share our knowledge with the men and women who work here. Hence, among other things, the superb training program on which you are about to embark.

Hence, also our famous Magic Lanterns, which encapsulate some of what we know about a wide range of subjects.

But the most precious asset we have is probably our ETHOS—the spirit which binds our offices together all over the world. It embraces:

Intellectual honesty—with our clients and with each other.
Thoroughness—as opposed to superficiality.
Professionalism—in everything we do; high standards.
Human decency—and good manners.
The emphasis we place on character—in choosing people for key jobs.
Pride in O&M—tempered by unrelenting discontent with our shortcomings.

You will find more on this subject in my Principles of Management.

BIBLIOGRAPHY
AND SOURCE NOTES

AUTHOR RESEARCH AND INTERVIEWS

Ogilvy was a prolific writer, almost beyond comprehension. He wrote books, memos, letters, notes, speeches, and presentations. When he retired to France, he donated his papers to the Library of Congress: over 30,000 items, mostly by him. He did not stop there, but continued writing for another 25 years. I went through all 87 containers at the Library, reviewed more than 2,000 pieces in my own collection, and surveyed still more books, films, and tapes that relate to him in some way.

Beyond the written record, I visited his birthplace in Surrey, the Fettes school in Edinburgh, Christ Church college at Oxford, Lancaster County, Pennsylvania, where he had two farms, and his homes in New York and France.

My major source of fresh material was 100-plus lengthy interviews, as well as many dozens of shorter phone conversations, letters, and e-mails.

BIBLIOGRAPHY

Unpublished Manuscript Collections and Papers

LIBRARIES AND ARCHIVES

American Association of Advertising Agencies, New York

Archives Center, National Museum of American History, Smithsonian Institution, Washington DC—*Barton S. Cummings papers*

British Library, Newspaper Library, London

British Library, Science and Reference Division, London

Churchill Museum and Cabinet War Rooms, London

Federal Bureau of Investigation, Washington DC

John W. Hartman Center for Sales, Advertising, and Marketing History, Rare Book, Manuscript and Special Collections Library, Duke University, Durham NC—*David B. McCall papers, Jock Elliott papers*

History of Advertising Trust Archive, Raveningham, Norwich, England

Imperial War Museum, London

International Spy Museum, Washington DC

Leo Burnett Company, Chicago IL—*Burnett-Ogilvy files*

Manuscript Division, Library of Congress, Washington DC—*David Ogilvy papers*

Museum of TV and Radio, New York

The National Archives, Public Record Office, London

National Library of Scotland, Edinburgh

The Roper Center for Public Opinion Research, Univ. of Connecticut, Storrs, CT

Wisconsin State Historical Society, Madison WI—*Rosser Reeves papers*

The University Club, New York

MANUSCRIPTS AND PAPERS

How to Make $50,000 a Year in Advertising circa 1957—Judson H. Irish
The Story of Ted Bates & Company 1965—Martin Mayer
How to Create Advertising That Sells 1964–198?—Ogilvy & Mather
Principles of Management 1968—David Ogilvy
My Creative Principles 1968—David Ogilvy
Reva Korda interviews David Ogilvy—*Viewpoint* November 1976
Corporate Culture—Ogilvy & Mather 6/24/85 *My Life* December 1986—David Ogilvy
Mr. David Ogilvy 1986—Stanley Piggott
A Gallup Through Our First 139 Years (1850–1989)—Joel Raphaelson
Interview with David Ogilvy—Lee Bartlett 10/30/91
David Ogilvy's Biography 1994—Joel Raphaelson
David Ogilvy's Last Crusade 2000—Kenneth Jacobsen interview
Alan Northcote Sidnam: Autobiography 2001
Flagbearer (various)—Ogilvy & Mather
Viewpoint (various)—Ogilvy & Mather

Author Interviews

Fettes: Michael Dawson
Christ Church, Oxford: Ronald Hilton, Margot Wilkie
Gallup: Alec Gallup, George Gallup Jr.
British Security Coordination: William Stevenson
Lancaster County: Annie Fisher, Gerry Lestz, John and Michael Ranck
O&M U.S.: Alex Biel, Bill and Gaile Binzen, Paul Biklen, Doug Bomeisler, Sue Buck, Julian Clopet, Helen DeKay, Fran Devereux, Jules Fine, Charlie Fredericks, Gene Grayson, Chuck Guariglia, Steve Hayden, Jim Heekin, Judson Irish, Abe Jones, Ian Keown, Reva Korda, Shelly Lazarus, Jane Maas, Peter Mayle, Bruce McCall, Jerry McGee, Edmund Morris, Shelby Page, Bill Phillips, Graham Phillips, Jerry Pickholz, Gary Press, Vel Richey-Rankin, Joel and Marikay Raphaelson, Elaine Reiss, Brendan Ryan, Nancy Schutz, Dick Seclow, Gloria Sidnam, Ted Shaw, Bruce Stauderman, Lee Thuna, Mike Turner, Emil Vaessen, Jack Walker, Ellie Watrous, Bill Weed, Bill Whitney
O&M U.K.: Clive Aldred, Don Arlett, Bernard Barnett, Jimmy Benson, Drayton Bird, Nick Evans, Richard Fowler, John Nettleton, Archie Pitcher, Harry Reid, Sir Anthony Tennant, John and Jill Treneman, Sheila Trevellyan, Mike Walsh, Peter and Susan Warren, John Williams
O&M International: Michael Ball (Australia), Luis Bassat (Spain), Neil French (Singapore), Tony Houghton (Canada), Ranjan Kapur (India), Barry Owen (Singapore), Robyn Putter and Bob Rightford (South Africa), John Straiton (Canada), Francois and Simone Tiger (France), Roger Winter (Thailand), Lorna Wilson (Paris)
Clients: Tony Adams (Campbell), Phil Carroll (Shell), Jean Clark (widow of American Express Chairman Howard Clark), Edgar Cullman (Culbro), Louis Gerstner (American Express, IBM), Louis den Hartog and Dr. J. F. A. de Soet (KLM), Jack Keenan (General Foods), Bob Lauterborn (International Paper), and, for the World Wildlife Fund, Harold Burson (Burson-Marsteller), Charles de Haes, David Mitchell, and Mac Stewart (McKinsey)
Advertising and Media: David Abbott and Michael Baulk (Abbott Mead Vickers), Cap Adams (Leo Burnett), Lee Bartlett (Cole & Weber), Jeremy Bullmore (J. Walter Thompson), Walter Cronkite (CBS), Burtch Drake (4As), Winston Fletcher (ASBOF), Lou Harris (Louis Harris Associates), Leo Kelmenson (Kenyon & Eckhardt), Gene Kummel (Interpublic), Bob Kuperman (Doyle Dane Bernbach), Dick Lord (Richard Lord Agency), Martin Mayer (author), Ed McCabe (Scali McCabe Sloves), Ed Ney (Young & Rubicam), Fred Pa-pert (Papert Koenig Lois),

Keith and Rose-Lee Reinhard (DDB), Randy Rothenberg (*Advertising Age*), Frank Stanton (CBS)

Friends/family: Louis Auchincloss, Louis Begley, Elly Elliott, Mary Lindsay, Herta Ogilvy

Published Books, Publications, Tapes
BY DAVID OGILVY
Confessions of an Advertising Man Atheneum 1963
Blood, Brains and Beer Atheneum 1978
Ogilvy on Advertising Crown Publishers 1983
The Unpublished David Ogilvy Ogilvy & Mather 1986—edited by Joel Raphaelson
The Unpublished David Ogilvy Crown 1986—edited by Joel Raphaelson
Dear Friend Fund Raising Institute 1990—Lautman and Goldstein, foreword by D.O.
Scientific Advertising Moore Publishing 1952—Claude Hopkins, 1993 preface by D.O.
David Ogilvy: An Autobiography John Wiley & Sons 1997
Tested Advertising Methods Prentice Hall 1997—John Caples, foreword by D.O.
Confessions of an Advertising Man Scribner 1988,—2002 foreword to new edition
Quotations of David Ogilvy Ogilvy & Mather London

FAMILY
The Fountain Overflows Penguin Books 1956—Rebecca West
The Scotch-Irish University of North Carolina Press 1962—James G. Leyburn
Rebecca West: a Life Alfred A. Knopf, Inc. 1987—Victoria Glendinning
Pigeon Holes of Memory Constable, London 1988—Edited by Christina Byam Shaw
The Story of West Horsley Manor St. Mary's Church P.C.C. 1993—Pam Bowley
Old West Horsley Horse & Tree Publications 2000—Pam Bowley
A Century of Change Horse & Tree Publications 2003—Pam Bowley
East Horsley Horsley Countryside Preservation Society 2006
Around & About Horsley Horsley Countryside Preservations Society, Spring 2007

STUDENT
A Keen Wind Blows: The Story of Fettes James & James Pub. Ltd. 1929—Roger Philp
Confessions of an Innkeeper Chatto & Windus, London 1938—John Fothergill
George: Autobiography of Emlyn Williams Random House 1961
Illustrated History of Oxford Oxford University Press 1993—Edited by John Priest
You Only Live Twice Jonathan Cape Ltd. 1964, Penguin Books 2003—Ian Fleming
A Hundred Years of Fettes T. and A. Constable Ltd. 1970—Edited by H. F. MacDonald
Cyril Connelly St. Martin's Press 1996—Clive Fisher
Christ Church Oxford Pitkin Pictorials 1991
The Fettes List 1870–1992 Fettes College 1993—George Preston
William Fettes Fettes College 1995—Lindsay, Cheetham, Clarke, Hughes, Rose
Orwell, Wintry Conscience of a Generation W.W. Norton Co. 2000—Jeffrey Meyers

SALESMAN
Aga: The Story of a Kitchen Classic Absolute Press 2002—Tim James

RESEARCHER
Increasing Profits with Audience Research ARI 1941—George H. Gallup, D.O.
George Gallup in Hollywood Columbia University Press 2006—Susan Ohmer
A Guide to Public Opinion Polls Princeton University Press 1944—George H. Gallup
Learning from Winners Taylor & Francis Group 2008—Raymond Pettit

SPY
Room 3603 Farrar, Straus and Company 1962—H. Montgomery Hyde
The Life of Ian Fleming McGraw-Hill Book Company 1966—John Pearson

A History of the British Secret Service Taplinger Publishing 1969—Richard Deacon
A Man Called Intrepid Lyons Press 1976—William Stevenson
Camp X Lester & Orpen Dennys Ltd., Toronto 1986—David Stafford
Secret Intelligence Agent Constable London 1982—H. Montgomery Hyde
"C": The Secret Life of Sir Stewart Menzies Macmillan 1987—Anthony Cave Brown
Desperate Deception Brassey's 1998—Thomas E. Mahl
British Security Coordination Fromm International 1999—Highet, Hill, Dahl
Ian Fleming: The Man Behind James Bond Turner Publishing 1995—Andrew Lycett
The Quiet Canadian H. Hamilton 1962—H. Montgomery Hyde
Spymistress: The Life of Vera Atkins Arcade Publishing 2007—William Stevenson
The Letters of Noël Coward Alfred A. Knopf 2007—Edited by Barry Day
The Irregulars Simon & Schuster 2008—Jennet Conant

FARMER
To Lancaster with Love Brookshire Publications 1992—Gerald S. Lestz
Amish Perspectives York 1998—Armstrong, Fisher, Klimeski, Lestz
A History of Salisbury Township 2002—Joan M. Lorenz

OGILVY & MATHER-RELATED
Murder Must Advertise HarperCollins 1933—Dorothy L. Sayers
My Lives: Francis Meynell The Bodley Head Ltd. 1971—Francis Meynell
OBM: 125 Years Ogilvy Benson & Mather London 1975—Stanley Piggott
How to Advertise St. Martin's Press 1976—Kenneth Roman and Jane Maas
Nobody Else is Perfect W.H. Allen, London 1980—Charles Hennessy
Writing That Works Harper & Row 1981—Kenneth Roman and Joel Raphaelson
Or Your Money Back Crown Publishers, Inc. 1982—Alvin Eicoff
Of Women and Advertising McClelland and Stewart 1984—John S. Straiton
Adventures of an Advertising Woman St. Martin's Press 1986—Jane Maas
Debevoise & Plimpton: The Autobiography of a Law Firm 1991—D. Bret Carlson
Having It All Signet 1992—Reva Korda
Dorothy L. Sayers: Her Life and Soul St. Martin's Press 1993—Barbara Reynolds
David Ogilvy as I Knew Him www.dnaml.com 2008—Michael Ball. Also www.ebook.com

ADVERTISING
Attention and Interest Factors in Advertising Printer's Ink Bookshelf—Harold J. Rudolph
The Hidden Persuaders D. McKay Co. 1957—Vance Packard
Madison Avenue U.S.A. Pocket Books 1958—Martin Mayer
Reality in Advertising Alfred A. Knopf 1961—Rosser Reeves
The New Advertising The Citadel Press NY—Robert Glatzer
Ad: An Inside View of Advertising Bachman & Turner 1973
Advertising the American Dream Univ. of California Press 1984—Roland Marchand
The Mirror Makers William Morrow and Co., Inc. 1984—Stephen Fox
The Benevolent Dictators Crain Books 1984—Bart Cummings
Advertising in America Harry N. Abrams 1990—Charles Goodrum and Helen Dalrymple
50 Years of TV Advertising—Advertising Age Special Collectors Edition Spring 1995
Whatever Happened to Madison Avenue? Little, Brown 1991—Martin Mayer
The Art of Writing Advertising NTC Business 1995—Denis Higgins
Adcult USA Columbia University Press 1996—James B. Twitchell
Conflicting Accounts: Saatchi & Saatchi Touchstone 1997—Kevin Goldman
Adweek 20th anniversary issue—11/9/98
Twenty Ads That Shook the World Crown Publishers 2000—James B. Twitchell
5 Giants of Advertising Assouline 2001—Philippe Lorin
Adland: A Global History of Advertising Kogan Page Limited 2007—Mark Tungate
Advertising of Today UK Quaritch
American Advertising 1800–1900 Chandler Press 1975—Myron Johnson

The 100 Greatest Advertisements 1852–1959 Dover Publications, Julian Lewis Watkins
Diary of an Ad Man Advertising Publications 1944—James Webb Young
The Care and Feeding of Ideas Times Book Division, Random House—Bill Backer
J. Walter Takeover Business One Irwin 1991—Richard Morgan
Powers of Persuasion: The Inside Story of British Advertising Oxford University Press 2008—Winston Fletcher

CLIENTS/COMPETITORS
The Beard and I David McKay Company 1965—Tommy Whitehead
Leo Leo Burnett Company Inc. 1971
Madame: Helena Rubinstein Weidenfeld and Nicolson 1971—Patrick O'Higgins
Marion Harper, An Unauthorized Biography Crain Books 1982—Russ Johnston
J. Walter Takeover Business One Irwin 1991—Richard Morgan
Leo Burnett: Star Reacher Leo Burnett Company 1995—Joan Kufrin
100 Leo's: Wit and Wisdom from Leo Burnett NTC Business Books 1995
Bill Bernbach's Book Villard Books 1987—Bob Levenson
Bill Bernbach Said DDB Needham Worldwide
The Power of the Obvious Palo Alto Press 1995—Aldo Papone
A Big Life (in advertising) Alfred A. Knopf 2002—Mary Wells Lawrence

OTHER
Obvious Adams Executive Development Press, Inc. 1916—Robert Updegraff
All out of Step Doubleday & Co., Inc. 1956—Gerard B. Lambert
The Supersalesmen World Publishing Co. 1962—Edwin P. Hoyt
The Pump House Gang Farrar Straus Giroux 1968—Tom Wolfe
Myself Among Others Dell 1971—Ruth Gordon
Americana Houghton Mifflin 1971—Don DeLillo
Gardens of France Harmony Books 1983—Anita Pereire and Gabrielle van Zuylen
Big Deal Warner Books 1998—Bruce Wasserstein
The Fifties Random House 1993—David Halberstam
The Longevity Factor HarperCollins 1993—Lydia Brontë, Ph.D.
The Tennessee Encyclopedia of History and Culture Thomas Nelson Inc. 1998—Tennessee Historical Society, Carroll Van West (Editor)
McKinsey's Marvin Bower John Wiley & Sons, Inc. 2004—Elizabeth Haas Edersheim

VIDEO AND AUDIOTAPES
Dr. George Gallup 1979 DO interview by John Crichton—4As
David Ogilvy Project—Frank McGee interview 1963
When to Take My Name Off the Door 1967—Leo Burnett
DO—*The View from Touffou* 1981
David Susskind interviews DO 1985
Ken Roman and Martin Sorrell at O&M U.S. officers' meeting 5/17/89
DO at O&M Worldwide Meeting October 1989
DO—*The Importance of Direct Marketing* 9/19/92
DO—*The Art of Persuasion* 9/18/92
DO—*David Ogilvy on Creativity* 9/18/92
Advertising on Ogilvy 1996
Booknotes—interview with Jeffrey Meyers 3/11/2001
HRH Prince Philip, Duke of Edinburgh (World Wildlife Fund) 11/19/06
David Ogilvy: Original Mad Man BBC Four 3/29/08

SOURCE NOTES
Unless otherwise indicated, papers are from the author's collection

Abbreviations
4As: American Association of Advertising Agencies
ANA: Association of National Advertisers
DO: David Ogilvy
FO: Francis Ogilvy
HC: Hartman Center
HOBM: Hewitt, Ogilvy, Benson & Mather
KR: Kenneth Roman
LB: Leo Burnett papers
LOC: Library of Congress
M&C: Mather & Crowther
O&M: Ogilvy & Mather
OBM: Ogilvy, Benson & Mather
OMW: Ogilvy & Mather Worldwide
TOG: The Ogilvy Group
WI: Rosser Reeves papers

Author's Note
xiii **The only thing that can be said in favor**—DO to Richard Thomas 6/10/68

Introduction: The King of Madison Avenue
1 **the conscience and catalytic agent**—*Printer's Ink* 1958
1 **No single figure**—Unidentified magazine 1958
2 **Is Ogilvy a Genius?**—*Fortune* April 1965
2 **if he should sue**—"Further Confessions," *Viewpoint* January/February 1989
2 **most sought-after wizard**—"The literate wizard," *Time* 10/12/62
2 **all-time agency team**—DO to Joel Raphaelson 9/18/85
2 **the best of the best**—Ed Ney to KR 10/22/99
2 **only civilized, literate and entertaining book**—Bruce McCall *7 Days*, NY 6/14/89
2 **He always made a big point**—*The Pump House Gang* p. 57
2 **listed Ogilvy with Pope Paul II**—DO to OMI directors 1/24/83
2 **came as close to being anointed**—*Advertising Age* 10/18/82
3 **Pope of modern advertising**—DO to OMI directors 10/21/82
3 **flowing black cape**—Ellie Watrous interview 4/5/06
3 **"pencil slim"**—*Printer's Ink* 1961
3 **"big agricultural hands"**—Peter Warren interview 5/25/99
3 **He looked a tiny bit like Rupert Brooke**—Margot Wilkie interview 3/12/06
3 **He was very, very sexy**—Jane Maas interview 4/11/06
4 **a movie star was in my little office**—Lee Thuna interview 12/8/06
4 **not a getter-upper**—Doug Bomeisler interview 6/30/06
4 **lay down his jacket**—Bill Phillips to KR
4 **Perhaps a bit of self-advertisement**—*Printer's Ink* c. 1957
4 **Ogilvy waited until the man had finished**—Archie Pitcher interview 5/23/06
4 **A speech consultant**—Dorothy Sarnoff to KR undated
4 **first job had been with BAT**—Elly Elliott interview 4/18/06
4 **told** *another* **CEO that his first job had been**—Elly Elliott interview 4/18/06
4 **Ogilvy's trouble**—*Printer's Ink* 1961
5 **oil situation in the Middle East**—Sue Buck interview 7/17/06
5 **How many flutes?**—Mike Turner interview 6/15/06
5 **books all over his house**—Mary Lindsay interview 9/26/06
5 **George V's stamp collection**—Drayton Bird interview 5/2/06

5 discussion of abstract painting—Fran Devereux interview 3/5/08
5 "culture" bored him—Bruce McCall interview 10/8/06
5 If there's anything David likes—Marikay Raphaelson interview 5/8/97
6 I wasn't going to play that game—DO to KR 1/25/93
6 We don't take people to the elevator—Elly Elliott interview 4/18/06
6 young writer had lost his parents—Devereux interview 3/5/08
6 pre-Christmas dinner—Warren interview 5/25/06
6 He was famous for his eccentricities—David McCall, HC McCall Box 1
7 which of two commercials to show first—Bruce Stauderman interview 8/26/06
7 He had a near-psychopathic hatred of laziness—Bruce McCall interview 7/14/06
7 see him working at his desk—Walter Cronkite interview 4/24/06
8 I went over 375 pieces of paper—Bill Phillips interview 5/29/97
9 Unless your advertisement is based on a Big Idea—*Autobiography* p. 139
9 resisted the use of "ads"—DO to staff 11/3/54 LOC Box 41

Chapter 1: An Eccentric Celtic Mixture
11 Our chairman is *definitely* descended—*Flagbearer* O&M NY c. 1964.
11 Empress Eugenie of France—DO to Joel Raphaelson 9/12/85
11 born in 1911—General Register Office, Guildford, Albury, County of Surrey
11 population of West Horsley had recently boomed—*A Century of Change*
12 Wix Hill—*Kelly's Directory* 1911
12 Wix Hill deed—Jane Lewis, Surrey County Council, to KR 3/14/07
12 a paradise of plover's eggs—*Autobiography* p. 1
12 "Come to Britain"—*Madison Avenue* 1958
12 upper middle to upper class—Winston Fletcher to DO 5/22/78
12 a glass of raw blood every day—*Autobiography* p. 5
12 "eccentric" father—Pam Bouley to KR Oct 06
12 didn't speak to him for 15 years—Stanley Pigott to KR 5/21/93
13 I was a mollycoddle—*DO Autobiography* p. 2
13 When you write a book about advertising—Mike Turner interview 6/15/06
13 the title was repulsive—DO to Winston Fletcher 2/22/95
13 "that eccentric Celtic mixture"—Peter Warren to KR undated
13 I'm a Celt—*Printer's Ink* 1953
13 his Highland relatives—Mary Lindsay interview 9/26/06
14 address to the St. Andrew's Society 11/30/62—LOC, DO papers
14 two spellings of the name—DO to Richard B. Ogilvie 3/10/67
14 father of the F.B.I.—DO to Richard B. Ogilvie 3/10/67
14 My name is David Ogilvy—David Airlie to KR 1/9/07
15 no known connection—Louis Auchincloss interview 10/5/06
15 a man of status—Tony Reid to KR 11/1/06
15 six servants—Registrar General for Scotland, Census Year 1861
15 1796 will—Reid to KR 11/1/06
15 this uneducated sheep farmer—*Autobiography* p. 16
15 "Gentlemen with brains"—*Autobiography* p. 17
15 had to call him "sir"—Emil Vaessen interview 5/18/06
16 saw Ogilvy as an intensely rational man—*David Ogilvy as I Knew Him*
16 Potter's famous gardener, Mr. McGregor—*A Century of Change* p. 6
16 "We were a very poor family"—*The Benevolent Dictators* p. 101
16 hard as nails—DO seventy-fifth birthday interview 1996
17 writ of fire and sword—*Pigeon Holes of Memory* p. 19
17 "perfervid" Mackenzie—DO to W.A. Stevenson Mackenzie 4/18/60, LOC
17 Highland Clearances—www.highlanderweb.co.uk/clearance.htm
17 Anglo-Irish—*Rebecca West: A Life* p. 9
17 lived in County Kerry for 400 years—*Madison Avenue* 12/58
18 a "Gentleman" (i.e.) rich—Tony Reid to KR 3/8/07

18 Dolly—Lorna Wilson interview 10/28/07
18 pocket Venus—Herta Ogilvy interview 9/30/07
18 18-year-old medical student—General Register Office, Marriage Certificate 6/20/1900
18 Dolly fulfilled her ambitions—*Madison Avenue* 1958
18 nutty as a fruitcake—Joel Raphaelson DO 75th birthday interview 1996
18 elder (by eight years)—Guildford Registration District (Vol 2a 90)
18 considered Christina the cleverest—Mike Walsh interview 5/25/06
19 Dolly left some inherited money—*Madison Avenue* 1958
19 Rebecca West . . . changed her name from Cicely—Tony Reid to KR 3/13/07
19 Rebecca was an incurable liar—DO to KR 1/25/93
19 stand outside the Waldorf-Astoria—Jules Fine interview 5/14/97
19 the reason I left Scotland—Bill Whitney interview 9/29/08
20 Zucky—DO to Mairi Ann Macleod 7/5/60
20 he was raised by his mother with help—Vaessen interview 5/18/06
20 That would be a dreadful school—David McCall, HC McCall Papers Box 1
20 made to wear a dress kilt—Clive Aldred interview 5/25/06
20 as a father was "a cruel, cruel mix"—Doug Bomeisler interview 6/30/06
20 What am I going to do—Bill Weed interview 12/13/06
20 advertising was never an option—Weed interview 12/13/06
20–1 proud of his later success—Weed interview 12/13/06
21 He puts a salve on everything—Weed interview 12/13/06
21 estranged for a period—Louis Begley interview 5/3/06
21 kissed when meeting—Walsh interview 5/25/06
21 He cared for his son—Auchincloss interview10/5/06
21 Fairfield flew to France from the United States—Vaessen interview 5/18/06
21 ninth-generation Melinda—Mary Huyck to KR 7/6/06

Chapter 2: "I Failed Every Exam"
23 a distinctly original mind—DO to Sue Brown 5/11/59, LOC
23 the crowning horror of his school years—Jeffrey Meyers on *Booknotes* 3/11/01
24 a bit Dickensian—Gayle Binzen interview 10/9/06
25 Orwell's views of the school—*Orwell, Wintry Conscience of a Generation*, p. 20
25 The horror was Mrs. Wilkes—*Autobiography* p. 12
25 "wretchedly homesick"—*Autobiography* pg 13
25 the Bible was taught intensively—DO 75th birthday interview 1996
26 fictional student, secret agent James Bond—*You Only Live Twice*, p. 201
26 an almost perfect combination—Ian Keown interview 7/12/06
26 "homework, homework, homework"—Keown interview 7/12/06
26 classic public school virtues—David Johnston to KR 7/19/06
27 delicious Scottish porridge—*Autobiography* p. 19
27 put him on "Big Side"—DO to S. Knox Cunningham 8/22/55, LOC
27 played the double bass—*A Hundred Years of Fettes*
28 taught by Walter Sellar—*Autobiography* p. 20
28 head fag—DO to Rosser Reeves, 3/13/? WI Reeves Box 1, Folder 3
28 too lazy to take classical studies—DO to A.H. Ashcroft 10/7/59
28 spoke with an upper-crust accent—DO to Winston Fletcher 5/14/78
28 a predominately "classics" school—Cameron Cochrane to KR 9/4/07
28 minor infractions were punished—George Preston to KR 9/9/07
28 should have studied the classics at school—Cameron Cochrane to KR 9/4/07
28 1968 Founder's Day oration—*Unpublished David Ogilvy* p. 95
29 Invited back in 1974—DO at Founder's Day 10/5/74, HL Jock Elliott files
29 an inventive litany of ideas—DO speech at Fettes 10/5/74 HC Jock Elliott papers
29 market the "Fettes Product"—DO to Cameron Cochrane 12/4/84
29 you are stinking rich—*A Keen Wind Blows*

29 Faced with choosing a school—DO to H. Glynne Newman, 4/19/55, LOC
30 top marks in modern studies—Fettes headmaster 11/6/29
30 a rare open history scholarship—DO to A. H. Ashcroft 10/7/59
30 produced more Prime Ministers—*Autobiography* p. 34
30 grandest, most aristocratic—Hilary Spurling in *New York Times Book Review* 7/29/07
30 first two Harry Potter movies—*Christ Church Guide to College and Cathedral,* p. 5
30 its founder, King Henry VIII—*The Illustrated History of Oxford University*
30 most aristocratic—*George: Autobiography of Emlyn Williams*
30 entered Christ Church in 1929—Judith Curthoys to KR 10/31/06
30 scholars sat in an area slightly higher—Ronald Hilton to KR 7/3/06
30 Scholars like Ogilvy wore—Ronald Hilton to KR 11/28/06
30 Did you go to a good school?—Ronald Hilton to KR undated
30 warm and friendly and "sort of odd"—Margot Wilkie interview 3/12/2006
31 perpetually late to classes—Harold Burson interview 5/9/06
31 always very self-dramatizing—Wilkie interview 3/12/06
31 lodged for a year in Cambridge—DO to Mairi Ann Macleod 7/5/60
32 surgery left a large hole behind his left ear—Herta Ogilvy interview 9/29/07
32 Although Oxford was demanding—Ronald Hilton to KR 7/3/06
32 He was sociable—Wilkie interview 3/12/06, 7/2/08
32 sent down—*Printer's Ink* 1961
33 boisterous, handsome and almost idiotic—*Confessions of an Innkeeper,* p. 83

Chapter 3: The Making of a Salesman

35 A very bad time—*Printer's Ink* 1961
35 A chef always has enough to eat—*Madison Avenue* 1958
35 through the parents of some pretty young girls—Herta Ogilvy interview 9/29/07
36 wanted a Scotsman like a hole in the head—Frank McGee interview 1963
36 then at 19 Avenue Kléber—Francois Tiger to KR 4/3/07
36 seized by Hitler—*New York Times* 12/1/06
36 where Le Duc Tho and Henry Kissinger—Ronald Hilton to KR 9/11/06
36 highest rating in the Michelin Guide—Tiger to KR 6/19/07
36 a "terrifying martinet"—*Autobiography* p. 41
36 a kitchen in the grand old manner—*Printer's Ink* 1961
37 vast repertoire of dishes—*Autobiography* p. 46
37 Working in underground kitchens—*Printer's Ink* 1961
37 If I can't have the boy doing those apples—Herta Ogilvy interview 9/29/07
38 "*That is the way to do it*"—*Autobiography* p. 45
38 passed the test as chef—John Nettleton interview 9/19/06, *Printer's Ink* 1961
38 found in better kitchens—Dawn Roads to KR 9/27/07
38 one of the agency's largest accounts—Jimmy Benson interview 5/23/06
39 as British as roast beef—Richard Bicknell in *Marketing* UK undated
39 created . . . by Gustav Dalen—*AGA: The Story of a Kitchen Classic*
39 threw it high in the air—Frank McGee profile 1963
40 sold more by offering six cooking lessons—*Madison Avenue* 1958
40 sold an Aga to the Roman Catholic Archbishop—*Autobiography* pg 50
41 not knowing of the secret help—DO 75th birthday interview 1986
41 Theory and Practice of Selling the Aga Cooker—1935, LOC
41 an amusing classic—DO obituary, Stanley Pigott 1989
43 might order a plate of ketchup—Vel Richey-Rankin interview 11/17/06
43 little interest in fine dining—*David Ogilvy As I Knew Him*
44 What is not perfect is bad—Pierre LaForêt in unidentified French magazine undated
44 Aga had "axed" him—DO to friend who had been fired 11/28/66
44 no chance Ogilvy was going to be a stove salesman—Bill Phillips interview 5/21/97
44 "I tasted blood"—*Autobiography* p. 55

Chapter 4: Who Was Mather?
45 best dressed man on Fleet Street—*Now and Then* O&M London Summer 2008
46 Is it 'Infra-Dig'—*OBM 125 Years* p. 12
46 Mather & Crowther rode the boom—*OBM 125 Years* p. 12
46 "electric advertising"—*OBM 125 Years* p, 18
47 Pickwickian style—Jimmy Benson interview 5/23/06
48 "An apple a day keeps the doctor away"—*OBM 125 Years* p. 32
48 Rising at 5 A.M.—Philip Riley *Now and Then* Winter 2005
48 In her 1933 novel—*OBM 125 Years* p. 37
49 but I was just the chap—*OBM 125 Years* p. 37
49 married an actress—M&C management paper undated, LOC Box 32
49 As recent as the 1950s—Don Arlett to KR 2/28/07
49 messenger would come scuttling in—Peter Warren interview 5/25/06
49 two buttons under the desk—Clive Aldred interview 5/25/06
50 Office hours were—Aldred interview 5/25/06
50 "Dirty old man"—Aldred interview 5/25/06
50 A bigger version of his brother—Aldred interview 5/25/06
50 rounder, reddish face—Gaile Binzen interview 10/9/06
50 bon vivant—Pitcher interview 5/23/06
50 attractive women in the office—John Straiton interview 6/7/06
50 wrote a headline in Latin—Aldred interview 5/25/06
50 Francis launched a youth movement—*The Advertising World* London undated
51 Francis tells me—*How to Make $50,000 a Year in Advertising*
51 Francis tended to blurt out—Anthony Tennant interview 11/27/06
51 listed his recreations as—*The Advertising World* London undated
51 ran a paternalistic agency—Jill Treneman interview 10/28/06
51 Part of the problem—Benson interview 5/23/06
51 gather bills from his bottom drawer—Warren interview 5/25/06
51 two roller-coaster marriages—Pitcher interview 5/23/06
52 I don't know how a man—John Nettleton interview 9/19/06
52 hated public speaking—Benson interview 5/23/06
52 "Creed for Copywriters"—*Synopsis* O&M London 1964
53 close but complicated relationship—Tennant interview 11/27/06
53 everything David wanted to be—Peter Warren to KR undated

Chapter 5: Lucre in America
55 hardbound, gold-blocked book—Archie Pitcher interview 5/23/06
55 "Old Masters in Advertising"—Dawn Roads to KR 9/24/07
55 Ogilvy was soon embarrassed—*Ogilvy on Advertising* p. 25
55 going to work in a morning coat—Margot Wilkie interview 3/12/06
56 In the section on Advertising—DO to Directors 5/7/64
56 although not yet considered a huge success—Pitcher interview 5/23/06
57 professed a grab bag of reasons—*New York* 2/6/78
57 curious how an Oxford classmate—Mary Huyck to KR 10/14/06
57 income was less than $1,000 a year—*Benevolent Dictators* p. 101
57 a far cry from being poor—David McCall, Frank McGee Profile 1963
57 said he had read every book—*Benevolent Dictators* p. 102
58 American advertising was years ahead—*Benevolent Dictators* p. 102
58 in steerage—Stanley Pigott obituary of DO 1989
58 where he could direct the action—*Vanity Fair* February 2001
58 Bull's motorboat hit the dock—*Myself Among Others*
61 I launched an attack—*Journal of Advertising History* undated
61 Meynell challenged him—*My Lives*
61 seen one mail-order advertisement actually sell—*Tested Advertising Methods* p. 4
62 My ideas about advertising—*Journal of Advertising History* undated

63 Gallup had made headlines in 1936—AScribe Newire 6/29/06
63 hired him as associate director—*Printer's Ink* 1961
63 had come to the same conclusion—Joel Raphaelson DO 75th birthday interview 1986
63-4 one of the best raconteurs—Gallup videotape 1979
64 A very beautiful and rich—DO to Joel Raphaelson 10/24/86
64 "Gallup Gestapo"—Gallup videotape 1979
64 going to Hollywood all the time—*Printer's Ink*
65 Gallup got much of the credit—Alec and George Gallup Jr. interview 2/21/07
65 467 nationwide surveys—DO to O&M General Foods group 3/5/74
66 everyone knew when he sneezed—Gallup interview 2/21/07
66 a disease called halitosis—*All Out of Step* p. 98
67 Probably the only other man—Gallup videotape 1979
67 ask Gallup to join him—Gallup interview 11/28/06
67 gave Ogilvy a new life—Margot Wilkie interview 3/12/06
67 hated him on sight—David Fairfield Ogilvy *David Ogilvy: Original Mad Man* 3/29/08

Chapter 6: The Farmer and the Spy
69 moonlighting since 1939—*Autobiography* p. 77
69 first client at Mather & Crowther—DO to KR 1/25/93
69 represent all British intelligence services—*British Security Coordination* p. ix
69 People often ask me how closely—*Room 3603* p. x
70 earns his double-O classification—*The Life of Ian Fleming*—p. 98–99
70 martinis, served in quart glasses—*The Life of Ian Fleming* p. 98
70 In Britain, short of arms—*A History of the British Secret Service*
70 "I shall drag the United States in"—*Desperate Deception* p. 1
70 alarmed to discover—*A History of the British Secret Service* p. 328
71 "British Passport Control"—*Camp X* p. 15
71 task of combining propaganda—*A History of the British Secret Service* p. 329
71 "Celebrity was a wonderful cover"—*The Letters of Noel Coward* pp. 402–403
71 perhaps the most remarkable of the younger men—*Room 3603* p. 195
72 criticized for not serving—Francis Ogilvy to Gordon Boggon 2/3/46 LOC Box 32
72 Asthma . . . afflicted him for the rest of his life—Herta Ogilvy interview 9/29/07
72 Francis was working in British Intelligence—*Desperate Deception*
72 complete with black hat—*Secret Intelligence Agent* pp. 57–58
72 Squadron Leader F. F. Ogilvy—Ian Ogilvy to KR 7/15/08
72 the Old Man would come down—James Benson interview 5/23/06
72 started his new job—interviews Bill Stevenson 12/12/06, Nick Evans 10/25/06
73 a master of the terse note—Joel Raphaelson obituary of DO 1989
73 Pray state this day—DO to *Flagbearer* 2/9/63
73 Instead of being parachuted behind enemy lines—*Autobiography* p. 82
73 Ogilvy was placed in charge of collecting—Herta Ogilvy interview 9/29/07
73 Ogilvy's experience with Gallup—*Room 3603* p. 198
74 Ogilvy's basic job—Richard Spence to KR 1/2/07
74 Espionage work sounds more romantic—*The Benevolent Dictators* p. 102
74 briefcase handcuffed to his wrist—Peter Hochstein to KR 6/10/08
74 questioning whether Intrepid was his code name—*Camp X* p. xix
74 Ogilvy remained Stephenson's admirer—DO to Roald Dahl 11/5/62
74 taught us everything we ever knew—Bill Stevenson to KR 9/12/08
75 Ogilvy's work on economic issues—DO to Gardner Cowles 5/3/62
75 resigned from the staff—DO to Alan Watson 1214/51, LOC Box 38
75 Unlike other parts—Interviews Herta Ogilvy 9/29/07, Stevenson 12/12/06
75 "blazingly indiscreet"—DO to Roald Dahl 7/27/64, LOC Box 38
75 one of several BSC "insiders"—*British Security Coordination* p. xiv
76 shared quarters in Washington's—*The Irregulars* p. 196
76 If I give myself Alpha for the work—*Autobiography* p. 94

76 Like so many others, after the war—*The Benevolent Dictators* p. 102

76 more cows than people—*To Lancaster with Love*

77 a storm came up—Annie Fisher interview 2/15/07

77 Denlinger Road—Deed 166 David W. Denlinger to David M. Ogilvy

77 a man who lived on a farm—Gerry Lestz interview 1/6/07

77 chewed Mail Pouch tobacco—DO to John S. Hewitt 5/7/62 WI RR Box 9 Folder 2

77 Michael Finnegan—Fisher interview 2/15/07

77 A self-appointed expert—DO to H. Connell 9/27/54, LOC Box 38

77 recommended a children's book—DO to Ronald Hooker 3/6/62, LOC Box 38

77 Amish-based musical—DO to Mrs. Cecil Preston 12/21/53, LOC Box 38

78 Amish call everybody who is not Amish—John Ranck interview 1/9/07

78 at the top of the stairs in a kilt—Ann Slaymaker O'Reilly to KR 1/4/07

78 disenchanted with city life—*Madison Avenue,* December 53

79 Why not start an advertising agency?—*Autobiography* p. 115

79 He proposed staffing the operation—DO to M&C 9/7/38 LOC Box 32

79 But David was not yet committed—DO to FO 7/18/45 LOC Box 31

79 started a trading company—DO to Anderson Hewitt 10/30/45

80 For four years, starting in 1945—DO to Joel Raphaelson 10/28/86

80 By 1946, David had made a sale—FO to DO 10/25/46 LOC Box 31

80 New York is a city of freaks—M&C board minutes 1946 LOC Box 32

80 a tiny two-room office—FO to M&C Board 4/29/46 LOC Box 32

80 "Thirty-Nine Rules"—DO to Rosser Reeves 7/22/47 WI RR Box 1 Folder 3

80 Ogilvy took credit for reorienting—DO to Fred ? 5/25/47, LOC Box 32

80 his "kindergarten instructor"—DO to Rosser Reeves 7/22/47

81 Ogilvy sold the farm—Deed 25914 David M. Ogilvy to Harvey L. Heller

81 prefer *not* to be a part—M&C meeting minutes 9/22/47 LOC Box 32

81 To those of you who are scared—DO to FO 5/6/47, LOC Box 31

81 "Benson & Mather"—M&C meeting report 1/14/47 LOC Box 32

81 hire an experienced American—M&C meeting report 1/14/47 LOC Box 32

81 "no clue" about the agency business—Charlie Fredericks 4/26/06

82 All-time All-American—*The Nielsen Researcher* WI RR Box 1 Folder 1 1947

82 a "likeable nut"—Paul Biklen interview 6/15/06

82 Ogilvy would be number two—M&C meeting report 1/14/47 LOC Box 32

82 Operation Overlord—DO to FO 9/9/47 LOC Box 31

Chapter 7: Big Ideas

83 bar of the Knickerbocker Club—Louis Auchincloss interview 10/5/06

84 mortgaged his home—*Printer's Ink* 1961

84 Audubon prints—Shelby Page *Viewpoint* January/February 89

84 green, red lights—Helen DeKay interview 10/9/06, Joel Raphaelson to KR 11/4/07

84 This is a new agency—DO to Anderson Hewitt, LOC Box 38

85 five clients he wanted most—Prime Target List 5/21/57, LOC Box 38

85 spent only $250,000—DO to Mather & Crowther London 8/4/48

85 Ogilvy the research director—DO John Crichton interview undated

85 text was by copywriter Peter Geer—DO to Joel Raphaelson 9/2/82

86 knew *nothing* about accounting—Shelby Page interview 5/4/06

86 impressed that his grandfather—Page *Viewpoint* January/February 89

86 I figured my job was to—Page interview 5/4/06

86 as if a Mafia contract—David McCall 1988 unidentified

86 hide of a rhinoceros—David McCall 1988 unidentified

87 Camelot—Mike Turner interview 3/1/06

87 had to discount the 15 percent—Page interview 5/4/06

87 running out of money—Page interview 5/4/06

88 fortune of over $100 million—*Wall Street Journal* 3/15/08

88 indulge her passion for jewels—Reva Korda interview 4/29/98

88 Enough of that crap—Bruce Stauderman interview 8/26/06
88 not paying enough attention—Bill Phillips to KR
89 No more could run until—*Tide* NY 4/28/50
89 resigned the Rubinstein business—Esty Stowell to Staff 8/25/64
89 Big Ideas—DO to Staff 7/19/55
89 never change a word—Reiss interview with DO 12/16/59, LOC Box 38
89 #9 in one, #18 in another—DO to Walter Weir 4/10/57
89 noble Spaniard from Málaga—*El Nacional* 2/11/55
90 discovered the concept of story appeal—Advertising Workshop Incorporated
90 imitated around the world—*Harper's Magazine* May 1955 p. 55
90 idea was prompted—DO to Ellerton Jette 5/17/51, Bomeisler interview 6/30/06
90 bigger than both of us—*Harper's* May 1955
90 a silk glove with a brick inside it—*Observer,* London 5/5/57
91 the "sockiest" copy in America—*Space & Time* NY 11/5/51
91 fed up with "shop window" accounts—DO to FO 3/7/52, LOC Box 38
91 "Plush it up"—DO staff memo 5/20/53, LOC Box 38
91 token show of diffidence—DO to Charlie Brower 3/27/59, LOC Box 38
92 Whitehead's bearded mug–DO to F. C. Hooper 7/2/53, LOC Box 38
92 "Aren't you that Schweppes guy?"—*The Beard and I* p. 58
92 "Mr. Schweppes"—*Daily Mail,* London, LOC Box 38
92 Gary Cooper asked—DO to Roy Whittier 1/20/55, LOC Box 38
92 initial sales were disappointing—Guy Mountfort to DO 7/31/53, LOC Box 38
92 more hard-hitting—F. C. Hooper 7/10/53, LOC Box 38
92 Teddy's hairy kisser—DO to Alfred N. Steele 6/9/53, LOC Box 38
92 look like a rabbi?–Joel Raphaelson to KR 2008
92 Sales leapt 600 percent—DO to Mr. Johnson 6/20/55, LOC Box 38
92 one of the most successful campaigns—*Financial Times* 11/18/55, LOC Box 38
92 Success of British Agency—*Times,* London December 1950, LOC Box 38
93 supported Adlai Stevenson—*The Fifties* p. 231
93 design derived from *Holiday*—Bill Binzen interview 10/9/06
94 Borgie was key—Binzen interview 10/9/06
94 excellence in layout, art, and typography—*Advertising Agency* January 1955
94 an island in renaissance—"My involvement in Operation Bootstrap" DO Feb. 1991
94 like calling Chippendale a carpenter—*Viewpoint* September/October 1990
95 "lit by Vermeer"—*Nobody Else Is Perfect* p. 242
95 dirty, squalid, unpleasant—*Viewpoint* Dec 1992, DO to Teodoro Moscoso 3/15/56
95 immortal photographs—Binzen interview 10/9/06
95 best client he had ever known—DO to KR 6/30/92
95 Agencies came with proposals—DO to R.A. Bevan 9/20/56, LOC Box 39
96 Haloid Xerox came to him—Fred Papert interview 4/26/06
97 stubbed his toe—twice—to KR 10/31/79
97 Rinso White or Rinso Blue?—*Confessions* p. 64
97 When he met Dove—DO to Robyn Putter 9/16/91
98 first "beauty bar" that is neutral—Jim Heekin interview 7/31/06
98 cleansing cream—David McCall *O&M Flagbearers* Fall 1988
98 Dove on horseback—Jules Fine interview 5/14/97
98 came to him in a dream—*Confessions* p. 134
99 over the dead bodies—*How to Make $50,000 a Year* p. 46
99 did not invent his eventual choice—John Crichton DO interview undated.
99 do something about our clock—*New York Times* 9/7/58
99 used in a 1933 ad—DO to Charlie Brower 8/21/58, LOC Box 39
99 stimulated more praise—DO to Staff 4/4/58, LOC Box 39
99 we dare not run it again—DO to Walter Guild 1960
100 wanted a Rolls-Royce—Page interview 5/4/06
100 OBM-2—Doug Bomeisler interview 6/30/06

100 trudging down Fifth Avenue—*Original Mad Man* 2008
100 resigned the account—DO to Dr. F. Llewelyn Smith 3/15/62, LOC Box 39
100 a miracle worker—DO to Rollo Waterhouse 4/14/59, LOC
100 force a confrontation—Page interview 5/4/06
100 fighting the whole time—*The Benevolent Dictators* pg. 103
100 was not working as hard—*Printer's Ink* 1961
101 Hewitt never had a chance—David McCall in *Viewpoint*
101 attitude toward sex—Joel Raphaelson to KR 2008
101 "Tidy desk, tidy mind?"—Jules Fine interview 5/14/97
101 National College of Advertising—"A Program of Reform" 11/24/54 LOC Box 78
101 weasel merchants—DO to ANA 1954
101 brand image—The Image and the Brand, DO to 4As 10/14/55 LOC Box 78
102 "apostle of the brand image"—*New York Times Magazine* 4/10/05 p. 20
102 something of a cheerleader—*Madison Avenue* 1958
102 successful nonrational symbol—*The Hidden Persuaders* pp. 47–48
102 "A Hidden Persuader Confesses"—DO 1957, LOC Box 41
103 he had studied every book on advertising—*Autobiography* p. 117
103 four men were independently trying—*McKinsey's Marvin Bower* p. 213
103 Who takes care—*The Unpublished D.O.* p. 99
104 devoted several Saturday training sessions—Mac Stewart interview 4/14/06
104 the red of his rich aunt's chic household—*Adweek* 11/23/92
104 tidiness—*Welcome to O&M* 1960s
104 *Play of the Week*—Winter Shanck to KR 9/11/07
104 sponsors were dropping out—DO to Staff, LOC Box 40
105 picked up the phone—"Honor among thieves" David McCall undated
105 decisive role to Ogilvy—Daily Close-Up, *NY Post* 1/21/60
106 "Crown Princes"—DO to Jock Elliott 11/4/75 HC
106 "high-flyers"—DO to OMI Directors 1/4/80 HC
106 "teaching hospital"—*The Unpublished David Ogilvy* p. 25
107 Training was made important—DO to O&M General Foods group 3/5/74
107 attended every training program—Paul Biklen interview 6/15/06
107 honing his advertising philosophy—DO to Staff "Creative Credo" 7/19/55
107 hungry little birds—O&M *Alumni Flagbearer* Spring 1989
107 Rayon Manufacturers Association—*Confessions* p. 50
108 Greyhound Bus account—*Confessions* p. 45
108 Nothing was left to chance—Julian Clopet interview 10/20/06
108 sent mailings—*How to Make $50,000 a Year* Chapter 8
108 wangled an invitation—DO to R.A. Bevan 8/27/56 LOC Box 39, Gerry Leszt interview 1/6/07
108 "Scotland, my native country"—DO to Donegal Society 6/23/56, LOC
108 Steuben Glass account—DO to R.A. Bevan 12/3/53, LOC Box 38
109 Act of Parliament clock—*The New York Times* 9/7/58
109 treated them both badly—Joy S. Wiley to KR, Louis Begley interview 5/3/06
109 photograph in *Life* magazine—Bill Phillips interview 11/13/06
109 real all-American girl—Louis Begley interview 5/3/06
109 had married a Cabot from Boston—Elly Elliott interview 4/18/06
110 noises in the adjoining wall—Walter Cronkite interview 4/24/06
110 maybe not every day—Cronkite interview 4/24/06
110 totally obsessed with one thing—Bill Phillips interview 5/29/97
111 18 "hydra-headed" clients—DO to John Rhodes 5/28/54, LOC Box 41

Chapter 8: The Philosopher Kings
113 planned to spend much of his summer—DO to Sue Brown 6/19/62
113 sugar-coated with anecdotes—Pasch 11/1/63 LOC Box 82
113 a way to attract new business—Jane Maas interview 4/11/06

114 days at the beach—DO to Bob Pasch 11/1/63, LOC Box 82
114 ten "super-salesmen"—*The Supersalesmen*
114 you won't be bored—Raymond Rubicam to DO 11/4/63, LOC Box 82
114 Claude Hopkins enriched—Rubicam to DO 10/10/63, LOC Box 82
115 stimulating, rewarding, brilliant—Leo Burnett to DO LB
115 highly literate, colorful—Rosser Reeves to DO 8/6/63 WI RR Box 9 Folder 6
115 rich in insights—Benjamin Sonnenberg to DO 6/13/63, LOC Box 82
115 swimming prodigiously—Rebecca West to DO 11/30/63, LOC Box 82
115 the illusion of maturity—Charlie Brower to DO 10/18/63, LOC Box 82
115 Dear girl—Maas interview 4/11/06
115 in the erotica section—Jules Fine interview 5/14/97
116 You cannot bore people into buying—*Confessions* p. 97
116 1.5 million copies—DO to KR 4/23/93
116 standard text—DO to OMI Directors 2/23/80
116 philosopher kings—Plato, Book VII of *The Republic*
117 Hammers pounding horribly—"The Man from Iron City," *New Yorker* 9/27/69
117 U.S.P.—*Reality in Advertising* p. 46
118 Scottish son of a bitch—Gene Grayson interview 6/6/06
118 gave me a typed copy—DO to Rosser Reeves 4/18/60, LOC Box 39
118 the same true church—DO to Rudi (unknown) 5/22/62, LOC Box 39
118 "Hard Sell vs. Product Image"—DO to S. H. Britt 2/1/60 WI RR Box 7 Folder 4
119 If the Rosser Reeves model . . . is true—Jeremy Bullmore interview 5/24/06
119 she's an idiot—Grayson interview 6/6/06
119 he taught me how to sell—DO testimonial tape, Advertising Hall of Fame 1993
119 greatest advertising campaign—Dick Lord interview 5/16/06
120 link to lung cancer—"Cancer by the Carton" *Reader's Digest* 1952
120 absolute gatekeeper of quality—Jack Keenan interview 5/21/06
120 most unprepossessing man—Alex Biel interview 8/2/06
121 Northwestern University Alumni Association—Keenan interview 5/21/06
121 When to Take My Name—Leo Burnett to staff 12/1/67 LB
121 mutual admiration society—Leo Burnett to staff 1/27/55 LB
121 mutual admiration society—DO to HOBM executives 9/25/50
122 best possible merger—DO to R. A. Bevan 4/16/54, LOC
122 Black Pencil Award—Gary Press to KR 12/21/06
122 Burnett went into shock—Gary Press to KR 12/21/06
122 all-out accolade—DO "The Leo Burnett I Knew" 10/21/91
122 greatest compliment—DO to Leo Burnett 7/27/64
122 ad ran only once—*The New Advertising*
123 Forget words like 'hard sell'—Bernbach to 4As 5/14/80
124 quiet and soft-spoken—Ed McCabe interview 5/26/06
124 Neatly dressed—Bob Kuperman interview 5/3/06
124 Picasso of our business—Alan Rosenshine *Agency* Spring 1992
124 Jews, Italians, and other minorities—Dick Lord interview 5/16/06
125 something *fresh*—Kuperman interview 5/3/06, Lord interview 5/16/06
125 Rules are what artists break—Reinhard interview 11/13/06
125 No Jew is ever—Martin Mayer interview 1/13/07
125 My first hero was David Ogilvy—David Abbott interview 5/22/06
126 the need to be noticed—David Abbott interview 5/22/06
126 Facts are not enough—Bernbach to 4As 5/14/80
126 You make the bread—Kuperman interview 5/3/06
126 target group . . . was themselves—Bullmore interview 5/24/06
127 Never in all recorded history—DO to Bill Bernbach 5/6/63 LOC Box 65
127 something of a craftsman—Kuperman interview 5/3/06
128 we must choose between irrational genius—DO to Esty Stowell 5/12/61
128 two schools of advertising—DO to Leo Burnett 7/27/64

128 where there is no dogma—*Time* 11/1/63 p. 98
129 I was never in your agency—DO to Raymond Rubicam 4/1/54
129 star of the all-American team—Raymond Rubicam to DO 4/16/54, LOC
129 *Thompson Blue Book*—Jeremy Bullmore interview 5/24/06
129 Marion Harper—DO to KR 1/26/83
130 when the eyes are closed—Fred Papert interview 4/26/06
130 *The Gallagher Report*—DO to Bob Pasch 2/25/64, LOC Box 83
130 Your client is you—Roald Dahl to DO Michaelmas Day 1963, LOC Box 82

Chapter 9: The True Church
131 For seven years we got every account—*The Benevolent Dictators* p. 104
131 on the cover of *Time*—"The Visible Persuaders" *Time* 10/12/62
132 top agencies in 1960—DO to Rosser Reeves 5/6/63 WI RR Box 9 Folder 6
132 the high-brows' darling—DO to Gustavo Agrait 5/15/58
132 packaged goods companies—DO to O&M General Foods group 5/5/74
132 needed big people—Bill Phillips interview 5/29/97
132 any key appointment—DO to General Foods account group 5/5/74
132 Esty made us respectable—*The Benevolent Dictators* p. 106
132 come in as executive vice president—DO to R. A. Bevan 12/27/56
133 brought in smart pros—DO to Hugh Cullman 11/12/58, LOC Box 57
133 some found him aloof—*How to Make $50,000 a Year* p. 5
133 "Tastes as good as it smells"—John Crichton, Bill Phillips interview 5/29/97
133 Maxwell House Hotel—*The Tennessee Encyclopedia of History and Culture*
134 new ethical drug—Gene Grayson interview 6/6/06
134 cultivated him over several years—DO to Max Burns 9/7/54, LOC Box 41
134 not unethical to pay your doctor—DO to O&M General Foods group 3/5/74
134 prefer to work on a fee basis—response to Shell questionnaire, LOC Box 61
134 None of his partners wanted to do it—Shelby Page interview 5/4/06
134 support from marketing leaders—DO to O&M Vice Presidents 2/1/61, LOC
134–5 We don't make love until we're married—Jules Fine interview 5/14/97
135 Thompson's TV cartoon ads—DO to Charlotte Beers 7/26/94 Joel Raphaelson
135 "I don't *read* the ads"—*How to Make $50,000 a Year* p. 56
135 the results they get—DO to Bob Pasch 8/15/63 LOC Box 64
135 flaunted his Scottish heritage—Jock Elliott talk to *Reader's Digest* 4/15/86
136 got her new husband interested—DO to Esty Stowell 2/15/62, LOC Box 43
136 didn't think he was interested—Jean Clark interview 9/12/06
136 increases almost wholly to advertising—DO to Elliott Detchon 5/28/64
137 terrified to go to General Foods—Bill Phillips interview 5/29/97
137 "Brahmins" of General Foods—Bill Phillips interview 5/29/97
137 more mink too—John Crichton, Dave McCall *Flagbearers* Fall 1988
137 research showed it was upgrading Sears's image—George Fanning to KR 9/29/08
137 invited Ogilvy to speak—Brendan Ryan interview 11/9/06
138 the only one who kept his word—*The Care and Feeding of Ideas*
138 so super-duper—Joel Raphaelson to KR 11/4/07
138 proposed an outhouse—Bruce Stauderman interview 8/26/06
138 kicked a nearby wall—Gene Grayson interview 6/6/06
138 wrote the initial ad—Interviews Ted Shaw 4/16/07, Sue Buck 8/1/06
138 The reliable airline—Louis den Hertog to KR 12/8/06
139 chapter on plagiarism—Dick Seclow to KR 1/14/08
139 U.S. offspring had now grown bigger—Jimmy Benson interview 5/23/06
140 gathered in London's Festival Hall—Peter Warren interview 5/25/06
141 two packs a day for 30 years—DO to Fay Stender 8/31/64
141 died of lung cancer—DO to Raymond Rubicam 4/30/64, LOC Box 41
141 *CBS Reports*—"Cigarettes: A Collision of Interests" 4/15/64, LOC Box 41
141 Royal College of Physicians Report—"Smoking and Health" 1962

141 **If he hadn't been Francis's brother**—Anthony Tennant interview 11/27/06
142 **never fully accepted him**—Bill Phillips interview 5/29/97
142 **man who won them over**—Clive Aldred interview 5/25/06
142 **Ogilvy & Mather International**—*The Wall Street Journal* 11/19/64
142 **50–50 merger was sold**—John Treneman interview 10/28/06
143 **condition of allowing the sale**—*Debevoise & Plimpton* p. 148
143 **couldn't afford the escalating salaries**—Fred Papert interview 4/26/06
143 **wanted to go public**—DO to Esty Stowell 1/7/64, LOC Box 85
143 **"All my eggs are in one basket"**—DO to Directors 2/18/63
143 **The only downside**—DO to Shelby Page 7/23/62, LOC Box 85
143 **THE OMNIBUS**—DO to Stowell, Page, Atkins 6/22/64, LOC Box 85
143 **public offering of Ogilvy & Mather**—*NY Herald Tribune* 3/25/66
144 **made little difference**—Shelby Page interview 5/4/06
144 **the fellow who has made more money**—Warren Buffett to KR 4/6/05
144 **"Mickey Mouse countries"**—Shelby Page interview 5/4/06
144 **bitterly opposed to the buyout**—Bill Phillips interview 5/29/97
144 **would be too adventurous**—Michael Ball to KR 5/18/08
146 **considered it a Ponzi scheme**—Shelby Page interview 5/4/06
146 **"One Agency Indivisible"**—DO to Ogilvy Group Board 10/24/85
147 **"barbarians who litter our streets"**—*Flagbearer* 9/15/99
148 **public awareness of the new arts complex**—Judith Johnson to KR 10/23/06
148 **boosted to 67 percent**—DO report to Lincoln Center Aug 1960
148 **Bernstein is Box Office**—Richard Wandel to KR 12/1/06
148 **seen as less honest**—DO to National Automobile Dealers Association 2/3/65
    LOC Box 78
148 **arch-symbol of tasteless materialism**—*The New York Times* 9/18/63
148 **opportunities for rapid advancement**—DO to Harvard Business School Club
    1/26/65 LOC Box 78
148 **Copywriters Hall of Fame**—*Advertising Age* 4/29/65
148 **12 ideas on how to run the college**—DO to Robert E. L. Strider 7/8/63
148 **HMG scorns the king**—DO to Kathleen Graham 1/25/65, LOC Box 56
149 **honored at Buckingham Palace**—C.B.E. Birthday Honours List 7/11/67
149 **"a mixture of incredulity, horror and amusement"**—*The View from Touffou*
149 *Roar Like a Dove*—IBDB Internet Broadway Database
149 **grandest evening of my life**—Harry Bauder to Bob Pasch 2/20/64, LOC Box 84
150 **bought a second farm**—Joan Lorenz to KR 1/24/08
150 **farmed for him by Ira's grandson**—Ira and Fannie Stoltfus to KR undated
150 **David Ogilvy Stoltfus**—Joan Lorenz to KR 4/29/08
151 **"Principles of Management"**—Jules Fine interview 5/14/97
152 **reminded some Catholics**—Chuck Guariglia interview 4/25/06
153 **a Belgian barber**—*Flagbearer* 9/3/66
153 **extricated from the Park Lane**—Emil Vaessen interview 5/18/06
153 **suggestions for a name**—*How to Make $50,000 a Year* p. 257
154 **You can't have him for dinner**—Elly Elliott interview 4/18/06
154 **When he's nice, he's very very nice**—*David Ogilvy: Original Mad Man* 2008

Chapter 10: The King in His Castle

155 **three jaunty tunes**—*Advertising Age* 5/3/71, Phil Carroll interview 7/28/06
155 *Il n'ya que deux châteaux*—Louis Auchincloss interview 10/5/06
155 *"folie de grandeur"*—"A Weekend with David Ogilvy" Tony Houghton undated
156 **didn't really get along with . . . English partners**—Bill Phillips interview 5/29/97
156 **never inviting him**—DO to chairmen 5/1/88, Stauderman interview 8/26/06
156 **loved France**—*Viewpoint* Sept/Oct 1986, Herta Ogilvy interview 9/29/07
156 **understood French**—François Tiger interview 11/7/06
156 **expected Russian tanks**—Tiger interview 11/7/06

156 **François I bedroom**—"Fortified Paradise" Carolyn Harrison, unidentified undated

156 **German soldiers billeted there**—"Fortified Paradise"

156 **counting the tourists**—Tony Houghton interview 1/9/07

156 **getting some money to buy Touffou**—DO to Board at Ham House 6/20/88

157 **bitter yellow liqueur**—Louis Begley interview 5/3/06

157 **a little list**—"David Ogilvy at 75" *Viewpoint* September/October 1986

157 **horns of countless deer**—Begley interview 5/3/06

157 **damp and cold**—interviews Begley 5/3/06, Jean Clark 9/12/06

157 **It doesn't travel very well**—Hank Bernhard *Flagbearer* 9/15/99

158 **featured in gardening books**—*Gardens of France* p. 142

158 **You have inherited my love of gardening**—*Autobiography* p. 8

158 **she was recently divorced**—Herta Ogilvy interview 9/29/07

159 **Come on, David**—Bill Phillips interview 11/13/06

159 **one storm to the next**—Bob Noble to KR Nov 2000

159 **stomping out of meetings**—Phillips interview 11/13/06

159 **a thoughtful host**—Drayton Bird interview 5/2/06

159 **appear on the château's second-floor balcony**—Carroll interview 7/28/06

160 **348 stayed at least two nights**—Herta Ogilvy interview 9/29/07

160 **put some houseguests to work**—Alex Biel to David Fairfield Ogilvy 8/16/99

160 **idyllic lunches**—Lee Bartlett interview 12/13/06

160 **full of energy**—Nick Evans interview 10/25/06, *David Ogilvy's Last Crusade*

160 **He hates me**—Bird interview 5/2/06

161 **his "spiritual home"**—*David Ogilvy's Last Crusade*

161 **could have been on the moon**—Herta Ogilvy interview 9/29/07

161 **often 30 to 50 a day**—Lorna Wilson interview 10/28/07

161 **snooze, read, and work**—Herta Ogilvy interview 9/29/07

162 **white nightcap**—Stauderman interview 8/26/06

162 **writing, writing, writing**—Herta Ogilvy interview 9/29/07

162 **continually *worried* about money**—Louis Auchincloss interview 10/5/06

162 **The Augustus is Disgustus**—Bill Phillips *Flagbearer* 3/15/05

163 **rich octogenarians**—"Down Under" DO to Board 4/1/78

163 **got off the plane**—Roger Winter 9/27/06, *David Ogilvy as I Knew Him*

163 **listing 17 criteria**—DO to OMI Directors 2/8/73

163 **non-playing captain**—DO to Angus Ross and Jimmy Benson 2/14/75

163 **nominated Jock Elliott**—*Advertising Age* 3/10/75

164 **You aren't selling whiskey**—DO at National Distillers Convention 4/10/72 LOC
    Box 78

164 **throwing him a bottle**—DO at Proprietary Association 5/12/70 LOC Box 78

164 **"Ogilvy's Farewell"**—*The New York Times* 5/20/74

164 **"as Frank Sinatra discovered"**—*Flagbearer* 5/21/74

164 **"bread-and-butter letter"**—DO to 4As 5/18/74

164 **attacked growth for the sake of growth**—DO to KR 10/24/82

165 *not by a stranger*—DO to Jock Elliott 1/9/80

165 **managed to impress security analysts**—DO to OMI Directors 4/6/78

165 **The analysts will guffaw**—DO to Jock Elliott 12/17/75

165 **resist starting a second network**—DO to Jock Elliott, Bill Phillips

165 **international "jamboree"**—DO notes for speech 4/4/84

166 **looks like an oil can**—DO to Campbell Soup Company 12/11/79

166 **David Susskind**—*Open End* WNTA-TV NY 1985

166 **World Wildlife Fund**—"David Ogilvy at 75" *Viewpoint* September/October 1986

166 **prestigious board**—David Mitchell interview 5/9/06

167 **This is my favorite**—DO to Bill Phillips 7/10/79

167 **contributed enormously**—HRH Prince Philip interview 11/19/98

167 **never seemed to get along**—Mac Stewart interview 4/14/06

167 **"a blithering idiot"**—Charles de Haes interview 6/3/05

167 **strong opinions**—Archie Pitcher interview 5/23/06
167 **center of attention**—Harold Burson to KR 4/27/05
167 **doing a fine job**—de Haes interview 6/3/05
168 **"The book of David"**—"On Madison Avenue" *New York* 8/22/83
168 **culture . . . *is* the game**—Lou Gerstner interview 7/28/06
169 **Fishmongers Hall**—DO to Ogilvy Group directors 6/24/85
170 **he hated T-shirts**—Robyn Putter interview 2/14/07
170 **It did not escape our notice**—Lee Bartlett interview 12/13/06
170 **wrote like an angel**—Dave McCall *Viewpoint* March/April 1990
170 **If I were a really creative writer**—DO to C. B. Larrabee 1/25/54, LOC
170 **never wrote an advertisement in the office**—DO to Ray Calt 4/19/55, LOC
171 **drafted in *pencil***—interviews Sheila Trevellyn 5/26/06, Wilson 10/28/07
171 **scribbled and rewritten**—Ian Keown interview 7/12/06
171-2 **People who think well**—DO "How to Write" recipients unstated 9/7/82
172 **"Naughty but nice"**—Winston Fletcher interview 10/26/06
172 **drew on his advertising background**—*Americana* pp. 84–85, 270–275
173 **Quack-quack.**—Peter Mayle interview, *David Ogilvy: Original Mad Man*
173 **copywriter on the "least glamorous" account**—Edmund Morris interview 7/9/06
173 **most influential car advertising**—Joel Raphaelson to KR 2008
173 **"Illiterate!!!"**—Bruce McCall interview 7/14/06
173 **"Not tan-tan-tara, *tin*-tan-tara"**—Ian Keown interview 7/12/06
174 **on the Métro (with suitcase)**—Tiger interview 11/7/06
175 **grew better with every visit**—Bob Rightford to KR 7/6/06
175 **treated like a god**—Graham Phillips interview 7/23/06
175 **"Maja Guru"**—Mani Ayer to KR 7/24/–08
175 **Car rides in India scared him**—Ayer to KR 7/24/08
175 **National Business Hall of Fame**—"Four Living Leaders" *Fortune* 3/36/79
175 **might have died of fright**—DO to Bill Phillips 3/21/1979
175 **L'etat c'est moi**—DO to Bill Phillips 3/12/70, DO to George Lindsay 7/5/78
175 **two attempts to capture his likeness**—DO to John Treneman 10/5/84
176 **fought for two days**—DO to KR 7/8/88, Herta Ogilvy interview 9/29/07
176 **left in tears**—DO to Bill Phillips 7/28/88
177 **last will and testament**—Bob Neuman to KR 1981
177 **I'm the most objective man**—"David Ogilvy at 75" *Viewpoint* Sept./Oct. 1986
178 **"close to paradise"**—"Fortified Paradise" unidentified magazine

Chapter 11: Megamergers and Megalomaniacs

180 **the "third Saatchi"**—"Buying American" *New York* 8/10/87
180 **the "Big Bang"**—*Advertising Age* 4/22/96
180 **Megamergers are for megalomaniacs**—*Viewpoint* September/October 1986
181 **JWT was undermanaged**—*Advertising Age* 6/29/87, 8/15/88
181 **Advertising agencies as an investment**—J. Walter Takeover
181 **I'm a buyer**—Dick Lord interview 5/16/06
181 **like an indentured servant**—Lord interview 5/16/06
181 **former Ted Bates executives**—*Advertising Age* 8/17/87
181 **criteria fit The Ogilvy Group**—*Chicago Tribune, London Times* 4/17/89
181 **no parallel with JWT**—*Fortune* 6/5/89 pp. 131–132
182 **If God went public**—*The Wall Street Journal* 3/20/87
182 **after years of doing well**—*Fortune* 6/10/85 pp. 220–221
182 **speculation continued**—*The New York Times* 1/11/89, *Chicago Tribune* 1/11/89
182 **stock price bounced around**—KR to Atkins, Brown, Rinehart 4/10/89
182 **brought up merger**—KR to TOG Executive Committee 2/10/89
182 **met with financial analysts**—*London Times* 5/1/89
183 **suggested we meet again**—Martin Sorrell to KR 4/25/89
183 **delivered my script**—KR notes 4/26–7/89

183 **destabilize his target**—"Is Sorrell bashing clients" *The Wall Street Journal* 10/10/06
184 **The "bear hug" arrived**—Martin Sorrell to KR 5/4/89
184 **no love letter**—*The New York Times* 2/5/08
185 **children being sold into slavery**—*Advertising Age* 5/8/89
185 **almost met Sorrell the prior year**—*Advertising Age* 5/5/1988
185 **EXCULPATE MY SIN!**—DO to TOG Board 1/17/89
185 **going private**—DO to KR 1/18/89
186 **"odious little shit"**—DO to Jonathan Rinehart 5/1/89
186 **"inaccurate and disingenuous"**—KR to Martin Sorrell 4/30/89
186 **Ads were prepared**—Joel Raphaelson to Bill Phillips 5/1/89
186 **explored defenses**—Shearson Lehman, Smith Barney to TOG Board 5/15/89
187 **firestorm of litigation**—DO to KR 5/9/89
187 **Sorrell's offer had risen**—Martin Sorrell to KR 5/5/89
187 **65 possible issues**—KR to TOG Directors, PR people 5/8/89
187 **drained by pressure and emotions**—KR to TOG outside directors 5/12/89
188 **didn't see the benefits**—Mike Perry to KR 4/27/89
188 **resembled Gordon Gecko**—*The New York Times* 4/4/93
188 **the Interpublic offer**—Phil Geier to KR 5/15/89
188 **had been suggesting he might be open**—DO to KR 5/1/89, 5/7/89
190 **pot of gold**—KR to TOG shareholders 5/16/89
190 **Sorrell had no quick fixes**—*Adweek* 11/18/91
190 **company's new owner**—KR and Martin Sorrell at O&M officers' meeting 5/29/89
190 **at the scene of an accident**—Randy Rothenberg interview 10/23/06
190 **accepted the invitation to be chairman**—DO to Martin Sorrell 5/19/89
191 **the value of brands**—Martin Sorrell *Viewpoint* August 1989
191 **merging with J. Walter Thompson**—Jock Elliott to KR 1/13/99
191 **"I like to count beans"**—"The Rise and Fall of the Ad Man" BBC Four 6/2/08
192 **accepted an offer**—KR to O&M officers 10/23/89
192 **effect of the takeover on Ogilvy**—Lorna Wilson interview 10/28/07
192 **had been kidnapped**—interviews Jerry McGee 6/5/06, Lorna Wilson 10/28/07
192 **one day, it was over**—David Fairfield Ogilvy *David Ogilvy: Original Mad Man*
192 **spent his life raising standards**—"Tribute to DO" Dave McCall 9/26/89
192 **bruising his already black-and-blue**—JE to DO 8/15/89
193 **Money erased his admiration**—DO to KR 7/22/93
194 **lost something from his prime**—Bullmore interview 5/24/06
194 **Why did he accept**—Marvin Sloves to KR July 1991
194 **sold his soul**—interviews Julian Clopet 10/20/06, Peter Warren 10/2/06
195 **The Joke**—O&M Worldwide Meeting Oct. 1989

Chapter 12: A Disease Called Entertainment
199 **ban Ogilvy & Mather people from entering**—DO to Staff 1/26/70
199 **The David Ogilvy Award**—DO at O&M Staff Meeting 12/14/70
200 **"show-case advertising"**—DO to O&M creative directors 12/25/79
201 **Alka-Seltzer fell into the same trap**—*Advertising in America* p. 9
203 **more bad advertising**—*The Wall Street Journal* 10/29/91
203 **as screwed up a sense of priorities**—"Brand Burning" Jim Jordan 10/28/91
204 **the most valuable I have ever heard**—DO at ANA 10/28/91
204 **unmitigated gall**—*Chicago Advertising & Media* 12/15/91
205 **time to stop scolding**—DO to Lee Bartlett 11/8/91
205 **Before the annual Cannes Festival**—Daniel Sicouri to KR 9/27/07
205 **none of them were dull**—Joel Raphaelson to KR 1/10/02
205 **guru of phony creatives**—*Adweek* 10/5/92
206 **left the Touffou Jamboree after lunch**—DO to Graham Phillips 6/19/92
206 **When he started appearing at its meetings**—Jerry Pickholz interview 5/17/06
206 **your work is accountable**—Pickholz interview 5/17/06

206 "We Sell. Or Else"—Jerry Pickholz to KR 7/3/06
206 ripping into the world—DO to Direct Marketing Hall of Fame 1986
208 "Why steal from anyone but the best?"—Pickholz to KR June 1990
208 "How do you know?"—Joel Raphaelson, *Admap* UK Oct 1999
209 short on self-esteem—Tony Adams interview 11/10/05
209 Ogilvy Research Awards—Adams interview 11/10/05, *Advertising Age* 2/19/96
209 specialists in television—DO to Advertising Research Foundation 4/9/94
209 Ogilvy Center—Biel interview 8/2/06, report "Life in the Twilight Zone" 5/30/89
210 return on investment—report "Converting Image Into Equity" Alex Biel 6/16/91
210 softer side of advertising—Biel interview 8/2/06
210 talking to the inner man—Biel interview 8/2/06
210 "promise" testing—Biel interview 8/2/06
211 what makes a great surgeon—DO to Jock Elliott 1/29/75
211 dug himself a deep hole—*The Economist* 10/19/91 pp. 80–85
211 "Wagons Are Circled at WPP Group"—*New York Times* 10/31/91
212 signed the 1991 WPP annual report—WPP Group Annual Report 1991
212 I don't want him out—DO to KR 5/16/92
213 little more than ornamental—*Advertising Age* 7/20/92
213 minimal influence—DO to Graham Phillips 7/23/92
213 "WPP begging bowl out again"—*Independent* London 3/12/93
213 insisted he be replaced—*The Wall Street Journal* 7/9/92
213 Did I hear Chairman?—Chris Simpson to KR 5/14/92
213 agreed to step down—*The Wall Street Journal* 8/7/92
213 I'd die of misery—DO to KR 5/16/92
213–4 some baboon in the New York office—DO to Nigel (unknown) 5/6/93
214 formalizing his creative philosophy—DO *"My Creative Principles"* DO 1968
214 sales person who suddenly bursts into song—Keith Reinhard interview 11/13/06
214 simply got up and left the room—Vel Richey-Rankin interview 11/17/06
214 changes were taking place in British advertising—Don Arlett to KR 2/27/08
215 It was David we wanted no part of—Ed McCabe to KR 2008
215 how to succeed in advertising—DO to INSEAD *Viewpoint* January-February 1994
215 "Bees in My Bonnet"—DO "15 Bees in My Bonnet" 7/14/93
215 Carnation milk is the best—*Confessions* p. 112
216 forced Maurice Saatchi out—"Master of Illusion" *The New Yorker* 5/15/95
216 make another acquisition—*The Wall Street Journal* May–June 1998
216 It was very unlike him—Bill Phillips to KR 3/28/95
216 anything except senility—Joel Raphaelson to KR September 1992
216 feeling my age—DO to KR 1/18/94
216 "hot as the hinges of Hell"—DO to KR 5/16/92
217 "My problem is poverty"—DO to Graham Phillips 7/19/93
217 ask Sorrell to rectify his pension—DO to Martin Sorrell 7/20/95
217 I am now OUT—DO to Graham Phillips 3/1/95
217 If anyone sings that dreadful song—Joel Raphaelson to KR June 1995
217 "a series of five friends"—DO to Graham Phillips 3/1/95
218 three years of increased meddling—Graham Phillips interview 7/23/06
218 found nothing to disagree with—DO to Lee Bartlett 5/7/92
218 She's the best chief we've had—DO to KR 5/16/92
218 didn't answer Ogilvy's memos—Herta Ogilvy interview 9/29/07
218 killed his "We Sell. Or Else"—DO to Graham Phillips 1/9/94, to KR 7/1/94
218 stop people from talking about the new O&M—DO to Charlotte Beers 6/2/94
218 major change in the corporate culture—DO to KR 7/1/94
218 has not brought in a single new account—DO to Graham Phillips 1/9/94
218 abolished everything which I think is valuable—DO to KR 5/9/95
218 promoting Shelly Lazarus to chairman—*The Wall Street Journal* 9/9/96
219 I called to find out how you are—Shelly Lazarus interview 11/16/06

219 remained fixated on the past—Alex Biel to KR Oct 1993
220 conspiracy against old men—DO to KR 4/14/91
220 Had he retired at 60—*Campaign* London 12/7/90
220 If you work to age 85—*The Longevity Factor* p. 204
220 he watched two movies over and over—Joel Raphaelson to KR 5/25/97
221 We wives came into his life—Herta Ogilvy interview 9/29/07

Chapter 13: The Burr of Singularity
223 A blessing—Herta Ogilvy interview 9/29/07
223 sneaked cigarettes—Steve Hayden interview 2/14/07
223 last advertising man whose death—Jerry Della Femina *Adweek* 7/26/99
223 Burnett agency placed—*The New York Times* 8/16/99
224 funeral scene at Touffou—Shelly Lazarus to OMW board 7/26/99
224 no pomp nor circumstance—Shelly Lazarus to O&M Family 7/21/99
224 you can change your mind—Joel Raphaelson to KR 8/4/99
224 put him in a cardboard box—Lorna Wilson interview 10/28/07
225 nice to have a television expert—Jules Fine interview 5/14/97
225 he never wrote a good TV commercial—DO at Touffou board meeting 5/11/94
225 not relevant today—interviews Ed McCabe 5/26/06, Barry Owen 2/7/07
225 "You reversed the body copy"—Neil French interview 10/18/06
226 Mount Rushmore—Jeremy Bullmore in *Marketing* London 7/29/99
226 Associated Press suggested—"Manager's Journal" *The Wall Street Journal* 8/2/99
227 consumerist before it had a name—Randy Rothenberg interview 10/23/06
227 the leading personal care brand—"Unilever to Cut" *Wall Street Journal* 9/22/99
227 100 "top" advertising campaigns—"The Advertising Century" *Advertising Age* 1999
227 most influential creative force—"The Advertising Century" *Advertising Age* 1999
228 consider a career in advertising—*Adweek* 4/12/04
228 greatest advertising mind—*Forbes* 5/9/05
228 the definitive 'how to' book—Jerry Della Femina *The Wall Street Journal* 3/18/06
228 I realized he was talking about me—Jerry Della Femina *Adweek* 8/2/99
228 winning side or the losing side—*The Economist* November 2006
228 Consider China—*The New York Times* 7/26/08
230 WPP started edging back—*The New York Times* 9/13/04
230 operate like a business—"path to creative success" *Financial Times* 10/28/04
230 one of his two major regrets—Emil Vaessen interview 5/18/06
230 Why he was passed over—Sir Michael Angus to KR 10/16/06
231 Jock Elliott—*The New York Times* 10/31/05
231 Hal Riney—*The New York Times* 3/26/08
231 creative geniuses like Hal Riney—*Adweek* Nov 1992
231 all that shiny paper—Joel Raphaelson to KR 3/26/08
231 Madison Avenue in the 1960s—*The New York Times* 5/30/06
231 inspired designer fashions—*Vanity Fair* June 2008 pp. 128–129
231 mock issue—*Advertising Age* 6/23/08
231 Original Mad Man—BBC Four 3/29/08
232 burr of singularity—*Confessions* p. 132
232 "the most American Brit"—Herta Ogilvy interview 9/29/07
232 the soul of Uriah Heep—Robyn Putter interview 2/14/07
233 "My Death"—"For David" Jock Elliott 9/15/99
233 Friendships can be more important—DO "My Life"
234 lines by Horace—Edinburgh newspaper 1984
234 done rather well for an immigrant—Margot Wilkie to KR June 1997

Afterword: (More) Unpublished David Ogilvy
235 fascinated by monkeys—to Howard Connell 12/17/53, LOC

236 **Jekyll/Hyde**—to Commander Whitehead 6/18/54, LOC Box 61
236 **limericks**—to Howard Baldwin 8/18/55, LOC
237 **CHRISTMAS CARDS**—to Staff 12/15/58, LOC
238 **on a salver**—to Randolph Churchill 7/25/61, LOC
238 **Burpee Seed Company**—to David Burpee 6/7/72
239 **HIS MASTER'S VOICE**—to OMI Directors 12/21/71
239 **the common foe**—to OMI Directors 7/27/72
240 **MOONLIGHTING**—to OMI Directors 1/17/73
240 **opulence of their offices**—to Bill Phillips 3/30/75
241 **GENERALISTS COST LESS**—to OMI Directors 8/20/75
242 **first person to look out for is the customer**—to OMI Directors 10/6/75
242 **Principles of Management**—to Ron Daniel 2/25/78
242 **PROMOTIONS**—to OMI Directors 11/10/75
242 **PRESENTATIONS**—to O&M executives 5/5/78
243 **JUMPERS**—to OMI Directors 3/31/79
243 **ARE YOU THE GREATEST?**—to Creative Directors 7/1/79
245 **HOW TO WRITE**—to Joel Raphaelson and Ken Roman 9/24/79
245 **ENGLISH**—to Joel Raphaelson 3/26/80
246 **ACQUISITIONS**—to Jock Elliott 2/28/80
246 **hoope of steel**—to Bill Phillips 10/11/81
247 **A GROWING NUISANCE**—to Ogilvy Group board 9/18/85
247 **King George's surgeon**—to Steve Gardner 9/22/77

ACKNOWLEDGMENTS

*D*avid Ogilvy and I have something else in common beyond events described in this book—we both collaborated with Joel Raphaelson on our writing. Someone described Joel's contribution to one Ogilvy book as "more David than David." Joel and I worked together on advertising campaigns, Ogilvy & Mather publications, and a book on writing. On this project, Joel (and his wife, Marikay) brought a sense of agency history, an intimate knowledge of Ogilvy the man, an analytical eye to every word I wrote, and some well-chosen editorial contributions of his own. I was blessed to have him as my collaborator again.

Before Joel saw anything, my wife, Ellen, had to signal thumbs-up or thumbs-down. She lived (and loved) my O&M life, and encouraged and contributed to all my work and writing. On this project, she mobilized her market research background, lived through my endless telling of Ogilvy anecdotes, critiqued all too many drafts of the manuscript, and deserves more credit than is due most members of author families. Our son Neil, rare among lawyers for his writing and editing skills, improved several drafts.

Every author should have a George Fabian. My pal and former client, George performed the combined roles of relentless cheerleader and informed outsider, as he reviewed my drafts.

Sue Buck added a pair of fresh eyes in editing the page proofs.

Many other people helped along the way.

Peter DeLuca struck the spark that reignited this project after it was stalled for seven years, by inviting me to talk about Ogilvy at The University Club in New York in 2004.

Tony Reid in Edinburgh worked genealogical magic in researching Ogilvy's Scottish roots. Jane Campbell Garratt promoted the book in her wonderful O&M U.K. alumni publication *Now & Then*, reaching a gold mine of agency history.

Clive Aldred, Jimmy Benson, Archie Pitcher, and Peter Warren were my guides to Ogilvy's brother, Francis, and the agency's history in England. John Treneman added to this and went beyond, helping me research Ogilvy's birthplace in Surrey. Vicky Surman and Francois Tiger made things happen for me in London and Paris respectively.

I was lucky to work with Alexia Lindsay, archivist at Fettes, not long before she died. She and other Fettesians—Dawn Beaumont, Paul Cheetham, former headmaster Cameron Cochrane, Adrian Hall, Robert Philp, George Preston, and former students Michael Dawson, David Johnston, and Simon Cameron—educated me on this great school. I was ready to enroll.

Judith Curthoys, archivist at Christ Church, Oxford, translated the customs and records of that towering institution. I was lucky again in finding Ronald Hilton, Ogilvy's Oxford classmate, who provided the perspective of a university contemporary before he died.

Gerry Leszt interviewed Ogilvy when he first moved to the Amish country, and was a unique source. Mick Ranck arranged my talks to the Hamilton Club and the Rotary in Lancaster, Pennsylvania, producing anecdotes and photographs. Joan Lorenz, historian of Salisbury Township, added to the picture with her meticulously researched history—and located his second farm. Ann Slaymaker O'Reilly knew Ogilvy in Lancaster and contributed colorful stories.

Intelligence experts and authors Bill Stevenson and Tom Mahl helped me understand the arcane British Security Coordination and other intelligence services.

More than 100 people who knew or worked with Ogilvy generously agreed to be interviewed at length. Their names are listed in the Bibliography. Ogilvy wrote and spoke so much about his life and career and the "bees in his bonnet," it is hard to believe they could tell much more than what is known. But they did. I hope I have reflected their comments accurately.

Along with interviews, transcribed impeccably by Betty Hunt, the trove of Ogilvy papers in the Library of Congress was a major source of fresh material. During my four two-day expeditions, the staff in the Manuscript Reading Room produced any of their 87 Ogilvy containers instantly. Bonnie Coles in the Library's Photo Duplication Services was a genial tiger in tracking down a key photograph.

At libraries I could not visit, several researchers filled in heroically. Stacey Erdman found what I needed in the Rosser Reeves collection at the Wisconsin State Historical Society. Lynn Eaton discovered gold in the David McCall and Jock Elliott papers at the Special Collections Library at Duke's John W. Hartman Center for Sales, Advertising and Marketing History. Wendy Shay produced helpful Bart Cummings papers from the Smithsonian Center for Advertising History.

Marsha Appel knows everything there is to know in the world of advertising, and mobilized the library at the American Association of Advertising Agencies. Jane Reed and her colleagues at The University Club in New York found books—and answers. Leo Burnett and Ogilvy had a mutual admiration society, and Carol Halamma with Cap Adams opened doors at the Leo Burnett Company. Eleanor Mascheroni delivered crucial photographs (and permissions) at Ogilvy & Mather.

Several people graciously turned over their personal D.O. files: Tony Adams, Lee Bartlett, Bill Binzen, Nick Evans, Richard Fowler, Ann Iverson, Bill Phillips, Graham Phillips, Joel Raphaelson, and John Straiton, among others.

Jock Elliott and George Lindsay were Ogilvy's friends as well as partners. Their widows, Elly and Mary, granted me vital interviews, encouraged me, suggested other interviewees, and (with O&M chairman Shelly Lazarus) were a bridge to the family.

Ogilvy's longtime colleagues Bill Phillips, my boss and tennis partner for 25 years, and the wise and painfully honest Jules Fine provided some of the most insightful comments.

Nobody understood Ogilvy better than his wife Herta, who invited me back to Touffou for two days of her special perspective.

Julian Bach, as much editor as literary agent, represented my first two books and believed in this one. When he retired, Jim Levine expertly took over as my agent and placed it with Palgrave Macmillan. Beyond her vote of confidence in the book, my editor Airié Stuart produced its title and striking cover and encouraged me to go beyond my material and tell a story. Her cheerful assistant Marie Ostby made everything run close to on time.

The cover photograph might not have happened without the intervention of my former colleagues Steve Harty and Parry Merkley. Parry's Annie Liebovitz campaign for American Express led to her visit to the château where this photo was taken.

In 1963, David P. Crane looked beyond my marginal credentials and hired me at Ogilvy, Benson & Mather—and thereby changed my life.

INDEX

THE KING OF
MADISON AVENUE

Designed by Andrew Berry

Composed by Letra Libre, Incorporated

in Adobe Garamond with display lines

in Adobe Caslon Pro and Trade Gothic

and accents in Shelley Andante Script

and Minion Ornaments